★ THE TEACHER'S CALENDAR OF ★

Famous Birthdays

Other Teacher Resources from *Chase's Calendar of Events*

The Teacher's Calendar

180 Creative Ideas for Getting Students Involved, Engaged, and Excited

★ THE TEACHER'S CALENDAR OF ★

Famous
Birthdays

The Editors of McGraw-Hill
With Luisa Gerasimo and
Sandy Whiteley

McGraw·Hill

New York   Chicago   San Francisco   Lisbon   London   Madrid   Mexico City
Milan   New Delhi   San Juan   Seoul   Singapore   Sydney   Toronto

Library of Congress Cataloging-in-Publication Data

The teacher's calendar of famous birthdays / the editors of McGraw-Hill with
Luisa Gerasimo and Sandy Whiteley.
        p.   cm.
    Includes index.
    ISBN 0-07-141230-1 (alk. paper)
    1. Birthdays.   2. Birthdays—Study and teaching.   3. Celebrities—
Miscellanea.   4. Biography—Study and teaching.   I. Gerasimo, Luisa.
II. Whiteley, Sandra, 1943–   III. McGraw-Hill Companies.

    D11.5.T43   2003
    920.02—dc21   2003041985

1 2 3 4 5 6 7 8 9 0   AGM/AGM   2 1 0 9 8 7 6 5 4 3

ISBN 0-07-141230-1

Interior design by Todd Petersen

This book is printed on acid-free paper.

CONTENTS

Introduction   vii

January   1
February   33
March   63
April   95
May   127
June   159
July   191
August   223
September   255
October   287
November   319
December   351

Index   383

INTRODUCTION

Welcome to *The Teacher's Calendar of Famous Birthdays*. For each day of the year, from January 1 to December 31, we've created a biographical profile of an influential person who was born that day. It might be a statesman, an artist, a sports hero, a scientist, an author—or someone quite unexpected. We pluck people out of the distant past as well as people living today. These are the people who have put a stamp on their times—and who will be of interest in the classroom to your students.

While there are some very familiar faces here—Mark Twain, George Washington, Eleanor Roosevelt, Lance Armstrong, and more—we've also chosen people who were famous within their particular field in their time or today but who may not always be on the front page of the newspaper. For example, Junko Tabei (born September 22, 1939) was the first woman to climb Mount Everest (in 1975). She still climbs and has established a foundation to protect mountain habitats. Or consider Benjamin Banneker (born November 9, 1731), the "first black man of science." Banneker, an astronomer and clockmaker, assisted in the survey of the District of Columbia in 1791. A devastating fire during his funeral destroyed his papers, and as a result less biographical information has been preserved in history than he merited.

Also included are some who have had an impact on children as illustrators, authors, or musicians. You'll find Maurice Sendak, Sterling North, Jean de Brunhoff, Walt Disney, Raffi, Maxfield Parrish, Louisa May Alcott, and more.

We've aimed for an entertaining and educational variety of people— not just presidents or other typical subjects from the history books. Inevitably, we've had days of the year when too many interesting people were born, and we've had to make difficult decisions on which of them to profile. When this dilemma has occurred, we chose the person not covered as thoroughly in reference books. August 1, for example, saw the birth of Herman Melville in addition to that of Maria Mitchell. We chose

Mitchell for her contributions to astronomy *and* because she is not profiled as often as Melville.

Each profile includes the birth date, birthplace, death date, and death place (if applicable). We've sketched in the major events and facts of each person's life and included some thoughts as to just what makes them significant in history.

For every day of the year, you now have a source of inspiration for yourself and your class. This book can serve as a catalyst for biographical assignments; a source of supplemental information for lesson plans on history, science, and more; a way to add spice to the day ("Guess who was born today?"); and a way to bring different kinds of accomplished people to your students' attention (see July 23 for the biography of chess grandmaster Judit Polgar, for example). At the very least, we hope that *The Teacher's Calendar of Famous Birthdays* is a fun read!

Please note: Practically all birthdays in this book reflect Gregorian calendar ("New Style") dates. Great Britain and its colonies adopted the Gregorian calendar in 1752, and Eastern Europe and other countries adopted it in the early twentieth century. This means that some of the people profiled here were born under Julian calendar ("Old Style") dates. For example, we list George Washington's birthday as February 22, 1732, but his Julian calendar birth date was February 11, 1731. When looking at other sources, you may see the Old Style date used for those born when the Julian calendar was still in effect.

JANUARY

PAUL REVERE

Born January 1, 1735
Died May 10, 1818

American patriot, metalworker, and maker of eyeglasses and surgical instruments, Paul Revere is best remembered for his April 18, 1775, ride from Boston to Lexington to warn Samuel Adams and John Hancock that British troops were coming. Adams and Hancock were wanted for treason; the warning may have saved their lives. The warning also prepared the Minutemen for the next day's Battle of Lexington, which launched the American Revolution. "The Midnight Ride of Paul Revere," a poem by Henry Wadsworth Longfellow, told the tale somewhat inaccurately, but when it was published in 1863 it vaulted Revere from relative obscurity to a new status as an American folk hero.

Paul Revere was born at Boston where he had a long and productive life that extended far beyond running information about British troop movements. The eldest surviving son of a large family, Paul used the family metal shop to support his mother and siblings when his father, silversmith Apollo Revere (originally De Revoir), died. Revere's name soon became synonymous with high-quality metal products ranging from simple spoons and cooking pots to magnificent works of decorative art. Eventually he branched into dentistry and went on to provide important metal items such as cannons and bells for his newly formed country.

As colonial discontent with Britain grew, Revere became active in rebel activities. He was one of the instigators of the 1773 Boston Tea Party and the lead rider of the Boston Committee of Safety. He also created the coinage for the Colonies and the official seal.

Paul Revere is an example of an American success story. Born the son of an immigrant artisan, he managed to serve the public while building a successful business that survives to this day.

JAMES WOLFE

Born January 2, 1727
Died September 13, 1759

Born at Westerham, England, Wolfe entered the British army in his mid-teens. At the outbreak of the French and Indian War, while he was still very young, he was selected for a command in Canada. This conflict between Prussia and Austria involved much of Northern Europe, with Britain supporting the Prussian king, Frederick the Great. France, which was fighting Britain in North America at the time, sided with Austria. In 1758 Wolfe showed both courage and skill in the capture of Louisbourg (Nova Scotia). He was then shocked and somewhat dismayed by his quick promotion to major general. Despite these misgivings, he gamely took command of an expedition up the St. Lawrence River to do battle against Quebec (which was held by the French) in April 1759.

On the morning of September 13, 1759, after negotiating the river and then a twisting path in full darkness, Wolfe and his men engaged General Montcalm's troops on the Plains of Abraham and won Quebec for the British, setting the stage for the British to seize Montreal. Both Montcalm and Wolfe were killed in this battle. Wolfe became a national hero because though mortally wounded he inquired how the battle was proceeding. When a soldier told him the French were on the run, he reportedly replied: "God be praised. I will die in peace." A monument to him was placed in Westminster Abbey, and a town was named for him in New Hampshire.

J. R. R. TOLKIEN

Born January 3, 1892
Died September 2, 1973

This man's unusual powers of imagination defined what we visualize today when we hear the words *wizard*, *elf*, or *dwarf*. John Ronald Reuel Tolkien was born at Bloemfontein, South Africa, but settled in England at an early age after the death of his father. He was a serious student of European languages. He also created complete languages all his own. His mother encouraged his love of language and imagination before her untimely death in 1904.

After graduating college, fighting in World War I, and marrying, he became a professor. One day while grading exams, he came across a mostly blank page where, for no apparent reason, a student had written: "In a hole in the ground there lived a hobbit." Being a man of great creative energy, and by then the father of small children, Tolkien proceeded to write a story to entertain his children about this hole-dwelling creature that had captured his imagination. A draft circulated for some time and eventually came to the attention of an employee at the London publisher George Allen and Unwin who asked Tolkien to expand it. He did, and the publisher's ten-year-old son convinced his father, Stanley Unwin, to publish the work. Published in 1937, *The Hobbit* was a surprise hit with both adult and juvenile audiences. Twenty years later Tolkien released a follow-up to *The Hobbit*, a trilogy called *The Lord of the Rings*, which was also a runaway hit—first in book form and, beginning in 2001, as a movie series.

Tolkien, who was rather amazed by his success, lived a long life of both scholarly and fictional writing. He died at Bournemouth, England.

LOUIS BRAILLE

Born January 4, 1809
Died January 6, 1852

The inventor of a widely used touch system of reading and writing for the blind was born at Coupvray, France. Louis Braille was permanently blinded at the age of three by a leatherworking awl in his father's saddle-making shop. He attended Paris's National Institute for Blind Children, where he stayed on as a teacher after completing his own studies in 1826. At that time blind people learned to read with actual raised letters. But then a soldier named Charles Barbier explained in a lecture his invention of "night writing," which was intended for the battlefield but was never adopted. In 1824, Braille developed a system based on Barbier's, which, ironically, used an awl-like stylus to make raised dots in paper that could be felt and interpreted by the blind. The Braille system is a code using one to six dots that fit within a six-part grid. The system was largely ignored until after Braille's untimely death from tuberculosis. He died in poverty at Paris. Although he had published information about his code, his own school didn't adopt it until 1854. In 1932, the United Kingdom and United States adopted an English version.

Today, blind children are taught to read the punch type we now refer to as Braille at an early age. People tell time on Braille watches, play music from Braille sheet music, choose elevator floors by touching Braille signs next to the buttons, and use Braille keyboards to compose notes or letters on computers. There is even a winery that sells wine with Braille labels.

JEANNETTE RIDLON PICCARD

Born January 5, 1895
Died May 17, 1981

On October 23, 1934, Piccard piloted the "Century of Progress," a hot-air balloon, 57,579 feet into the stratosphere with her husband Jean-Felix Piccard to become the first woman in space. This scientific couple teamed up to do research. They were responsible for advances in plastic film and polyethylene balloon materials, which eventually led to ascents of more than 100,000 feet.

Jeannette Piccard earned two bachelor's degrees from Bryn Mawr, a master's degree in organic chemistry from the University of Chicago, and a Ph.D. in education from the University of Minnesota. For many years she served NASA as a manned-flight consultant. To top off these accomplishments she became one of the first women ever to be ordained an Episcopal priest (1976). Born at Chicago, Illinois, she died at Minneapolis, Minnesota. The Piccard Gondola is a part of the permanent collection at Chicago's Museum of Science and Industry.

CARL SANDBURG

Born January 6, 1878
Died July 22, 1967

The bard of the American heartland—following in the poetic tradition of Walt Whitman—Carl Sandburg was born at Galesburg, Illinois, the son of a Swedish immigrant. Leaving school as a youth, he traveled the United States and worked at odd jobs. After brief military service in the Spanish-American War (1898), Sandburg enrolled in Galesburg's Lombard College and began publishing poetry in journals and pamphlets. After college, he began a journalism career and was an organizer for the Wisconsin Social Democratic Party. In 1908 he married Lillian Steichen (sister of photographer Edward Steichen). In 1913 Sandburg moved his new family to Chicago where he began work for the *Chicago Daily News*. He also began to contribute his work to *Poetry* magazine.

With the acclaimed publication of *Chicago Poems* in 1916, Sandburg arrived on the literary scene. From the now famous "Chicago," Sandburg gave that city the nickname it still bears: "City of the big shoulders." Other important volumes of poetry, including *Cornhuskers* (1918) and *Smoke and Steel* (1920), quickly followed. In 1922 Sandburg published the children's book *Rootabaga Stories*. Through years of work and research Sandburg produced one of the great American biographies, *Abraham Lincoln: The Prairie Years* (1926), which was a critical and popular success. The four-volume *Abraham Lincoln: The War Years* finally followed in 1940; this towering work won Sandburg the Pulitzer Prize. In his later years, Sandburg continued to write poetry as well as a novel, a memoir, and two collections of folk songs. He won a second Pulitzer Prize in 1951 for his *Complete Poems*. Sandburg died at his home in North Carolina.

JACQUES-ÉTIENNE MONTGOLFIER

Born January 7, 1745
Died August 2, 1799

Orville and Wilbur Wright might be the most famous brothers of early flight but the Montgolfier brothers of France made history more than a hundred years earlier. Jacques-Étienne and his older brother Joseph-Michel conducted important experiments with paper and fabric bags filled with smoke and hot air. These November 1782 experiments led directly to the invention of the hot-air balloon and humankind's first flight.

The first passengers in the flimsy balloon and basket rigs were ducks, chickens, and sheep. Then, on November 21, 1783, in front of a crowd of onlookers that included the king and queen of France, the Montgolfiers sent two brave human passengers into the air over Paris for a five-mile flight. This event started what quickly became a balloon flight craze. Not long after, J. A. C. Charles, a physicist, successfully flew a balloon filled with hydrogen. As people all over the country began launching their own balloon variations (with varying degrees of success), suspicious farmers, seeing giant bags of gas coming down at them in their fields, would sometimes attack the balloons. Early aviators found they had better landings if they plied folk with drink upon coming down or crashing.

Born at Annonay, France, Montgolfier died at Balaruc-les-Bains. By then he was an honored member of the French Academy of Science.

ELVIS PRESLEY

Born January 8, 1935
Died August 16, 1977

Born into a poor family in Tupelo, Mississippi, Elvis Presley became a pop music sensation in his early teens. He became known as the king of rock and roll, and at the time of his death, his recordings had sold more than 600 million copies. By 2003, his records had sold more than one billion copies. He had 131 songs or albums certified gold, platinum, or multi-platinum. His three television specials were among the most highly rated programs of all time. He also made thirty-three feature films. His good looks, sensual moves, and original singing style gained him a very loyal teen following. Girls fainted when he came onstage—at times he could not be heard over the screaming of his fans.

He was drafted in 1958 and stationed in West Germany, where he met his wife Priscilla. When Elvis's term of duty ended, he and Priscilla lived at Graceland, his estate in Memphis, Tennessee. In his middle age, Presley became extremely overweight and struggled with addictions to various prescription medications. He died of a heart attack brought on largely by drug abuse. He was buried at Graceland, which opened as a tourist attraction several years later. More than 750,000 fans visit each year, especially during the week of August 16, the anniversary of his death. For years after his death people claimed to have seen him or talked to him. Although his body is gone, his music lives on—not only in his recordings but also in the memories of his devoted fans and in the work of the many musicians he influenced.

JOAN BAEZ

Born January 9, 1941

Joan Baez's family moved to California from Staten Island, New York, in the early 1950s. In 1958 Baez graduated from Palo Alto High School and recorded her first demonstration album, which studio executives promptly shelved. When her father accepted a post at the Massachusetts Institute of Technology, the family moved back east and Baez got into the coffeehouse folk music scene in Cambridge. Her guitar playing and singing won her a large and lively audience. By the early 1960s she had been discovered by a number of famous musicians. She played at the Newport Folk Festival, recorded a number of successful albums, and embarked on what would become a lifetime of political activism.

Known for her gorgeous voice, unique guitar style, and narrative songwriting, Joan Baez used her talents to help people all over the world. Her first efforts were on behalf of the civil rights movement when she announced a strict "no discrimination, no segregation" concert policy. She also protested U.S. involvement in Vietnam and actually served a short jail sentence for taking part in a protest against the draft. Baez sang "We Shall Overcome" to an estimated crowd of 30,000 people at the civil rights march on Washington in 1963. By the late 1960s many of her recordings had gone gold; she had sung at the Woodstock Festival and appeared on film. Working for humanitarian goals, she visited a number of Latin American countries in the 1980s and released a Spanish-language album. Despite pressure from many governments, including her own, she continued to let her conscience be her guide and to speak for those who had no voice. Joan Baez has received many humanitarian awards including the French Legion d'Honneur and two honorary doctoral degrees. She continues to play music, write poetry, and paint. She has even used her considerable talents in a comedy cabaret.

WILLIAM TOOMEY

Born January 10, 1939

Born at Philadelphia, Pennsylvania, Bill Toomey was one of America's greatest athletes. Competing in the pentathlon and decathlon, he was at his prime in the 1960s. From 1960 to 1964, he won five consecutive Amateur Athletic Union (AAU) pentathlons; from 1965 to 1969, he won five consecutive AAU decathlons. To date, no one has broken the AAU pentathlon consecutive-wins record. But his goal was to take the gold medal at the Olympics, where the decathlon winner is considered the best all-around athlete in the world.

The 1968 Olympics were in Mexico City, Mexico, where the high altitude added to the challenges of all the athletes. Nevertheless, Toomey won the gold medal after a tough two-day competition in the 100 meters, long jump, shot put, high jump, 400 meters, 110-meter high hurdles, discus throw, pole vault, javelin throw, and 1,500 meters. He placed first in all but two events—in those he placed second. *Time* magazine wrote, "The man who wins the Olympic decathlon well deserves to be known as the finest athlete in the world. That man last week was William Anthony Toomey." (Coincidentally, another January 10 birthday athlete also won a gold medal at the 1968 Olympics—boxer George Foreman.)

After the Olympics, Toomey went on to set world records in the decathlon and pentathlon. His 1969 pentathlon world record of points still stands. Upon retirement from competition, Toomey has remained active with the U.S. Olympic Committee and with the international committee. He is also a broadcaster and motivational speaker. He was elected into the National Track & Field Hall of Fame in 1975 and the Olympic Hall of Fame in 1984.

ALDO LEOPOLD

Born January 11, 1887
Died April 26, 1948

Considered by many to be the father of wildlife ecology, Leopold was a fine scholar, writer, teacher, and philosopher. He is best known for his book *A Sand County Almanac*, in which his poetic prose gave many readers reason to pay attention and learn more about the patch of land they occupy. The many hours Leopold spent tramping and observing Midwestern fields, forests, and streams led him to live in harmony with nature. He saw the natural world as a series of communities. He came to believe that the tools of nature's destruction could instead be used to rebuild the environment.

After working for the U.S. Forest Service in the Arizona Territories, in 1924 he accepted a transfer to a forest-products laboratory in Wisconsin. He began teaching at the University of Wisconsin in 1928, and in 1933 he published *Game Management*, an important work that combined biology, forestry, zoology, agriculture, forestry, education, communication, and ecology. Soon after, Leopold was appointed to serve as the first chair of the newly created Department of Game Management. In 1935 Leopold put some of his theories into practice when he bought a run-down farm in an area of Wisconsin known as the sand counties. There Leopold refurbished an old chicken coop and used it as both a retreat for writing and research and a place to host family, friends, and students. The many essays he wrote as he tried to rebuild the land became *A Sand County Almanac* (1949), a lovingly written book that profoundly influenced the budding environmental movement in the United States and abroad.

Born at Burlington, Iowa, Leopold died at Madison, Wisconsin.

JACK LONDON

Born January 12, 1876
Died November 22, 1916

A novelist and short-story writer, London was born at San Francisco during the booming years of the late 1800s. Before he became a writer London was a fisherman, hobo, sailor, and gold prospector. Later he would use his own adventures as the basis for many of his stories. *The Cruise of the Snark* (1911) was an account of his experiences in the South Pacific. Many of his classic works depict the often antagonistic relationship between humans and the natural world—for example, *The Son of the Wolf* (1900), *The Call of the Wild* (1903), *The Sea Wolf* (1904), *White Fang* (1906), and *Burning Daylight* (1910).

Although his works often were criticized as rough and overly realistic (some readers of his day were shocked by his gruesome descriptions), he continues to be one of America's most often translated and widely read authors. A number of his fictional works, such as *The Call of the Wild*, have been made into gripping movies.

A prolific writer, he managed to finish fifty works of fiction and nonfiction in only seventeen years. He died of gastrointestinal uremic poisoning at his Glen Ellen, California, ranch. He wrote: "I would rather that my spark should burn out in a brilliant blaze than it should be stifled by dryrot. . . . The proper function of man is to live, not to exist."

HORATIO ALGER

Born January 13, 1832
Died July 18, 1899

Born at Chelsea, Massachusetts, Alger studied under Henry Wadsworth Longfellow and originally intended to become a poet. Rejected by the Union Army on account of asthma, he became a correspondent for the *Boston Transcript* and the *New York Sun*. Later he became a Unitarian minister. His adventure stories for young people (for example, *Ragged Dick* and *From Canal Boy to President*) centered on the poor-boy-makes-good theme. In fact, Americans often use the phrase "a real-life Horatio Alger story," when referring to the theme of rags to riches.

Alger's heroes were nearly always kind, industrious, diligent, brave, and generous. The stories emphasized the notion that everyone can better themselves, do their best, and become successful by working hard and making good choices. This formulaic approach to story writing worked well for Alger and his bestselling books influenced both children and adults. More than 250 million copies of his books have been sold worldwide. His novels of faith, courage, and the worth of an honest day's work reflect what many people consider traditional American values.

Alger died at Natick, Massachusetts.

ALBERT SCHWEITZER

Born January 14, 1875
Died September 4, 1965

Born at Upper Alsace, which was then part of Germany and later a region of France, Schweitzer became a prolific writer. By the age of twenty-nine he had already published three books. He was a noted theologian, medical missionary, organist, philosopher, and world authority on Bach. In 1913, at the age of thirty-seven, Dr. Schweitzer and his wife, Helene, established a hospital in the province of Gabon in what was then French Equatorial Africa. This area lacked any access to medicine, and the Schweitzers saw the need for a modern facility. The acclaimed hospital they built continues to receive international support and recognition today.

Schweitzer's reverence for life was evident in his 1923 work *Philosophy of Civilization*. In it he stressed the interdependence of all living things and paved the way for the environmental and animal welfare movements. Schweitzer was awarded the Nobel Prize for Peace in 1952. In his Nobel lecture he stated, "Inspired by humanitarianism we are true to ourselves and capable of creating." He spent his later years working at his hospital and writing about the dangers of nuclear energy, testing, and the arms race between superpowers. After he retired as a surgeon he continued to oversee the hospital until his death at age ninety in Gabon.

MARTIN LUTHER KING JR.

Born January 15, 1929
Died April 4, 1968

The great American civil rights leader and clergyman was born at Atlanta, Georgia, to a Baptist clergyman father. King received his first bachelor's degree from Morehouse College at the age of nineteen, then received a bachelor of divinity degree from Crozer Theological Seminary and a doctorate from Boston University. He became pastor at Dexter Avenue Baptist Church in Montgomery, Alabama, in 1954 and copastor with his father at Ebenezer Baptist Church in Atlanta in 1960.

In 1957, King was elected president of the Southern Christian Leadership Conference, a leading civil rights organization that he had helped found. King was a student of nonviolent civil disobedience principles as articulated by Henry David Thoreau and Mohandas Gandhi, and he put them into practice during the 1950s and 1960s as a charismatic leader of Southern African Americans seeking to overcome prejudice and segregation practices. The first phase of much nonviolent civil disobedience was economic boycotts against bus, restaurant, and other services that segregated black customers. The next phase involved sit-ins and protest marches, culminating in the famous 1963 march to Washington, D.C., where under the Lincoln Memorial King proclaimed, "I have a dream . . ." *Time* magazine named him Man of the Year 1963. The next year, Congress passed the Civil Rights Act of 1964, and King received a Nobel Peace Prize (he donated all his prize money to the civil rights movement). He was the youngest person to receive the honor. The Voting Rights Act was passed in 1965.

During all his efforts, he and his family were subjected to threats, assaults, arrests, a house bombing, and other such abuse, but he became a beloved figure worldwide and a valued consultant to American presidents Kennedy and Johnson. Tragically, his life was cut short by an assassin's bullet while he was in Memphis, Tennessee.

Today, the third Monday of January is observed as a national holiday in honor of his birth.

ANDRÉ MICHELIN

Born January 16, 1853
Died April 4, 1931

Born at Clermont-Ferrand, France, André Michelin became a powerful industrialist. In 1889 he and his brother Édouard started the Michelin Company, a factory that manufactured agricultural rubber products. In 1891, the company began to make removable bicycle tires—a major innovation at the time. Michelin later become the first company to mass-produce detachable pneumatic tires for cars.

After Édouard noticed that a stack of tires could resemble a human form, André commissioned a commercial artist to design a man made of tires. The artist came up with the Michelin Man (or Bibendum) in 1898. The Michelin Man is still one of the world's most recognized advertising characters; it has represented the company in more than 170 countries. André was also responsible for the development of the Michelin guides, which catered to a new group of consumers: traveling motorists. The *Red Guide* was published in 1904. Later guides initiated the often-copied ratings system for restaurants and hotels.

BENJAMIN FRANKLIN

Born January 17, 1706
Died April 17, 1790

The eldest person to sign both the Declaration of Independence and the American Constitution, Ben Franklin was a self-made, self-educated man. Incredibly bright and inventive, Franklin played a number of influential roles over the course of his long life, including scientist, inventor, diplomat, philosopher, philanthropist, and social reformer. As the author, printer, and publisher of *Poor Richard's Almanac*, he managed to produce ideas and phrases that not only caught on during his time, but also are still used today. ("A penny saved is a penny earned" and "An ounce of prevention is worth a pound of cure" are just two examples.) His inventions, such as efficient wood-burning stoves and his Philadelphia fire insurance cooperative live on. His simple, pithy speech and writings were often aimed at ordinary citizens and were meant to be entertaining as well as educational.

He was wildly popular both in the United States and in France where he served as an able U.S. diplomat. More than 20,000 people attended his funeral in Philadelphia. Years before, in 1727, he had written an epitaph for himself: "The Body of Benjamin Franklin/Printer/Like a Covering of an old Book/Its contents torn out/And stript of its Lettering and Gilding,/Lies here, Food for Worms;/But the work shall not be lost,/It will (as he believ'd) appear once more/In a New and more beautiful Edition/Corrected and amended/By the Author."

DANIEL WEBSTER

Born January 18, 1782
Died October 24, 1852

Born at Salisbury, New Hampshire, Webster was a lawyer and served in the House of Representatives and the Senate. He was opposed to the War of 1812, and after a short term in the House of Representatives he moved to Boston and began winning important constitutional cases before the Supreme Court. As secretary of state he negotiated the Webster-Ashburton Treaty, which settled the northeast boundary between the United States and Canada. He ran for president many times but never won.

As a politician he worked hard to keep the country together and was a great orator, famous for such sayings as "Liberty and Union, now and forever, one and inseparable!" When the Southern states were pushing to expand the territories where slavery was legal, and the North was fighting to abolish all slavery he favored the Compromise of 1850, which meant supporting the Fugitive Slave Act. As secretary of state it was his job to enforce this highly controversial act requiring people in the Northern states to return runaway slaves to the South. His efforts helped hold the country together for a few more years, but eventually mounting pressures resulted in the Civil War. He died at Marshfield, Massachusetts, only a few years after gaining the passage of the compromise.

AUGUSTE COMTE

Born January 19, 1798
Died September 5, 1857

The founder of positivism and the coiner of the term *sociology*, Comte was born at Montpellier, France. Positivism is a philosophical system (and some say secular religion) that looks at facts and phenomena. Unlike many philosophies popular during Comte's time, positivism did not concern itself with issues of ultimate causes or origins. He wrote a six-volume masterwork, *Cours de philosophie positive*, as well as a rather strange four-volume work about society and religion, which was generally dismissed because of his growing mental illness. His views on the systematic religion of humanity even featured priests and a calendar of saints.

Comte is seen by many as the father of the social sciences. Early social scientists believed that natural human behavior obeys laws just as strict as those that govern physics. Comte, and many of the other social scientists who followed him, firmly believed that if they could discover these laws, they would be able to eliminate moral evils—the moral equivalent of medical scientists' attempts to uncover the ways in which diseases work as a way to prevent, control, or cure them. The goal of these scientists was to use logic and reason to eliminate human suffering.

PATRICIA NEAL

Born January 20, 1926

Born at Kentucky, internationally acclaimed stage and film actress Patricia Neal starred in Broadway productions such as *Another Part of the Forest* and *The Miracle Worker*, and in films such as *The Fountainhead* (1949) and *Hud* (1963), for which she won an Academy Award for Best Actress.

In 1966 Neal was making the film *Seven Women* when she suffered a series of sudden massive strokes. After surgery she was unable to speak and was completely paralyzed on one side. Her amazing recovery is a chapter in the archives of stroke rehabilitation.

Guided by her own recovery and experiences, she and her husband devised a system to assist other recovering stroke victims. This system was very successful and has been internationally recognized. Her recovery was complete. Two years after her illness she was able to go back to work. She starred in *The Subject Was Roses* (1968), which garnered her an Academy Award nomination. In recognition of her courage, President Lyndon Johnson gave her the Heart of the Year Award in 1968. She also received the Women's International Center Living Legacy Award in 1986. She is still active in her profession and devotes much of her time to the Patricia Neal Rehabilitation Center in Knoxville, Tennessee.

THOMAS "STONEWALL" JACKSON

Born January 21, 1824
Died May 10, 1863

American Civil War Confederate leader best known for his skillful and relentless war tactics. Born at Clarksburg, West Virginia, Jackson attended the U.S. Military Academy at West Point and served in the Mexican-American War. He resigned from the army in 1851 to teach at the Virginia Military Institute. In 1861, when the fighting between the North and the South began, Jackson was made a colonel and quickly became a general.

The name "Stonewall" was given to him for his determination and discipline at the bloody Battle of Bull Run. His many victories included battles at Cedar Run, Manassas, and Harpers Ferry. Jackson's surprise attack on the Union army in 1863 played a large part in the Confederate victory against General Joseph Hooker at Chancellorsville. However, Jackson was shot when one of his men mistook him for a member of the federal calvary. He died eight days later at Guiney Station, Virginia.

WILLA B. BROWN

Born January 22, 1906
Died July 18, 1992

Willa B. Brown was the first African-American woman to receive a commercial pilot's license in the United States. She began her career as a schoolteacher in Gary, Indiana. After a divorce and a change of heart about teaching, she moved to Chicago, Illinois, in 1932. That's when she became involved with aviation pioneer Bessie Coleman (see January 26). After taking flying lessons she became a member of two flying clubs: Challenger Air Pilot's Association and the Chicago Girls Flight Club. She was a dedicated student of flight and even purchased her own plane. In 1937 she received her pilot's license and a master's degree from Northwestern University.

Brown cofounded the National Airman's Association of America with her flight instructor Cornelius Coffee—one of the organization's goals was the promotion of African-American flight. Brown and Coffee started their own flight school in 1938, where they trained over 200 pilots in the next seven years. Some of these men went on to become a part of the famed Ninety-Ninth Pursuit Squadron at the Tuskegee Institute, where they were known as the Tuskegee Airmen. Brown's efforts to get the U.S. government to include African Americans in the Civil Pilot Training Program and the Army Air Corps put her in the spotlight. In 1942 she became the first African-American member of the Civil Air Patrol. A tireless promoter of flight to people of all backgrounds, she was selected to be a member of the Federal Aviation Agency's Women's Advisory Committee in 1972.

JOHN HANCOCK

Born January 23, 1737
Died October 8, 1793

Known to most Americans as the fellow with the biggest signature on the Declaration of Independence, Hancock played a pivotal role in a number of early dramas in U.S. history. Born into an upper-class family in the town of Quincy, Massachusetts, young Hancock was sent to live with his uncle after his father's death. His uncle, Thomas Hancock, was a successful merchant and a benefactor to Harvard University. Upon his death, John Hancock inherited Thomas's estates and at the age of twenty-seven became perhaps the richest man in New England. He was known for his love of fashionable clothing and wildly colorful carriages, but he also showed restraint and was a fair and kind employer and a good citizen. His political actions often put his considerable assets and investments at risk.

Though never regarded as a person of genius, he soon blossomed in circles of debate and discussion with the likes of Samuel Adams. It was the seizure of one of Hancock's vessels that led to the placement of British troops in Boston. Friction between citizens and soldiers led in 1770 to the Boston Massacre. This event touched off an underground revolt that featured Hancock as a brave and vocal player giving an impassioned speech to the governor asking for the removal of the troops. This speech, which made him a target for British reprisal, undid any doubts the local citizenry may have had about this wealthy man's loyalty to the cause. By 1765 Hancock had been elected selectman for the town of Boston, by 1766 he was a member of the Massachusetts House of Representatives. Gaining support from citizens and political leaders alike, he became the president of the Continental Congress in 1775. He distinguished himself by keeping the peace and moving the debate along to create the document that launched the new nation. Hancock also served as governor of Massachusetts for eleven years.

MARY LOU RETTON

Born January 24, 1968

Almost a decade after her fabulous performance at the 1984 Olympics, the Associated Press named this gymnast the Most Popular Athlete in America. Known for her enthusiasm and glowing smile, Retton has won many awards for gymnastic performances on the uneven bars and the vault and as a member of the American women's gymnastic team. In fact, she won five medals at the 1984 Olympics, the most awarded to any athlete that year. She was the first American woman ever to win a gold medal in the all-around exercise category—and scored perfect 10s in two events.

Born at West Virginia, Retton began training at the age of four. Like many committed athletes, she gave up a normal childhood to be the best. In Retton's case, she moved to Houston, Texas, at age fifteen to train with famed gymnastics coach Bela Karolyi. Mary Lou Retton's list of championships make the head spin: 1983 American Cup, 1983 American Classics, 1983 Chunichi Cup, 1984 American Cup, 1984 American Classics, 1984 U.S. Championships, and 1985 American Cup. These performances and others led to her induction into the United States Olympic Committee's Olympic Hall of Fame. She was the first gymnast to receive this honor. In 1997 she was elected into the International Gymnastics Hall of Fame.

ROBERT BOYLE

Born January 25, 1627
Died December 30, 1691

Often called the father of modern chemistry, Boyle was born into a very wealthy and aristocratic family at Lismore Castle in Munster, Ireland. The grandson of the Earl of Court, he was a great favorite of King Charles II. Though he lacked a university degree, his private tutors, years at Eaton, and more than a decade of living at Oxford and rubbing shoulders with great minds must have given him a good foundation for his work. He wanted to establish chemistry as a mathematical science based on a mechanistic theory of matter. To this end he studied hydrostatic pressure, sound, and gravity. His studies of the recently invented air pump led to improvements of the design and also to the theory now known as Boyle's law. This law states that if the temperature and quantity of a gas remain constant, the volume varies inversely with pressure.

He was also one of the founders of the Royal Society of London (1663). A man of many interests, he published books on a wide variety of subjects. Because he was chronically ill he followed medical advances very closely and did experiments of his own looking for cures to his ailments. He also attempted to develop a process for distilling fresh water from salt water at sea. His great wealth ensured that he never needed to pursue paying work. Instead he worked on whatever drew his interest and supported a number of other great thinkers and scientists who lacked financial backing.

BESSIE COLEMAN

Born January 26, 1893
Died April 30, 1926

A woman who refused to take no for an answer, Coleman had to travel to Europe when she was denied the right to become a pilot in the United States because of her race and gender. She worked as a manicurist until she could earn enough to travel to France. In Paris she was accepted to the Fédération Aéronautique Internationale, where she earned an international pilot's license in 1921. She was the first American woman to do so.

A woman of uncommon daring, she thrilled audiences upon her return to the United States where she took part in acrobatic air exhibitions. "Queen Bess" soon became well known for flying figure eights and other stunts. She avidly encouraged women and nonwhites to take up aviation. She died when she was thrown from her open cockpit during a midair practice session at Jacksonville, Florida. She was only in her midthirties at the time and her many fans mourned her passing. The budding students of aviation she inspired took up the mantle, however, each generation encouraging the next.

MIKHAIL BARYSHNIKOV

Born January 27, 1948

One of the world's most famous and arguably finest classical ballet dancers, Baryshnikov defected from the former U.S.S.R. in June 1974—running to a waiting car after a performance in Toronto. After joining the American Ballet Theatre, he found a new audience—not just of fans of ballet but also of moviegoers. He played important roles in *The Turning Point* (1977) and *White Nights* (1985). Ironically, *White Nights* tells the story of an African-American tap dancer who defects to the Soviet Union from the United States. Baryshnikov was nominated for an Academy Award as Best Supporting Actor for his work in *The Turning Point*.

Born at Riga, Latvia, "Misha" Baryshnikov was a popular soloist (starting at age nineteen) with the internationally acclaimed Kirov Ballet from 1966 to 1974. He was principal dancer with the American Ballet Theater from 1974 to 1978 and with the New York City Ballet from 1978 to 1979. He also served as the American Ballet Theater's artistic director for many years. Always intrigued by modern dance, he collaborated with choreographer Twyla Tharp often. Together, they created "Baryshnikov by Tharp," an Emmy Award–winning TV special (1985). After retiring from ballet, Baryshnikov has gone on to explore modern and jazz dance with his White Oak Project dance company—also to great acclaim.

ALICE NEEL

Born January 28, 1900
Died October 13, 1984

This famous portrait artist worked with the Federal Art Project, which was part of the U.S. Works Progress Administration's (WPA) effort to employ some of the millions of people who had been left jobless by the Great Depression. Neel promoted radical social and cultural reform at the WPA from 1933 to 1943. Her haunting portraits revealed the complex emotions and personalities of her subjects. One of her best-known works, *Harlem*, painted in 1940, depicts the effects of tuberculosis on an urban ghetto.

Neel was the daughter of a railroad clerk. She grew up in the small town of Colwyn, Pennsylvania. During a summer session at an art school, she met Carlos Enriquez, a wealthy Cuban painter. They were married after she graduated. The two had a daughter and moved to Cuba, and then returned to New York, where their daughter died of diphtheria. Neel and Enriquez had a second daughter in 1928. Shortly thereafter, Enriquez took the child, abandoning Neel, who then had a nervous breakdown. Following treatment, Neel returned to New York, where she continued to paint portraits, often of people living in poverty, as well as landscapes. Her style of painting was very different from what was considered fashionable in New York in the middle of the twentieth century. Her work did not gain much of a following until the 1960s, when the artist was in her sixties.

JOHN D. ROCKEFELLER JR.

Born January 29, 1874
Died May 11, 1960

Known mostly as a philanthropist, John D. Rockefeller Jr. was the son of the wealthy industrialist John D. Rockefeller Sr. He was born at Cleveland, although he spent most of his life in New York City. Rockefeller joined his father's business, but he also created the Rockefeller Institute for Medical Research, the General Education Board, the Rockefeller Foundation, the Laura Spelman Rockefeller Memorial, and the International Education Board. His interest in the conservation of historical resources led to the restoration of colonial Williamsburg, which has become one of the most popular historic attractions in the United States.

In the 1930s, Rockefeller helped create Rockefeller Center, an international business and entertainment hub in New York City. His 1946 gift of $85 million to the United Nations made it possible for the UN to build its headquarters in New York City. Over the years Rockefeller's gifts created new programs, buildings, and services that brought aid to people all over the world. His children and grandchildren have continued in his philanthropic spirit in New York City and across the nation.

FRANKLIN DELANO ROOSEVELT

Born January, 30, 1882
Died April 12, 1945

The thirty-second president of the United States, Roosevelt served from 1933 to 1945; he was the only president ever to be elected four times. (The Twenty-second Amendment to the Constitution, which was ratified in 1951, limited presidents to a maximum of two terms in office.) He was born at Hyde Park, New York, to a patrician family—a distant cousin of Theodore Roosevelt. In 1921, Roosevelt fell ill with polio and was paralyzed for some time, eventually gaining enough movement to walk with braces. Because his disability made travel difficult, his wife, Eleanor, often appeared as his representative at events around the country. She became one of the most important female leaders of the 1930s and 1940s, reporting back to Roosevelt what she learned in her travels.

Roosevelt's fierce determination saw the country through the difficult times of the Great Depression (1929–1940) and led to his success as one of the leading figures of World War II. Before the United States even entered the war he supported the Allies by supplying them with war materials through the Lend-Lease Act. After the Japanese bombed the U.S. naval base at Pearl Harbor, Roosevelt (along with Russia's Joseph Stalin and Britain's Winston Churchill) became involved in broad decision making that impacted the direction of the war against Nazi Germany. Roosevelt also helped lay the groundwork for the United Nations before his sudden death in 1945 at Warm Springs, Georgia.

FRANZ (PETER) SCHUBERT

Born January 31, 1797
Died November 19, 1828

This Austrian composer, born at Nussdorferstrasse, shaped the art song, or German *lied*, and thereby brought about a new art form. Schubert showed musical talent from a very early age and won a scholarship with the Vienna imperial organist and composer Antonio Salieri at the age of eleven. While still in his midteens, he composed the song "Gretchen am Spinnrade," based on a poem by Goethe, and a new musical form was born. A few years later he performed one of his works publicly for the first time. The *Italian Overture in C Major* was a big hit, and he went on to compose works that gained him even more notice. *Piano Sonata in A Major, D.644* and the *Trout Quintet* are among his best-known compositions.

In 1822 Schubert contracted a serious illness, but he continued to create music. In 1828, at the age of thirty-one, already weakened by the previous illness, he contracted typhoid fever and died after several weeks. There has always been speculation about how much more this creative genius would have contributed to the music world had he lived another thirty years.

FEBRUARY

LANGSTON HUGHES

Born February 1, 1902
Died May 22, 1967

Born at Joplin, Missouri, James Langston Hughes was one of America's great poets. He was a leading light of the Harlem Renaissance, a flourishing of African-American artistic activity in New York in the 1920s and '30s. The contributions made by black musicians, writers, and painters of Harlem continue to impact American culture today.

Hughes published his first book of poetry, *The Weary Blues*, in 1926, and he soon became known as a passionate chronicler of the black experience. And as jazz, with its color and new rhythms, grew in popularity, it became a vital influence in his work.

Hughes produced a vast amount of work in many forms—novel, autobiography, short story, and drama—in addition to the moving poetry for which he is so well known. Among his works are the poetry collections *Shakespeare in Harlem* (1942) and *Montage of a Dream Deferred* (1951); the novel *Not Without Laughter* (1930); and the autobiographies *The Big Sea* (1940) and *I Wonder as I Wander* (1956).

The street on which he lived for so many years—East 127th Street—is now named "Langston Hughes Place," and his former home there has been designated a New York landmark.

STAN GETZ

Born February 2, 1927
Died June 6, 1991

Born at Philadelphia, Getz began playing music at age thirteen and went on to become a world-famous tenor saxophone player. His first professional job came with Jack Teagarden's band at age sixteen, and he went on to play with Stan Kenton, Jimmy Dorsey, Benny Goodman, and Woody Herman throughout the 1940s and '50s. He had a golden sound, and his services were in high demand. The darker side of his rise to fame was that, like many musicians of his time, Getz struggled with drug and alcohol addiction most of his life.

Getz was known for taking a song and making it his own—he had a way of not losing the melody while embroidering it with subtle jazz shadings using the high register of his instrument. He influenced a whole generation of young jazz greats, including John Coltrane. Getz began playing Brazilian music in the early 1960s. He recorded the incredibly popular song "The Girl from Ipanema" in 1963. By that time he had international recognition. He was the driving force behind the bossa nova craze in the 1960s and '70s. He died at Malibu, California.

NORMAN ROCKWELL

Born February 3, 1894
Died November 8, 1978

This beloved American artist and illustrator was born at New York City. He chose the artistic life while still a youth. Halfway through high school, he dropped out to attend art school full-time. While still a student, Rockwell got a job illustrating children's books. Shortly after, he began illustrating *Boy's Life* magazine and was eventually given the position of art director.

In 1916 Rockwell sold his first painting to George Horace Lorimer, editor of the *Saturday Evening Post*, for that magazine's cover. It was the start of a long-term relationship with the magazine. His realistic (often both sentimental and humorous) depictions of everyday American life (such as getting a first haircut or celebrating a Thanksgiving dinner) have become iconic. His *Rosie the Riveter* and *The Four Freedoms* were popular morale-boosting images during World War II. Rockwell received the Presidential Medal of Freedom in 1977. He died at Stockbridge, Massachusetts, at the age of eighty-four.

36

CHARLES LINDBERGH

Born February 4, 1902
Died August 26, 1974

Pioneering aviator born at Detroit, Michigan, Lindbergh was raised in Minnesota. He started flying while in college and enlisted in the army in 1924 so that he could continue his training to become a pilot. His first flying job involved running mail from St. Louis to Chicago and back. He raised money from St. Louis businessmen to construct a single-winged plane that allowed him to compete for a $25,000 prize offered to the first pilot to complete a solo trip across the Atlantic. In 1927 he flew his new plane, the *Spirit of St. Louis*, from California to New York breaking all previous transcontinental records. He went on to cross the Atlantic in thirty-three hours and thirty minutes, landing outside Paris. He was given a ticker-tape parade upon his return and awarded the Congressional Medal of Honor and the Distinguished Flying Cross.

In 1929 he married Anne Morrow, who became a pilot and copiloted their plane to set a new transcontinental speed record. The kidnapping and subsequent murder of their infant son in 1932 caused the Lindberghs to move to Europe to escape the press. As war clouds loomed, Lindbergh came out publicly as an isolationist. He changed his isolationist stance after the bombing of Pearl Harbor. In 1944 he went to the Pacific as an adviser to the military and flew combat missions despite his civilian status. He went on to write a successful autobiography, which won a Pulitzer Prize in 1954. Lindbergh died at the age of seventy-two at his home in Hawaii.

HENRY "HANK" AARON

Born February 5, 1934

A powerful baseball hitter who shattered previous records, Aaron also had to shatter the game's stereotyping and racial prejudice. His record speaks for itself: 755 home runs, the most ever by a major leaguer. He also had a knack for hitting in runs (2,297). His lifetime hitting average is an amazing .305. Born at Mobile, Alabama, Aaron made fans wild when he hit for the Braves, first in Milwaukee and later in Atlanta. He said that the thing he liked about baseball was that it really came down to ownership: if he hit a run it was *his* run, if he goofed it was *his* mistake.

In 1974 he performed the unthinkable: he hit his 715th career home run, which meant he surpassed Babe Ruth's record. The lead-up to this event was marked by what today seems an impossible level of racism. Aaron was hitting very well in 1973 and there was increasing speculation about his beating Ruth's record. The mail he received also increased to an estimated 3,000 letters a day. Sadly, much of this mail was written by racists, some of whom threatened to kill him. On April 8, 1974, as the Braves played for their largest crowd ever (over 53,000), his fans and teammates went crazy as he rounded the bases to break the record.

Years later he is a busy baseball and media executive who still keeps the letters because they remind him not to be surprised or hurt by the way people can be.

BOB MARLEY

Born February 6, 1945
Died May 11, 1981

An influential reggae singer and songwriter who performed for many years with his acclaimed group the Wailers, Marley was born at Rhoden Hall in northern Jamaica. He became a follower of the political/religious Rastafarian movement. Rastafarians see the late Ethiopian emperor Haile Selassie I as a holy leader. Selassie was formerly known as Ras Tafari, hence the name of the movement. Rasta is closely associated with reggae music, which features a Caribbean-accented style. Bob Marley was the first artist to popularize this style of music; he brought it to the attention of a whole generation of pop musicians and rappers both in the United States and abroad. Influential albums include *Exodus* (1977) and *Uprising* (1980).

Marley is also known for his lyrics of love and redemption in the midst of chaos and poverty. Jamaican elections throughout the nation's history have been marred by violence. In the 1970s Marley wrote a tune for his country at election time asking for everyone to come together. Marley's subsequent 1978 "One Love" concert—during which he invited opposing party leaders to come up onstage together—is fondly remembered by peace-loving Jamaicans everywhere. Bob Marley died of cancer at an early age but left musical children, including eldest son Ziggy Marley, to keep the family musical tradition alive.

LAURA INGALLS WILDER

Born February 7, 1867
Died February 10, 1957

Wilder turned her memories of growing up in the 1870s and '80s into a series of wildly popular books for children, heartwarming tales of a pioneer family in the woods and plains of the Midwest. Her first book was *Little House in the Big Woods*, which was loosely based on her early childhood near Pepin, Wisconsin, on the Mississippi River in what was at that time a very dense and dark forest. Wilder went on to write *Little House on the Prairie*, a closely observed depiction of life in rural Kansas; *On the Banks of Plum Creek*, which tells of life in rural Minnesota; and *By the Shores of Silver Lake*, the story of life in South Dakota.

Her sweet and sometimes sad tales have touched generations of readers and continue to inspire festivals, parades, plays, poems, and artwork on the theme of the Ingalls family. Since the author's death, picture books written by others have opened up the world of Laura, Mary, Ma, and Pa to an even younger audience. Fans wanting to know more about the life and times of the early pioneers often visit the towns mentioned in her books, which has led to flourishing historic sites, museums, and reenactments. Perhaps the best-known outgrowth of Ingalls's works was the 1970s TV adaptation of *Little House on the Prairie*, starring Michael Landon as Charles Ingalls. The show was immensely popular and is still running in syndication.

JULES VERNE

Born February 8, 1828
Died March 24, 1905

Known as the father of science fiction, Jules Verne was born at Nantes, France, to a seafaring family. As a young man, he studied law in Paris and then spent several years traveling in Europe and America. He was fascinated with science, technology, and geography. In particular, he was interested in the future of transportation. This fascination came across in his works of fiction such as *Five Weeks in a Balloon* (1863), *A Journey to the Center of the Earth* (1864), *The Adventures of Captain Hatteras* (1866), *20,000 Leagues Under the Sea* (1870), and his best-known book, *Around the World in Eighty Days* (1873).

These novels explored the possibility of traveling to every corner of the Earth—through the air, over water, under water, and through the surface—in a plausible manner. *From the Earth to the Moon* (1865) was one of the earliest imaginings of space travel. His writing generally focused on an imagined future containing new technologies and machines; it gave birth to a new genre of writing: science fiction. It is thought Verne's writings, like those of today's science fiction writers, inspired engineers and mechanics to think in new ways. Verne died at Amiens, France.

ALICE WALKER

Born February 9, 1944

Born the eighth child of Georgia sharecroppers, Walker lost sight in one eye when one of her brothers shot her with a BB gun. Her visual impairment did not keep her from excelling in high school, where she graduated valedictorian. She went on to Spelman College. From there she went on to Sarah Lawrence College in New York where she became active in the civil rights movement. Much of Walker's writing explores issues of domination and submission, and the sometimes violent relationships between black men and women.

Walker has a long list of poems, novels, and awards to her credit. Her writings are required reading in many high school and college literature classes. She is perhaps best known for her Pulitzer Prize–winning book *The Color Purple* (1982), which also won the American Book Award and was made into an Oscar-nominated movie by Steven Spielberg. Walker continues to write and to speak out on issues that concern her, such as the women's movement, the antinuclear movement, and civil rights. In 1984 Walker started her own publishing company, Wild Trees Press.

FRANCES MOORE LAPPÉ

Born February 10, 1944

Vegetarian activist and writer Lappé was born at Pendleton, Oregon. Lappé's book *Diet for a Small Planet* created shock waves in some communities—and hardly a ripple in others. Her book advocated vegetarianism, and while it was a cookbook, it was much more than that. Lappé's book was a wakeup call for the West to see how many resources are wasted by our meat-heavy diet. A large number of people gave up meat after reading her book, and vegetarian items started showing up on restaurant menus and grocery store shelves. Of course, many people went on eating as they always had, but the word was out: eating lighter is good for the body and the planet.

Lappé cofounded the organization Food First and recently authored an influential work called *Hope's Edge*, which gives examples of food and politics, health and poverty, environmental disaster and recovery from all over the world. Her philosophy that we don't have to accept a continuing decline in the quality of our air and water, that we don't have to give up on feeding the hungry, and that people's choices make big changes possible have made her a hero to many. Her little movement of eating clean, organically raised foods proved persuasive to world-class chefs, business executives, school lunch program administrators and politicians.

LYDIA MARIA CHILD

Born February 11, 1802
Died October 20, 1880

Born at Medford, Massachusetts, Child became a strong advocate of social reform. She authored *The Frugal Housewife* (1829), which was very popular among women of her day and was published in many editions. In 1836, seeing a need for positive reading material for children, she founded the *Juvenile Miscellany*, the first American magazine for children. A fervent abolitionist, she and her husband published *An Appeal in Favor of That Class of Americans Called Africans*, which called for the education of blacks, a revolutionary idea at the time. They also edited a weekly newspaper called the *National Anti-Slavery Standard*. Child wrote on other social issues as well, such as feminism and capital punishment. Her writings and teachings influenced many important policymakers as well as common citizens. She lived and wrote into her late seventies. She died at Wayland, Massachusetts.

CHARLES ROBERT DARWIN

Born February 12, 1809
Died April 19, 1882

One of the most influential scientists in history, this biologist, botanist, geologist, and author, born at Shrewsbury, England, changed the way the world thinks about the development of life on Earth. His theories were presented in his masterwork, *On the Origin of Species by Means of Natural Selection, or the Preservation of Favoured Races in the Struggle for Life* (1859), and in *The Descent of Man* (1871).

Born into a prosperous family, the young Darwin was attending Cambridge when he was offered the chance to sail with the HMS *Beagle* on a five-year voyage (1831–1836) to explore South America. Spirited by recent theories of geology and the age of the earth and by new fossil discoveries, Darwin joined the trip as an expedition naturalist and collected thousands of animal and fossil specimens. Darwin's journals written during the trip were published to critical and popular acclaim.

His observations sparked questions that upon deliberation formed the basis for his later theory: Why had certain animal forms become extinct? What explained variations in species? During his voyage, on a visit to the Galapagos Islands, Darwin noted the differentiation in the ground finches of the island that had come from the mainland many generations back. Darwin observed that natural variations, such as beak shape, created advantages for certain birds, who were more likely to thrive (survival of the fittest) and pass on those advantageous traits to their offspring. Over many generations, that trait became more common and eventually led to the creation of a new species.

His theory of "natural selection" created a public furor when *On the Origin of Species* was published November 22, 1859 (the controversy extended into the twentieth century—see August 3, for information on the "Monkey Trial"). While the media and public debated the implications of Darwin's work, the man himself continued studying and writing, while battling ill health, for the next several decades. Given awards and medals by scientific societies and nations for his vast studies, Darwin was honored upon his death by burial in London's Westminster Abbey.

GRANT WOOD

Born February 13, 1892
Died February 12, 1942

A uniquely American artist known for his powerful realism and satirical paintings, Wood was born near Anamosa, Iowa. In addition to being a gifted painter, he was also a high school and college teacher, woodworker, printer, and sculptor. His best-known works include *Fall Plowing* and *Stone City*. The scene from his most famous painting, *American Gothic*, is familiar to almost everyone. It depicts a gaunt elderly couple (actually a brother and sister): a tired-looking man in overalls holding a pitchfork with a serious-looking woman by his side in front of a farmhouse. This scene has been used for hundreds of oddball and humorous projects in print and electronic media; it is one of the most copied paintings in the country.

Wood was a compatriot of Thomas Hart Benton and John Steuart Curry; together they represented what came to be known as the school of the Regional American Landscape. They all enjoyed great success during the Depression, when the nation was naturally attuned to American problems and strengths. Wood's popularity waned as the economy improved. He died at Iowa City, on the verge of giving up painting, just one day before his fiftieth birthday.

MARY ANN ("AUNT MARY") PROUT

Born February 14, 1801
Died 1884

Mary Ann Prout was born at Baltimore, Maryland. There is some debate in historical circles about whether or not she was born a slave. However, the record is clear on her talents as a social activist, humanitarian, and teacher. Prout founded a day school in 1830. Actively involved in her church, Prout founded a secret society in 1867 that became the Independent Order of St. Luke. This fraternal order was organized to provide assistance to needy African-American families for everything from medical care to burial services. By 1900, this organization had expanded to 1,500 chapters across the country.

A solid example of the ripple effect created by Prout's work is the story of Maggie Walker, the first female bank founder in the United States. Walker joined the Order of St. Luke at fourteen, at which point she was exposed to the ideas of self-help and race solidarity. After gaining financial experience as a treasurer, Walker began to see how black money in Baltimore could be put to use for the improvement of the black community. She went on to found the St. Luke Penny Savings Bank, which was an immediate success. People lined up the first day to deposit thousands of dollars. The bank provided a safe way to save for Christmas, retirement, or other future expenses and it proved an unbiased institution from which to borrow for business or personal needs. This bank is still in existence today as the Consolidated Banks and Trust and has assets totaling approximately $116 million. "Aunt Mary" Prout died at Baltimore in her late eighties.

ERNEST SHACKLETON

Born February 15, 1874
Died January 5, 1922

British Antarctic explorer, born at Kilkea, Ireland, known for his excellent leadership abilities and his role in one of the greatest adventures in the history of polar exploration. When Shackleton was preparing to cross the Antarctic via the South Pole, he put a help-wanted advertisement in a paper in London asking for strong men willing to work long hours in dangerous conditions for low wages. All he promised was adventure and possible recognition upon their unlikely return to civilization. It had the highest response rate of any ad in the paper's history! He hired an unusual crew; many of his hiring decisions seemingly were based on nothing more than hunch. The crew set sail in August of 1914 on the ship *Endurance*, which was named for Shackleton's family motto.

In 1915, the ship was caught in drifting ice in the Weddell Sea. The men tried everything they could think of to try to free the vessel from the ice, but finally they were forced to abandon ship. They saved all they could and, packing themselves into three lifeboats, they headed 100 miles to Elephant Island, which they reached after a series of life-threatening events, in April 1916. From there Shackleton decided to travel 900 miles to a whaling camp at South Georgia to get help for his crew. He chose their best boat and best sailors. These five men in a tiny open boat braved violent storms, with almost no navigational readings. They suffered raging thirst, utter exhaustion, and constant wet and cold. Against the odds, by a combination of luck and skill, they arrived at the coast of their destination in just fourteen days. They still had to hike 150 miles and climb glaciers to find the whaling station on the far side. Shackleton returned with a rescue party to save the rest of the crew. He did not lose a single member of the expedition. Because his photographer hauled the heavy equipment through the whole trip, today we can see what they saw on one of the greatest adventures of all time. Shackleton died at Grytviken, South Georgia, during his fourth expedition.

LEVAR BURTON

Born February 16, 1958

Known for his role as Kunta Kinte in the award-winning TV miniseries *Roots*, and as Geordi La Forge in *Star Trek: The Next Generation*, Burton also hosts the award-winning public TV show *Reading Rainbow*. Only nineteen years old in 1977 when he took a starring role in *Roots*, Burton's career was firmly launched. *Roots* told the story of one family from Africa to American slavery and beyond in a series that lasted eight nights and brought in an almost unheard of 71 percent viewership. Perhaps as many as 130 million Americans were glued to their sets. For the first time they saw gripping images of Africans ripped from pastoral villages, crammed into the gruesome holds of slave ships, whipped, beaten, and humiliated, and somehow surviving. Burton and others expected a sea change in the TV industry for blacks after *Roots*, but they were disappointed. Burton set his sights on becoming a producer, writer, and director in the hopes of making needed changes in the industry.

Years later a highly successful actor, LeVar Burton has also succeeded in breaking some barriers in the TV and movie industries where he has landed a number of directing and production jobs. He narrates many popular books on tape and children's films, including the *Children's Penny Theatre*. His PBS show was nominated for eight daytime Emmy Awards, and he received a National Association for the Advancement of Colored People Image Award.

ARCANGELO CORELLI

Born February 17, 1653
Died January 8, 1713

Popular violinist, conductor, and composer Arcangelo Corelli was born into a distinguished family at Fusignano, Italy. He established himself in Rome in the 1670s, where he attracted the patronage of many prominent citizens, among them Queen Christina of Sweden.

Corelli is known for popularizing the *concerto grosso*, which involves a small group of soloists with full orchestra. (This type of music was popular right up until the advent of the solo concerto, which was fixed in its classical form by Mozart.) Corelli also published a small but exquisite collection of sonatas and concertos. He had a reputation for mentoring students in a violin technique that disdained showy virtuosity. He died at Rome, Italy.

TONI MORRISON

Born February 18, 1931

Born Chloe Anthony Wofford, in the town of Lorain, Ohio, Morrison was the second of four children in a black working-class family. Morrison showed an early interest in literature and studied humanities at Howard and Cornell universities before taking academic posts at a number of universities including Howard, Yale, and Princeton. Her first novel, published in 1970, won praise from readers and critics alike. Her writing is powerful, bold, and poetic; no matter what the topic, her dialogue rings true. She depicts the joys and agonies of characters in the black community, making them the friends, relatives, or enemies of the reader. She brings her internal world into the mind of the reader so that her powerful images become an unshakable part of the mind's scenery.

Toni Morrison has published many novels: *The Bluest Eye, Sula, Song of Solomon, Tar Baby, Beloved,* and *Jazz.* Her academic essays concern race, ethnicity, and gender and are often required reading for college students in literature and ethnic studies courses. Morrison has also worked as an editor, critic, and public lecturer. The British Broadcasting Corporation (BBC) selected Morrison as one of the century's 100 greatest artists. In 1993 she won the Noble Prize for Literature. The committee wrote that Toni Morrison "in novels characterized by visionary force and poetic import, gives life to an essential aspect of American reality." In the speech introducing the prize Morrison was praised for her ability to see humor even when it is surrounded by a situation of great gravity. Morrison, whose topics can be painful, sad, beautiful, and haunting, says her writing "rises from delight, not disappointment."

NICOLAUS COPERNICUS

Born February 19, 1473
Died May 24, 1543

Born at Torun, Poland, Copernicus attended university in Bologna, Italy, where he studied ancient Greek astronomers' works and became fascinated by the movements of the heavenly bodies—the planets and the sun. He came to believe that the sun is the center of our planetary system, a premise that was considered religious blasphemy at the time. Copernicus returned to Poland after his graduation and worked as a priest but continued to make detailed observations of the planets. Given the limited tools available to him, his calculations were truly astounding. He was convinced his theory was correct. Confident he could prove it, he corresponded with other great thinkers of the day. Friends encouraged him to publish, but he refused because he felt he could not go publicly against the teachings of the church.

In 1543, on his deathbed, he relented and allowed publication of his book, *On the Revolutions of the Celestial Spheres.* This single work of scientific observation and calculation changed the way the Western world viewed Earth's place in the heavens. Until this time everyone thought that the stars and sun revolved around Earth, which was the center of the universe. His book is widely considered to be one of the most important books ever written.

ANSEL ADAMS

Born February 20, 1902
Died April 22, 1984

This world-famous photographer and conservationist was born at San Francisco, California. He came from a wealthy background and was training to be a concert pianist when photography took his fancy. A tireless advocate for the protection of U.S. natural parks and wilderness areas, he worked for the Sierra Club from the age of seventeen, eventually serving as its director and as its environmental spokesman for land protection before Congress. He moved to Yosemite in 1937 and later Carmel, California. He continued to be the country's best spokesman for the preservation of open lands.

Adams's painstaking control of the photographic process created incomparable prints. He managed to show the vastness of his subjects while preserving the intimacy of detail. Black-and-white photographs of national parks and western and southwestern landscapes gained him worldwide recognition. He helped create the photography department of the Museum of Modern Art in 1940, the first such department in a museum. In 1943 he documented the conditions of Japanese Americans forced into internment camps during World War II. He taught photography for decades and wrote a number of books on the subject. In 1984, the year of his death, the U.S. Congress created the Ansel Adams Wilderness Area between Yosemite National Park and the John Muir Wilderness Area. He remained active into his eighties and died at Carmel, California.

ERMA BOMBECK

Born February 21, 1927
Died April 22, 1996

Writer, humorist, homemaker, and teacher, Bombeck overcame many hurdles on her way to success. Her father died when she was young, leaving his struggling family in near poverty. Bombeck managed to get to college to study journalism only to discover she had a serious kidney disease that would likely cause her to suffer kidney failure. Many faculty members at that time were not encouraging women to pursue careers of any sort, much less journalism. After college she set out to prove them wrong and worked for five years as a reporter for the *Ohio Journal Herald*. By this time she had married and wanted to start a family. She left writing for a while to be a homemaker and mom to her three kids.

Her children provided her with plenty of funny stories. When the youngest started school Bombeck asked an editor of a local paper to give her a daily column. It took her months to persuade him. In 1964, he finally gave in and agreed to pay her $3 per column. He was amazed by the readers' response to her column, which she called "At Wit's End." Other papers soon asked to run her column. By 1965, Bombeck's humorous column was syndicated and ran in more than 500 newspapers across the country. She became a popular speaker and published books with titles that reflected her special brand of humor: *Family: Ties That Bind and Gag*; *A Marriage Made in Heaven . . .Or Too Tired for an Affair*; *Motherhood: The Second Oldest Profession*; *When You Look Like Your Passport Photo, It's Time to Go Home*; *If Life Is a Bowl of Cherries What Am I Doing in the Pits?*; and *The Grass Is Always Greener over the Septic Tank*. Her writing was a source of support to many women struggling with one of the hardest and worst-paying jobs on earth—homemaking. Bombeck spent her final years battling breast cancer and kidney failure. Born at Dayton, Ohio, she died at San Francisco, California, at the age of sixty-nine.

GEORGE WASHINGTON

Born February 22, 1732
Died December 14, 1799

The first president of the United States, Washington was "first in war, first in peace, and first in the hearts of his countrymen," according to Henry "Light Horse Harry" Lee. Born at Westmoreland County, Virginia, Washington was educated at home where he lived until his midteens when he went to work as a surveyor. His father owned several parcels of land and when he died, a plantation called Mount Vernon passed to Washington's older half-brother and eventually to Washington himself. This land beckoned him back from war and duty, but despite wishing for a quiet country life, Washington would serve his young country over and over.

By the 1770s Washington had served in the Virginia Militia where he was promoted to colonel. He had also been elected to represent Virginia at the first and second Continental Congresses. In 1775 the delegates unanimously elected him as commander-in-chief of the armed forces when it appeared military action against the British was inevitable. The war went on for many years, and Washington continued to inspire his troops and the American cause. After Britain was defeated, Washington returned to his plantation thinking his era of public service had ended. As Congress wrangled over the Constitution, Washington was again drawn in and served Virginia as a delegate. In 1789 his fellow delegates unanimously elected him president of the United States of America. He was charged with seeing to the organization of a whole new government, strained relations with Britain, angry Indian tribes, and a drained treasury. Washington rose to the challenge and created executive policies so sound that presidents still follow them today. He served two terms; despite pressure to serve a third, he refused. He believed that a person's role as president should be short-term so that no president would be tempted to become a king. Shortly after helping raise an army to fight the French, Washington retired in 1796. He enjoyed very little time at his beloved Mount Vernon before dying from a severe throat infection in 1799.

W. E. B. DUBOIS

Born February 23, 1868
Died August 27, 1963

An American educator and leader of the movement for black equality, DuBois was born William Edward Burghart DuBois at Great Barrington, Massachusetts. The only child of a disabled, impoverished mother, Dubois showed signs of greatness from his early days and went on to attend some of the finest universities of his time. He completed a Ph.D. from Harvard and a famous study of black Philadelphia. This study led to his theory of the Talented Tenth, in which he suggested that the black elite should help lift up others in their community. In 1909 he wrote: "The cost of liberty is less than the price of repression." He published a famous book of essays entitled *The Souls of Black Folk* (1903), in which he examined the idea of "double consciousness," his theory that black people must work to reconcile their need to be black and their need to assimilate. He was often in conflict with Booker T. Washington and other moderate black leaders of his time. He joined ranks with other progressive blacks to form the National Association for the Advancement of Colored People (NAACP) in 1909. Black leaders of the 1920s criticized him for being out of touch with common folk.

A committed socialist, he had a falling-out with his party on account of their racist policies. He also bickered with the communists, but after he wrote *Black Reconstruction* he found himself more in agreement with them. McCarthy-era politics victimized DuBois—his passport was revoked due to his refusal to sign a government statement condemning communism. He advocated pan-Africanism and spent time abroad gathering support for a pro-Africa movement. In his later years he moved to Ghana where he died at the city of Accra at the age of ninety-five.

JOHANNES GUTENBERG

Born February 24, 1400
Died February 3, 1468

A metalworker and talented craftsman who was born and died at Mainz, Germany, Gutenberg was the inventor of movable type. From about 1434 to 1455, Gutenberg labored in secret to develop metal type that could be moved and used over and over to create printed pages. Printers then used his press almost without change until the twentieth century.

One of his first works was the forty-two-line Bible known as the Gutenberg Bible or Mazarin Bible. Because his type was constructed of durable metal instead of hand-carved wood, each letter could be moved and reused to form new words. His press revolutionized the printing world. Previously books were the result of months or even years of painstaking labor. Because of Gutenberg's invention, written works, which had been until then something only the very rich could afford, became something almost everyone could afford. Today the industrialized world is experiencing a similar revolution in the written word, as computer technology may one day make obsolete books printed on paper.

MILLICENT FENWICK

Born February 25, 1910
Died September 16, 1992

Born Millicent Hammond at New York, New York, in the era before women were allowed to vote, Fenwick was a fashion model and author of a book on etiquette before she turned to politics. Like many women, she started her political career by serving on a school board. She later served as a member of the New Jersey General Assembly and as a United States congresswoman. A fiscally conservative Republican with liberal views on human issues, she was hard to categorize. Over the years Fenwick supported many important causes but she pointed to her sponsorship of the 1975 Helsinki human rights accords as her proudest achievement. She also fought for civil rights, peace in Vietnam, aid for the poor, reduction of military programs, gun control, and restrictions on capital punishment. Her charming upper-class manners combined with a variety of personal quirks (she publicly smoked a pipe) made her unusually popular—she even served as the inspiration for cartoonist Garry Trudeau's *Doonesbury* character Lacey Davenport. Her leadership provided inspiration to the generation of female politicians who followed her.

JOHN HARVEY KELLOGG

Born February 26, 1852
Died December 14, 1943

Born at Livingston County, Michigan, Kellogg was a surgeon and health propagandist who advocated good health through a strict vegetarian diet. He ran a sanitarium (health institution) in Battle Creek, Michigan, where he established an experimental food laboratory in an effort to develop more nutritious edible products. In the early 1890s, he developed the first flaked cereals, first of wheat, then of corn and rice. Up until this time, families ate only oatmeal or other slow-cooked hot grains if they wanted cereal for breakfast.

With his brother Will, Kellogg brought the cereals to the market, where they gained in popularity. The brothers established what would eventually become a cereal dynasty. John and Will had a falling-out that resulted in a legal battle, and Will won the right to sell the cereal under the Kellogg name. John died at Battle Creek, where the Kellogg Company is still headquartered.

MARIAN ANDERSON

Born February 27, 1897
Died April 8, 1993

Considered one of history's finest contraltos, Anderson was known for the wide range, rich color, and tonal purity of her voice as well as for her interpretive ability. She excelled in a wide range of musical genres. After hearing her sing in 1953, famed conductor Arturo Toscanini told her, "Yours is a voice such as one is privileged to hear only once in a hundred years." She began her career singing in church, and in 1925 her church entered her in a contest to appear with the New York Philharmonic Orchestra. She won the contest in a field of 300 contestants. Her early career was fraught with disappointments and frustration, as many bookings were denied to her on account of her race. She took her career to Europe where she studied with some of the finest teachers and was warmly received by the public.

Anderson received wide publicity back home in the United States when, in 1939, the Daughters of the American Revolution refused to let her sing at Constitution Hall in Washington, D.C., because she was black. Many of its most prominent members, including First Lady Eleanor Roosevelt, resigned in protest. Eleanor Roosevelt helped arrange for Anderson to sing on the steps of the Lincoln Memorial on Easter Sunday. An estimated crowd of 75,000 showed up to hear her sing that day, and many more listened to the live broadcast. The beauty of her voice and the dignity with which she performed held the nation spellbound. In 1957, at the age of sixty, she broke another barrier when she became the first African American to perform with the New York Metropolitan Opera. She was later chosen to sing the national anthem at President Kennedy's inauguration, and in 1963 President Lyndon Johnson awarded her the Presidential Medal of Freedom. Born at Philadelphia, Pennsylvania, she died at Portland, Oregon.

LINUS PAULING

Born February 28, 1901
Died August 19, 1994

Award-winning chemist born at Portland, Oregon, Pauling was best known for his study of molecular structures in connection with quantum mechanics. He formed the theory of electronegativity that explained the behavior of electrons in a covalent bond.

Pauling's mother tried to keep him away from school when he was a young man, because she wanted him to help support the family after his father's death. He refused to quit school, sometimes working as many as a hundred hours a week in a wide variety of jobs in addition to attending school. Much of what he learned was self-taught since he often knew more than his teachers. Before he could finish college he was hired to teach. Over the years, his research, teaching, and publishing gained him a reputation as a maverick genius who stayed true to himself.

He was called to testify before the Senate where he denounced the idea that Americans should be forced to sign loyalty oaths. Even though he clearly was not a communist and had no connections to communism, McCarthy-era politicians took away his passport—they claimed that he hadn't denounced communism "strongly enough." His options were curtailed when he couldn't leave the country. However, he regained his passport with only two weeks to spare after being notified of his first Nobel Prize in chemistry in 1954. Pauling's second Nobel Prize (for peace) came in 1962. He and his wife remained committed to peace even when it wasn't popular to do so, and this adherence to their beliefs cost them personal and job security. Pauling continued to teach and also to research diverse topics. He studied the chemistry of the mind to better help mentally retarded people. He studied the effects of high doses of vitamin C in the hope of curing the common cold and facilitating cancer prevention and recovery. A person of wide-ranging interests combined with great energy and high standards of ethics, Pauling is one of the greats of his century. He died at his ranch in Big Sur, California, at the age of ninety-three.

MARCH

DONALD "DEKE" SLAYTON

Born March 1, 1924
Died June 13, 1993

Donald Kent Slayton, born at Sparta, Wisconsin, was one of the original seven astronauts picked by NASA for Project Mercury in 1959, a program dedicated to the U.S. race against the Soviets to explore space. He had spent years serving his country in World War II as an Army Air Corps bomber pilot (he flew sixty-three combat missions), pilot instructor, test pilot, and member of the National Guard.

Slayton was to be America's second astronaut in orbit. He was diagnosed with an irregular heartbeat, however, and so was held back. Despite the disappointment, Slayton persevered and became an invaluable member of the operations team at Johnson Space Center. He worked diligently to improve his health through diet and fitness, and in 1972 his condition was upgraded to "flight status." On July 15, 1975, at the age of fifty-one, Slayton finally made his flight into space as pilot on the *Apollo* module that linked up with the Soviet *Soyuz 19*. *Apollo* and *Soyuz* docked, and for the first time Americans and Soviets met in space. After this historic flight, Slayton continued with NASA as a manager. He later operated his own private commercial rocket company (the first such company ever) from 1982 until his death in 1993 at League City, Texas.

THEODOR SEUSS GEISEL ("DR. SEUSS")

Born March 2, 1904
Died September 24, 1991

Theodor Seuss Geisel was born at Springfield, Massachusetts. He launched his creative career doing commercial art and then worked in propaganda for the United States during World War II. He became a children's author with *And to Think That I Saw It on Mulberry Street* (1937), which he submitted to twenty-seven publishing houses before it was accepted by Vanguard Press. Dr. Seuss, as he came to be known, went on to publish many outstanding books for young children including *Hop on Pop*, *The Cat in the Hat*, *How the Grinch Stole Christmas*, *Horton Hears a Who*, and many more.

Geisel did his own illustrating. He created works that amused children and adults alike. His books often contained important messages about paying attention to folks of all sizes, the environment, the dangers of being too complacent, and even about nuclear war. In 1984, he received a Pulitzer Prize "for his contribution over nearly half a century to the education and enjoyment of America's children and their parents." Geisel was also a filmmaker: with his wife he won two Academy Awards for documentaries, and on his own he won an Oscar in the animated-short category. He died at La Jolla, California.

ALEXANDER GRAHAM BELL

Born March 3, 1847
Died August 2, 1922

The inventor of the telephone, Bell was born at Edinburgh, Scotland. His family enjoyed a reputation as leading authorities on elocution, or clear speech. His father was a teacher of the deaf. Bell followed in his father's footsteps by teaching the deaf through the use of visual devices. After the family moved to Canada in 1871, Bell's research into speech and hearing led to the development of the vibrating membrane he later used to invent the telephone. His experiments with electricity led to the invention of the harmonic telegraph, a device to transmit many signals over one wire. This, combined with his knowledge of the mechanics of human speech and hearing, enabled him to work with technicians to invent the telephone. He was granted a patent for his invention in 1876.

On March 10, 1876, Bell spoke the first electrically transmitted sentence to his assistant in the next room: "Mr. Watson, come here, I want you." Bell and two financial backers formed the Bell Telephone Company in 1877. This company outperformed all expectations and grew to such size and scope that the U.S. government finally broke it up into smaller, regional "Baby Bells" to stop it from being a monopoly. Bell's other accomplishments include refining Thomas Edison's phonograph and creating the first successful phonograph record, ailerons, and the audiometer. He continued research into the causes and nature of deafness. He served as president of the National Geographic Society from 1896 to 1904. He died near Baddeck, Nova Scotia, Canada.

CASIMIR PULASKI

Born March 4, 1747
Died October 11, 1779

A hero of the American Revolution, General Kazimierz (Casimir) Pulaski was born at Winiary, Mazovia, Poland, the son of a count. He was a patriot and military leader in Poland's fight against Russia from 1770 to 1771, and he was forced into exile when Poland was partitioned in 1772. He found a cause he could believe in and sailed to America in 1777 to join the Revolution, where he fought bravely alongside General George Washington at Brandywine. He also served in the famous military actions at Germantown and Valley Forge.

Using his background in underdog warfare, he organized and trained the Pulaski Legion to use guerilla tactics against the better-armed British forces. He was mortally wounded in a heroic charge at the siege of Savannah, Georgia, and died aboard the warship *Wasp*. To honor one of the greatest fighters of the American Revolution a number of states— including Nebraska, Massachusetts, Illinois, Indiana, and Wisconsin— celebrate Pulaski Day. Throughout the United States his name is used for schools, roads, parks, and towns.

GERHARDUS MERCATOR

Born March 5, 1512
Died December 2, 1594

Born Gerhard Kremer at Rupelmonde, Belgium, Gerhardus Mercator is the Latin form of his Flemish name. A mathematician, cartographer, geographer, and chair of cosmography at Duisburg, Germany, he dedicated himself to improving the quality of maps and invented a more accurate way to draw them. What became known as the Mercator projection first appeared on one of his maps in 1568 where it provided an accurate ratio of latitude to longitude. Although it distorts the relative size of landmasses, the Mercator projection is still used on maps today.

This projection explains why Greenland looks roughly the same size as South America, despite the fact that South America is actually eight times larger. The poles cannot be shown in this projection. So why do we use this way of making maps? The answer is that way the lines of latitude and longitude remain perpendicular across a flat piece of paper and the shapes of landmasses are preserved, making the map easier to use for navigation. Mercator also coined the term *atlas* for a collection of maps. In 1585 he began a great atlas, which was published by his son in 1594. Mercator died at Duisberg, Germany.

MICHELANGELO

Born March 6, 1475
Died February 18, 1564

Born Michelangelo di Lodovico Buonarroti Simoni, at Caprese, Italy, this prolific painter, sculptor, architect, and poet is the most revered Italian artist of the sixteenth century. He started as an apprentice to a painter but soon moved to a school supported by the wealthy Medici family. In 1496 Michelangelo moved to Rome, where he completed a sculpture called the *Pietà* in 1497. After moving to Florence, he produced the famed statue of *David* from a single huge block of marble (finished in 1504) before heading back to Rome at the request of the Pope. There he began one of the most astonishing works of art in the Western Hemisphere: the decoration of the Sistine Chapel. From 1508 to 1512 Michelangelo painted ceiling frescoes depicting great scenes from the Bible. In 1537, he returned to paint *The Last Judgement* on the altar wall. He then turned his attention mostly to architecture as he began producing plans for the dome of St. Peter's, the great basilica in Rome. He held the post of architect for this project from 1542 until his death in 1564. His powerfully rendered masterpieces continue to inspire people as much as they did centuries ago.

LUTHER BURBANK

Born March 7, 1849
Died April 11, 1926

A plant breeder and horticulturist, Burbank was born at Lancaster, Massachusetts. Over the course of his career Burbank introduced more than 800 new varieties of plants, including fruits, vegetables, grains, and flowers. In 1871 he moved to California, where he believed the climate would be ideal for growing. Of his experimental farm, Gold Ridge, near Sebastopol, California, Burbank said "I firmly believe, from what I have seen, that this is the chosen spot of all this earth as far as Nature is concerned." He launched into large experimental plantings, sometimes running three thousand experiments involving millions of plants at a time.

Best known for the development of the Burbank potato and the Shasta Daisy, Burbank helped turn plant breeding into a modern science; his work advanced the science of plants and the study of genetics by great leaps. In 1930 Thomas Edison testified in favor of changing patent law, specifically saying that allowing plants to be patented would create more Luther Burbanks. Once the law was changed Burbank was granted a total of sixteen posthumous patents. His methods and results were described in detail in his books *How Plants Are Trained to Work for Man* (1921) and, with Wilbur Hall, *Harvest of the Years* (1927) and *Partners in Nature* (1939). His plant varieties can still be purchased today. Burbank died at Santa Rosa, California.

KENNETH GRAHAME

Born March 8, 1859
Died July 6, 1932

The Scottish author of *The Wind in the Willows* and other children's stories, Grahame was born at Edinburgh. When his mother died of a fever
in 1864, and his father (who was an alcoholic) proved incapable of caring for them, the children were sent to live with a grandmother in the
town of Cookham Dene in Berkshire. The scenic surroundings of the
countryside became the backdrop for his later children's book featuring
the beloved characters Mole, Ratty, Badger, and the car-crazed Toad.
Grahame was a banker, who started as a gentleman-clerk and was eventually promoted to the post of secretary to the bank in 1898. Some claim
that he wrote light fiction as an escape from an unhappy marriage.

Much of *The Wind in the Willows* was originally written in the form
of a letter to his only son, Alistair, who had been born the year after Grahame's marriage in 1900. By the time the story was published as a book
in 1908, Grahame had been forced into early retirement due to ill health.
The book was not an immediate success, but a stage version created by
Winnie the Pooh author A. A. Milne in 1930 helped the book gain popularity. Grahame's other writings were well received by critics of his time;
some of them featured an imaginary family of five children that he
invented during his own childhood. He spent long periods in Italy after
his retirement and died at home in Pangbourne, England.

LELAND STANFORD

Born March 9, 1824
Died June 21, 1893

American railway builder, governor, senator, and philanthropist Stanford was born at Watervliet, New York. He began his career as a lawyer in Wisconsin. In 1856 he moved to California where he quickly became involved in politics and the early days of the railway industry. He believed that the public should not interfere with private railroads. He served as governor of California from 1861 to 1863.

Eventually he became president of the Central Pacific Company and drove the famous golden spike that joined the Union and Central Pacific Railroads. He founded Leland Stanford Junior University in 1885, as a memorial to his son who died at age fifteen. This university was one of the first of its kind on the West Coast and grew into what is now Stanford University. Leland Stanford re-entered politics and served as a California senator from 1885 to 1893. A rich and powerful man, he died at his home in Palo Alto, California.

CLARE BOOTH LUCE

Born March 10, 1903
Died October 9, 1987

Playwright and politician Clare Booth Luce was born at New York, New York, where she later wrote for and edited both *Vogue* and *Vanity Fair* magazines. In 1935 she married publisher Henry Luce. She penned a series of successful plays: *The Women* (1936), *Kiss the Boys Goodbye* (1938), and *Margin of Error* (1939). *The Women*, in particular, was an excellent vehicle for Luce's acid wit. This story of a group of upper-class New York matrons became a classic film starring the leading actresses of 1930s Hollywood.

During World War II, Luce became a war correspondent and wrote an article on Libya, which proved so influential that it is credited with changing Winston Churchill's Middle Eastern military policy. Luce was a political conservative who served in the U.S. House of Representatives from 1943 to 1947. From 1953 to 1956, she was ambassador to Italy, the first woman to be appointed to a major European diplomatic post. For her many years of service to the United States, Luce was awarded the Presidential Medal of Freedom in 1983. She died at Washington, D.C.

BOBBY MCFERRIN

Born March 11, 1950

Unconventional musician and ten-time Grammy Award winner Robert McFerrin Jr. was born to opera singer parents at New York City. McFerrin's father was the first African-American male soloist ever to perform at the Metropolitan Opera. The family moved to Hollywood in 1958 so that he could take a singing job for the movie *Porgy and Bess*. Young Bobby played clarinet until he got braces on his teeth, which he said got in the way. He took up piano and keyboards. In 1977 McFerrin came out from behind the piano to sing. He was soon singing with a number of bands and traveling across the country. Inspired by the improvisations of musicians such as Keith Jarrett, McFerrin launched into wild solo vocals. Audiences and critics loved it. Throughout the decades of the eighties and nineties, McFerrin amazed and amused audiences with solo vocal concerts and recordings. He became known for his zany, infectious, and audience-interactive performances and for his astounding vocal versatility.

When he released a simple, joyful tune called "Don't Worry Be Happy" (which he came up with off the top of his head one day in a recording studio), he won both Record of the Year and Song of the Year awards. It flew off all charts to become one of the most popular songs of the late twentieth century. McFerrin's wild popularity seemed to cause him to switch gears; he launched another highly successful career as a classical conductor. He has also recorded with famed cellist, and friend, Yo-Yo Ma. McFerrin has been creative director with the St. Paul Chamber Orchestra and is a promoter of music education programs.

CHARLES BOYCOTT

Born March 12, 1832
Died June 19, 1897

Born Charles Cunningham Boycott at Norfolk, England, this man has a name that, although he did not intend it, became part of the English language. Back in 1880 the Tenant's Land League of County Mayo, Ireland, was trying to help the many poor people who were having trouble paying their rent in the face of poor harvests and dire economic conditions. They appealed to Boycott, an estate agent, to reduce the rents. He responded by serving eviction notices to the tenants. They retaliated by refusing to deal with him from then on.

Charles Stewart Parnell, who was president of the National Land League and an agricultural reformer/agitator, decided to go one step further. He devised a simple yet powerful tool involving economic retaliation and social ostracism that came to be called a boycott. Most modern boycotts involve people refusing to purchase items sold, or manufactured by, a specific company. The goal is to bring about a change of company policy. Today boycotts are used against major corporations, employers, and even whole industries. When fueled by strong emotion and organized with enough publicity, boycotts are an effective tool for change even when used by people who seem relatively powerless. Boycott died at Suffolk, England.

HELEN CANDAELE ST. AUBIN

Born March 13, 1929
Died December 8, 1992

Known as Helen Callaghan during her baseball days, Helen Candaele St. Aubin was born at Vancouver, British Columbia, Canada. St. Aubin and her sister, Margaret Maxwell, were recruited for the All-American Girls Professional Baseball League, which flourished in the 1940s when many male major leaguers were off fighting World War II. She first played at age fifteen for the Minneapolis Millerettes, an expansion team that moved to Indiana and became the Fort Wayne Daisies. The women in these leagues were recruited from all over the country and came from all walks of life. They took charm-school lessons, traveled with chaperones, and were expected to act ladylike while playing fiercely competitive baseball. Team owners even insisted they play ball wearing uniforms with short skirts and bare legs. Because of this policy, women injured themselves while sliding into base or diving for balls.

For the 1945 season, St. Aubin led the league with a .299 average and twenty-four extra-base hits. In 1946 the left-handed outfielder stole an unprecedented 114 bases in 111 games. People who came to make fun of the "dames" went away fans. St. Aubin's son Kelly Candaele's documentary on the women's baseball league inspired the film *A League of Their Own*. St. Aubin, known as the Ted Williams of women's baseball, died at Santa Barbara, California.

ALBERT EINSTEIN

Born March 14, 1879
Died April 18, 1955

Possessed of one of the finest theoretical minds of our age and best known for his theory of relativity, Einstein was born to middle-class Jewish parents at Ulm, Germany. As a young child Einstein was not fond of school, which emphasized memorization. On his own, he read philosophy, physics, and mathematics books. He earned mediocre grades at university, and had trouble getting an academic job upon graduation. Finally, he was hired at a patent office in Switzerland, where he spent many of his off hours working on research and writing. In 1905 he published three important papers. The first claimed that light could behave like a stream of particles with discrete energies or "quanta." The second dealt with the theory of heat. The third brought forth the idea of relativity and offered a solution for a major puzzle for physicists—the connection between electromagnetic theory and ordinary motion. As a result of these papers, Einstein was hired by a number of universities.

By 1914 he accepted a research post in Berlin. In 1915 he released his general theory of relativity, which changed the way scientists interpret time and space. Einstein won the Nobel Prize in 1921. When Germany went to war, he supported pacifism and advocated forming a new government. He was attacked both for his beliefs and for his Jewish ancestry. In the 1930s he gave up on Germany and turned away from strict pacifism, warning President Roosevelt of the possibility of German nuclear capability. In 1939 he became a U.S. citizen. He moved to New Jersey where he continued to speak out for peace and became an ardent supporter of nuclear disarmament after World War II. His research focused on finding a unified field theory to explain nature in scientific terms. In 1955, while writing a speech for newly formed Israel, he died at his home in Princeton, New Jersey.

In an essay called "The World as I See It," Einstein once said: "I am satisfied with the mystery of life's eternity and a knowledge, a sense, of the marvelous structure of existence—as well as the humble attempt to understand even a tiny portion of the Reason that manifests itself in nature."

ISABELLA AUGUSTA GREGORY

Born March 15, 1852
Died May 22, 1932

Isabella Augusta Persse was the twelfth of sixteen children born to a wealthy family in County Galway, Ireland. From an early age she had a fondness for books and Irish folklore, but she was not encouraged in these pursuits until her marriage in 1880. When she was later widowed with a son to support, the great writer William Butler Yeats encouraged her to write. She began with a biography of her late husband, Sir William Gregory, and then, with more urging from Yeats, she collected and published Irish folklore and mythology taken from the oral narratives of the peasants of Galway.

With Yeats, she wrote dozens of short comedic plays that were performed at the Abbey Theater (which had been founded largely due to her efforts), where she was a codirector. Her home at Coole Park was a frequent gathering place for the authors of the early days of the Irish literary renaissance.

Over the years, she took political stances that, though unpopular with the upper classes, made her a heroine of sorts to the commoners in Ireland. She devoted herself to the theater and wrote a total of twenty-seven plays, in addition to her many volumes of folk history. A strong supporter of Irish nationalism and the Irish literary movement, and a fine writer in her own right, she died at Coole Park, County Galway.

CAROLINE LUCRETIA HERSCHEL

Born March 16, 1750
Died January 9, 1848

Born at Hanover, in what is now Germany, Herschel is considered the first significant female astronomer. Her father was a talented musician and while he himself had little formal education, he wanted his children to be educated. He schooled the boys but had to fight his wife to let Caroline receive any training aside from household chores. In fact, her mother controlled her every move and treated her like a servant. After her father's death, she escaped to England in 1722 to live with her brother, astronomer Sir William Herschel. Once there, he offered to teach her to sing and tutored her in English and mathematics. As he became more interested in astronomy she focused on a budding career in music—but she also took time to organize his notes, performed the more tedious routine calculations, and prepared his papers for publication. He observed her talent and continued her training in mathematics. He even encouraged her to do her own research, which eventually resulted in her discovery of eight comets and three nebulae.

She gained considerable fame after her first discovery and became a popular visitor to the Royal Family. She was described in an article as small, modest, gentle, and bright. In 1787 King George gave her a salary to serve as an assistant to her brother. In the 1790s she revised, corrected, and updated the standard star catalog of the day (Flamsteed's), adding a total of 560 stars that had previously been omitted. She produced a catalog of 2,500 nebulae in 1828, a project for which the Royal Astronomical Society awarded her a gold medal. After taking a few decades to educate her nephew, she returned to Hanover, where she continued doing research that won her many awards. She stayed spry and energetic, even entertaining visiting royalty on her ninety-seventh birthday. In 1889, many years after her death at Hanover, a planet was named Lucretia in her honor.

BAYARD RUSTIN

Born March 17, 1910
Died August 24, 1987

A Quaker who worked in many important organizations and served jail time for his beliefs, Rustin was born at West Chester, Pennsylvania. He was an excellent student, musician, and athlete. After college and a successful musical career, he began a long association with the Fellowship of Reconciliation, where he toured the country running race relations institutes meant to facilitate better understanding and communication among races. He was involved in many struggles for fairness and justice, including the American Friends Service Committee's efforts to protect the property of Japanese Americans held in detention camps. In 1943 he went to jail as a conscientious objector. In 1946 he was part of the Journey of Reconciliation, a protest that served as a model for the Freedom Rides of the 1960s. He was arrested in North Carolina and spent thirty days on a chain gang. His reports of his experiences were published in the *New York Post* and helped to bring about the end of the chain gang system in North Carolina.

As the director of A. Philip Randolph's Committee Against Discrimination in the Armed Forces, he played an important role in getting President Truman to sign a desegregation order for the military. He assisted Dr. Martin Luther King Jr. in the beginning of the Montgomery bus boycott and organized the prayer pilgrimage for freedom (1957) and the national youth marches for integrated schools (1958 and 1959). In 1963 he was the chief organizer of one of the largest demonstrations in our country's history: the march on Washington for jobs and freedom. He continued to devote his life to voter registration, worker rights, and democracy at home and abroad. In the 1980s he worked for human rights in many nations. His work has been recognized by many awards and also he has received more than a dozen honorary doctorates. At his death he was serving as cochairman of the A. Philip Randolph Institute, chair of the Social Democrats USA, and United States Holocaust Memorial Council member. He also sat on a number of boards and committees. He died at New York, New York.

BONNIE BLAIR

Born March 18, 1964

Speed skater Blair was born at Cornwall, New York, into a large supportive family that loves skating fast. Her father skipped going to the hospital to await her birth because he was a timer at a speed-skating event; he figured his wife could manage the birth, as it was her sixth baby. During the skating event the public address system announced that the Blair family had just added another skater.

After the family moved to Champaign, Illinois, the little girl strapped on her skates and went on to become one of the fastest skaters in the world, and the owner of five gold medals. A skater who performs well under pressure, in the 1988 Calgary Olympics she skated in the 500 meter right after her East German rival had set a world record. Blair took to the ice to break that record in an astounding 39.1 seconds, a record that remained unbroken for five years until Blair herself broke it in 1994.

At Albertville in 1992, Blair again triumphed and collected her second gold and her fourth Olympic medal overall. In 1994 in Lillehammer, Norway, more than sixty of her family and friends, known as the Blair Bunch, showed up to support her as she once again swept the races. She took home two more gold medals—one for the 500 meter and another for the 1,000 meter. A modest and confident athlete, she remains a favorite with fans and the press. On her thirty-first birthday she set an American record and had a personal best in a 1,000-meter race. She then retired from skating at the peak of her career and now spends her time doing motivational speaking and helping a variety of charities through the Bonnie Blair Charitable Fund.

WYATT EARP

Born March 19, 1848
Died January 13, 1929

Earp once stole a horse and was arrested, and then one year later he became a policeman in Kansas before he made his name as a deputy U.S. marshal. Born at Monmouth, Illinois, he is remembered particularly for the famous shoot-out at the OK Corral in Tombstone, Arizona Territory. On October 26, 1881, Wyatt Earp, his brothers Virgil and Morgan, along with Doc Holliday, settled a feud in a gunfight against the Clanton Gang; three members of the gang were killed.

Like many men of the Wild West, Earp tried his hand at many jobs in his lifetime, including some that seem contradictory: farmer, horse thief, police officer, gambler, gunslinger, railroad hand, miner, and real estate investor.

He became the stuff of legends and was immortalized in books, film, and even a television series, all of which showed him shooting a gun for justice. The truth is much more complicated; Earp fought most often with his fists or used his gun as a club. He was also not always on the side of justice. He died at Los Angeles, and was not really seen as a hero until after the release of a series of movies and books that immortalized (and fictionalized) his life.

HENRIK IBSEN

Born March 20, 1828
Died May 23, 1906

Ibsen is considered the father of modern drama. He was born into a wealthy family in Skien, Norway. The family fortunes went awry, however, and after his father's bankruptcy in 1836 Ibsen was out on his own at fifteen. He became a druggist's apprentice. He failed the math and Greek sections of an entrance exam at the University of Christiana in 1850. Ibsen saw his first Shakespearean play in 1852. He began to explore the theater and served as apprentice in the Bergen National Theater. Later, he served as an artistic director before becoming a playwright.

Ibsen spent many years away from his Norwegian home. His fame rests on his later work, beginning with *Peer Gynt* in 1867 and continuing with *A Doll's House* (1879), *Ghosts* (1881), *Hedda Gabler* (1890), and *The Master Builder* (1892). Ibsen's works were unique because they featured realistic themes and ideas. Each work illustrated an individual's search for meaning in the world, and many of these plays are still popular today. Ibsen died at Christiana (now Oslo), Norway.

JOHANN SEBASTIAN BACH

Born March 21, 1685
Died July 28, 1750

Regarded as one of the greatest composers of the Western world, Johann Sebastian Bach was born into a musical family at Eisenbach, Germany. He learned music from his father and uncle. He started as a choir singer and organist—his teacher at the keyboard was famed composer Johann Pachelbel. During his nine years as court organist at Weimar, Bach composed several religious cantatas. A deeply religious man, he became cantor and music director of St. Thomas Church at Leipzig, a position he held from 1723 until his death.

While employed at St. Thomas Church he composed the *St. John Passion* and the *Mass in B Minor*. Other masterpieces include the *Brandenburg Concertos* and *The Well-Tempered Clavier*. Bach married twice and fathered twenty children, several of whom went on to become composers. Other classical composers enjoyed more popularity in their lives, but Bach is now regarded among the greatest.

MARCEL MARCEAU

Born March 22, 1923

Acclaimed as the world's foremost mime, Marceau was born at Strasbourg, France. As a child he imitated with silent gestures everything that took his fancy. He was exposed to great actors of the silent screen era such as Buster Keaton, Charlie Chaplin, Laurel and Hardy, and Harry Langdon, and found their use of body language very inspiring. As a student in a school of dramatic art in Paris, he studied with the great dramatic master Etienne Decroux. One of Decroux's former students, Jean-Louis Barrault, noticed Marceau's talent and made him a member of his theater company. Marceau's appearance in the first ever "mimodrama" won him great acclaim and set in motion his career as a mime.

Marceau developed a clown character named Bip whose wild misadventures made him a favorite with audiences around the world. He also performs classic routines such as "Walking Against the Wind," "The Cage," and "In the Park." His satires have been described as pure genius. After winning a prize in 1949, Marceau established his own mime troupe, Compagnie de Mime Marcel Marceau, which was the only pantomime company in the world at that time. He has produced more than fifteen mimodramas. In the 1950s Marceau toured the United States performing in increasingly larger theaters as the word spread. He appeared on television a number of times in the 1970s, and his performance on *Your Show of Shows* won him an Emmy. He was recognized by the French government, which made him an Officier de la Legion d'Honneur. He has reopened his international school and continues to make public appearances performing at sold-out venues.

MARQUIS PIERRE-SIMON DE LAPLACE

Born March 23, 1749
Died March 5, 1827

French astronomer and mathematician, Laplace was born at Beaumount-en-Auge, Normandy. He was a professor of mathematics at the École Militaire in Paris. On the basis of Sir Isaac Newton's gravitational theory, he studied the movements of the planets and other celestial bodies. His five-volume work *Mécanique céleste* (*Celestial Mechanics*) came out in 1799 to 1825. The work used mathematics to determine the exact properties and motions of comets, the moon, and some planets. His research results, along with those of Joseph Lagrange and earlier mathematicians, placed Newton's theory beyond doubt once and for all.

Laplace also developed a differential equation in physics on the gravitational attraction of spheroids. His research into the origins of the universe led him to a nebular hypothesis, which he published in *Exposition du systéme du monde* (1796), a book that turned out to be even more popular than his masterwork. Many generations of seafaring and coastal fishing folk have used Laplace's studies of tides. His research into gravitational attraction and the movement of bodies in space has provided a starting place for space researchers today. Laplace died at Paris, France.

JOHN WESLEY POWELL

Born March 24, 1834
Died September 23, 1902

Born at New York City, Powell was an explorer and geologist. His family moved west to Illinois, and though considering a career in the ministry, he was attracted to naturalist pursuits on the Great Plains. After serving in the Civil War (during which he lost his lower right arm at the Battle of Shiloh) and spending some years as a university professor, Powell began a new career. In 1869 he led a boat expedition through the Grand Canyon on the Colorado River. He told the story of his dangerous 900-mile trip on the huge untamed river in his 1875 book *Explorations of the Colorado River*. He also made anthropological observations of American Indian tribes and was the first to create a workable classification of Indian languages.

In later years, he shared his knowledge of American Indians with other researchers and became the first director of the Smithsonian's Bureau of American Ethnology in 1879. His efforts led to the formation of the U.S. Geological Survey, which he headed from 1881 to 1894. He died at Haven, Maine.

GUTZON BORGLUM

Born March 25, 1867
Died March 6, 1941

Born John Gutzon de la Mothe Borglum at Bear Lake, Idaho, this famed sculptor of Mount Rushmore was the son of Mormon pioneers. He studied at the San Francisco Art Academy and in Paris at the École des Beaux-Arts. His first major work was the statue of President Lincoln, which is still on view in the rotunda of the Capitol in Washington, D.C. Other works from his early days include a statue of Henry Ward Beecher in Brooklyn, New York, and the apostles for the Cathedral of St. John the Divine in New York City. He was known as a man of strong opinions, which often led him to conflicts with those close to him. In 1916, he designed and began carving a Confederate memorial on Stone Mountain, Georgia. His work was interrupted by the outbreak of World War I, but he continued in 1924, only to get into a disagreement with the Stone Mountain Memorial Association. He quit work on the project and destroyed his models.

Not long afterward, in 1927, Borglum became the supervisor of a huge project at Mount Rushmore, South Dakota. One of the largest sculptures ever undertaken, the Mount Rushmore National Memorial features the heads of four U.S. presidents, each one sixty feet high, carved into a steep rock face. The memorial represents a great feat of engineering as well as being a great work of art. Borglum and his crew worked at great heights in all kinds of weather. Unfortunately, Borglum died before he could finish the monument. After his death, his son Lincoln Borglum took over to finish what his father had started. Gutzon Borglum died at Chicago, Illinois, a few weeks short of his seventieth birthday.

BETTY MACDONALD

March 26, 1908
February 7, 1958

Born Elizabeth Bard at Boulder, Colorado, she was the author of the laugh-out-loud book *The Egg and I* and the Mrs. Piggle-Wiggle series, among others. She married Robert Heskett and the two of them lived on a rustic chicken farm on the Olympic Peninsula. She found this life challenging. She had no running water or electricity, a broken-down house, and plenty of hard labor. The marriage didn't last very long, but the experience gave Bard some great ideas for books. *The Egg and I* was a million-dollar bestseller in the 1940s and '50s. Later she married Don Macdonald and *The Egg and I* was turned into a movie starring Claudette Colbert and Fred MacMurray and then the Ma and Pa Kettle movies.

Macdonald's Mrs. Piggle-Wiggle books came out of bedtime stories she told her children. These tales are well loved for their zany premises and child-friendly writing style. Mrs. Piggle-Wiggle lives in an upside-down house and knows everything there is to know about childrearing. Parents call her when their children have driven them to the brink and Mrs. Piggle-Wiggle comes up with humorous "cures," such as planting bean seeds in the ears of kids who won't bathe, or feeding a kid with a sweet-tooth nothing but sugary foods for days on end. Betty Macdonald had to overcome many hardships in her short life, including tuberculosis (which she wrote about in *The Plague and I*), divorce, and finally cancer, which ended her life at age forty-nine. She died at Carmel Valley, California.

PATTY SMITH HILL

Born March 27, 1868
Died May 25, 1946

Born at Anchorage, near Louisville, Kentucky, Hill was a schoolteacher, author, and education specialist. She is best known for writing the lyrics to the song "Good Morning to You All," which later became known as "Happy Birthday to You." The song was composed by Hill's older sister Mildred and was first published in 1893 as a classroom greeting in the book *Song Stories for the Sunday School*. A stanza beginning "Happy birthday to you" was added in 1924.

The song's authors reportedly made very little from its sales, but it later generated more than $1 million a year for its copyright owner. It has for many years been the song of choice at birthday parties. It is expected to enter the public domain upon the expiration of its copyright in 2010. Patty Smith Hill died at New York, New York.

SAINT JOHN NEUMANN

Born March 28, 1811
Died January 5, 1860

"The Little Bishop" was born the son of a German factory owner and a Czech mother at Prachititz, Bohemia (now the Czech Republic). Small and quiet, he took to his studies and was drawn at a young age into the religious life. After seminary school he headed for America. When he arrived in Manhattan in 1836, there were 200,000 Catholics in New York and New Jersey but only thirty-six priests. Neumann took a post in a rural area and proceeded to build a log cabin. He rarely lit a fire, slept and ate very little, and used all his talents and energies to help his parishioners. He walked miles from farm to farm to meet settlers from many countries. Neumann's facility with languages (he spoke twelve fluently) allowed him to minister to a wide variety of people.

He joined an order called the Redemptionists at Pittsburgh, Pennsylvania, in 1840. He became rector of Saint Philomena in Pittsburgh and was called to be bishop of Philadelphia in 1852. Under his care a cathedral was begun, fifty churches were built, almost a hundred schools were opened, and the number of parochial students grew from 500 to 9,000. He was an active bishop; he wrote newspaper articles and two catechisms. He did much of his writing in German, which at that time was one of the most common languages in Pennsylvania. He died at Philadelphia, in 1860, at the age of forty-nine. In 1963 he was beatified; he was canonized in 1977 and thereby became the first male saint from the United States.

KAREN ANN QUINLAN

Born March 29, 1954
Died June 11, 1985

Born at Scranton, Pennsylvania, Quinlan became the unwitting center of a legal, medical, and ethical controversy over the right to die. At a party, Quinlan, who was then twenty-one years old, ingested a combination of alcohol and tranquilizers that rendered her irreversibly comatose on April 14, 1975. When it became clear that she would not recover and was in what the medical community terms a persistent vegetative state, her parents petitioned the New Jersey Supreme Court in 1975 for permission to discontinue respirator use, which they thought would allow their daughter to die with "dignity and grace." They could not have been prepared for the publicity and the heat of the public's reaction to this request. The media was saturated with experts weighing in on who had the right to decide a comatose patient's life.

In 1976 Quinlan's parents' petition was upheld and her life support was removed. Ironically, Karen Quinlan began to breathe on her own. She lived for nearly a decade in a nursing home, still unaware of her surroundings. She died of pneumonia in 1985. Her plight brought attention to the ethical dilemmas of advancing medical technology—the need for a new understanding of life and death; the right to die; and the role of judges, doctors, and hospital committees in deciding when not to prolong life.

VINCENT VAN GOGH

Born March 30, 1853
Died July 29, 1890

The Dutch postimpressionist painter was born at Zundert, Netherlands, the son of a Protestant pastor. He worked in his uncle's art gallery and as a teacher and preacher, but he eventually gave up his possessions to be an evangelist among poor coalminers. He turned to art in 1880, doing paintings of peasants such as those in his famous work *The Potato Eaters* (1850). In 1886 he moved to Paris to live with his brother Theo, an art dealer. Van Gogh became influenced by the new art movements of the time: Impressionism and modern Japanese printmaking. Always feeling the pull of nature and the countryside, he left the city to live in the Provence countryside in 1888.

The bright sun, colors, and rustic life of southern France inspired him. But he didn't find much of an audience among art buyers—in fact, he sold only one painting in his lifetime. It was also in the south of France that van Gogh began using the strong, swirling brush strokes characteristic of what would become his best-known works, such as *Starry Night* and *Sunflowers*. Burdened by poverty and mental illness, van Gogh suffered a number of breakdowns, at one point even cutting off his right earlobe. Eventually he committed himself to an asylum, where he produced a large number of paintings. He shot himself and died two days later at Auvers-sur-Oise, France.

CESAR CHAVEZ

Born March 31, 1927
Died April 23, 1993

Chavez was born on a farm in the North Gila Valley near Yuma, Arizona. The Great Depression took its toll on Chavez's family and they were forced to become migrant farm workers in California. Chavez dropped out of school in the eighth grade (after attending thirty-two different grammar schools) to work in the fields. He noticed that landowners and labor contractors exploited the workers, who were paid very little and had to live in shacks or dormitories that lacked running water and electricity. He tried reasoning with owners, and tried to excite his fellow workers to make changes. But the owners had no economic incentive to make changes and the workers feared retaliation. In 1948, after a stint in the Navy, he married Helen Fabela, a woman who shared his concern for the workers. They began teaching Mexican farm workers to read so that they would be able to apply for citizenship. They figured that once the workers became Americans they would be more likely to help him in his fight.

A community service organization hired Chavez part-time to help the workers register to vote. He was highly successful, and the organization hired him to work full-time teaching workers about their rights. In 1962, Chavez decided to form a union. His wife had to pick fruit to put food on the table for their children while Chavez went from field to field and *la Causa* (the Cause) was born. He founded the National Farm Workers Association in 1962, which later became the United Farm Workers Union. He organized protests and consumer boycotts to bring greater public attention to the wretched working conditions of migrant workers. It was a bitter dispute; union members, including Chavez, were repeatedly thrown in jail. After many workers went on strike and grapes rotted on the vine, and after consumers stopped buying lettuce because they sympathized with the workers, the union at last succeeded in getting contracts signed by grape growers. He won collective-bargaining rights for farm workers through unions of their choice in 1975. Chavez died at San Luis, Arizona. He received the Presidential Medal of Freedom posthumously in 1994.

APRIL

JAGJIVAN RAM

Born April 1, 1908
Died July 6, 1986

Born into a family of the so-called untouchable caste in the town of Chandwa, in the Bihar region of India, Jagjivan went on to shatter all expectations of a person of his class. Ram showed an early delight in learning and was one of the first people of his caste to attend school. Not only did he graduate from high school, he also managed to get accepted to a university. After graduation his activities on behalf of others of his caste gained him the reputation as the spokesman for India's 100 million untouchables. For centuries this had been a class of people who were not allowed jobs other than those that were the least desirable. They were not allowed to fraternize with people of higher castes or marry out of the caste.

He took a leadership role in politics, eventually becoming a coworker to famed Indian independence leaders Jawaharal Nehru and Mohandas Gandhi. He served in a variety of ministerial cabinet posts and was twice a candidate for prime minister. Ram lived a long and productive life. He was present as his country gained its independence from Great Britain and as it struggled to become a democracy. He died at New Delhi, India.

HANS CHRISTIAN ANDERSEN

Born April 2, 1805
Died August 4, 1875

This beloved Danish author is best remembered for his more than 150 fairy tales, many of which are regarded as classics of children's literature. Born at Odense, Denmark, Andersen was the child of a poor shoemaker and a washerwoman. He left home at age fourteen hoping to find theater work in the city of Copenhagen. Although he had no luck finding a job, his poetry gained him entry to an advanced school, and eventually he caught the notice and financial support of the Danish king Frederik VI.

Andersen wrote travel books, adult novels, and children's stories such as *The Princess and the Pea*, *The Snow Queen*, and *The Ugly Duckling*. Many of his imaginative and often touching stories came from his fascination with traditional folktales. He usually published them first as little pamphlets. Compiled into books, presented as plays, translated into many languages, made into animated films, turned into movies and TV programs, Andersen's creations have far exceeded any expectation the author may have had for them. Hans Christian Andersen died at Copenhagen, Denmark.

JANE GOODALL

Born April 3, 1934

Naturalist and expert on chimpanzees Jane Goodall was born at London and grew up at Bournemouth on the southern coast of England. Goodall showed an early interest in animal behavior. One childhood story tells of her sitting in a henhouse for hours waiting to see how the eggs came out of the hens. The family thought the four-year-old was lost and called the police, but when Jane later ran up to the house, she was not scolded—her mother listened to her tale of discovery. Early family support allowed Goodall to take a nontraditional life path. At age twenty-three, determined to go to Kenya, she worked as a waitress to earn the boat fare. Once there, she met the world-famous paleontologist and anthropologist Dr. Louis Leakey, who was impressed with her understanding of Africa and its creatures. He hired her as an assistant on a fossil-hunting expedition to the Olduvai Gorge. When Leakey mentioned the possibility of studying a group of chimpanzees near Lake Tanganika, Goodall jumped at the chance. She now says of those days, "I wanted to learn things that no one else knew, uncover secrets through patient observation. I wanted to come as close to talking to animals as I could."

Goodall went on to set up a camp at the Gombe Stream Reserve in 1960. When authorities balked at a young Englishwoman camping out on her own, Jane's mother came to live with her for the first three months. Despite early difficulties getting close to the chimps, Goodall's patient manner eventually earned their trust and led to some startling discoveries, including a more complex primate social life than was previously thought. She was the first to observe chimpanzees using tools and hunting other animals for food. Her research has been instrumental in protecting wild chimps and improving care of those in captivity. Today Goodall writes and speaks on the importance of conservation and on her research. Her foundation, the Jane Goodall Institute, focuses world attention on the plight of chimpanzees. She lives in Dar es Salaam, Tanzania, where she has started an innovative environmental awareness program, open to children from around the world, called "Roots and Shoots."

DOROTHEA DIX

Born April 4, 1802
Died July 17, 1887

Born at Hampton, Maine, Dorothea Dix left home at the age of ten to escape a bad family situation. She became a teacher in her early teens. Later, while touring a jail where she was to teach Sunday school classes, she was horrified by the wretched conditions to which the mentally ill prisoners were being subjected. At the time it was common practice to put the insane into filthy, dark, and often unheated prisons. Women and children were mixed with violent criminals and people too destitute to pay their bills. Dix traveled across the northeast to research jails and insane asylums and lobbied legislatures for upgraded living conditions for the mentally ill.

She played a pivotal role in the founding of thirty-two mental hospitals; fifteen schools for the mentally disabled; a school for the blind; numerous training facilities for nurses; and libraries in prisons, mental hospitals, and other institutions. Although she had no formal training, she was appointed the superintendent of Union Army nurses at the outbreak of the Civil War. After the war, she returned to her lifelong crusade for psychiatric reform. In her era women were not allowed to make speeches or to be too strident about their causes, so she had to cultivate friendships with wealthy industrialists and other influential men of her time. With their help, Dix got her research noticed by lawmakers. Her reforms, when considered together, are among the biggest institutional change ever brought about by a single person. She died in a hospital at Trenton, New Jersey, that she herself had founded.

JOSEPH LISTER

Born April 5, 1827
Died February 10, 1912

Born at Upton, Essex, England, Lister studied medicine at the Glasgow Royal Infirmary. He studied the coagulation of blood in injuries and surgical wounds and noted that despite efforts to keep rooms clean there was a very high incidence of infection. He followed in the footsteps of Louis Pasteur (who proved that bacteria cause infection) by beginning the practice of spraying carbolic acid on surgical instruments, wounds, and surgical dressings.

By today's standards hospitals lacked sanitary practices. Maternity wards provide a good example. The traditional birthing practice up until Lister's time was home delivery assisted by a midwife. Midwives traditionally washed hands and only dealt with one woman at a time in her own home. When doctors started taking over, women delivered their babies in large open wards in close proximity with other women. Doctors commonly went from one to the next without properly washing their hands. Many women in hospitals died because of this practice, which the mystified medical establishment called childbed fever.

Lister insisted that doctors wash hands thoroughly, clean the area of operation, and use sterilized instruments. His methods reduced surgical mortality to 15 percent by the year 1860. The medical community was skeptical of his findings at the time, but they later became widely accepted. While his method, based on the use of antiseptics, is no longer used, his principle—that bacteria must never gain entry to an open wound—remains the basis of surgery to this day. Lister also developed absorbable ligatures and the drainage tube, both of which are used today. He was made a baronet in 1883 and raised to the peerage in 1897. He died at Walmer, Kent, England.

ROSE SCHNEIDERMAN

Born April 6, 1882
Died August 11, 1972

A pioneer in the battle to increase wages and improve working conditions for women, Rose Schneiderman was born at Saven, Poland, and immigrated with her family to the United States at the age of six. Ten years later, Schneiderman began work at a factory in New York City's garment district where she quickly became a union organizer. Opposed to the open-shop policy, which permitted nonunion members to work in a unionized shop, Schneiderman organized a famous 1913 strike that involved 25,000 women workers.

She also worked as an organizer for the International Ladies Garment Workers Union (ILGWU) and for the Women's Trade Union League (WTUL), serving as president for more than twenty years. During the Great Depression, her work was noticed by President Roosevelt. He appointed her to his labor advisory board—she was the only female member. She became a voice for the thousands of underpaid and overworked women laboring over machines in hot, cramped, and often dangerous shops in cities all across the nation. Her demands made work a more humane place and brought a measure of security to thousands of women who had been afraid to ask for needed changes. She died at New York, New York.

WILLIAM ELLERY CHANNING

Born April 7, 1780
Died October 2, 1842

Influential abolitionist and leader of the Unitarian movement in the United States, Channing was born at Newport, Rhode Island. He was a pivotal figure in the literary and religious life of the nineteenth century. An outspoken opponent of slavery and a powerful public speaker, his writings and sermons challenged opinions of the day and influenced such great minds as Longfellow, Emerson, and Thoreau.

Channing preached in the Boston area from 1803 until his death. His 1819 sermon "Unitarian Christianity" was really a manifesto that established the liberal Congregationalists as Unitarians apart from their more conservative brethren. The Unitarians were established in 1820 and became a powerful voice for the abolition of slavery; they influenced many politicians of the time. Channing also was a pacifist and helped start the peace movement in the early 1800s. He wrote about the miseries and crimes of war, the causes of war, and how war could be abolished. He believed that war gives governments dangerous powers and corrupts the morals of society and that Christians should refuse war and if necessary submit to prison or execution instead of killing. Channing died at Bennington, Vermont.

LEWIS MORRIS

Born April 8, 1726
Died January 22, 1798

Born at Morrisania Manor at Westchester County, New York, to an upper-class family of considerable wealth and land, Morris entered Yale at the age of sixteen where he quickly earned a good reputation. After graduation he returned to his father's plantation, married, and had ten children. Morris held many state positions in New York and New Jersey and despite his comfortable and wealthy life believed in his heart that the American colonies must separate from Britain.

When it appeared war was imminent in 1775, Morris served on a committee with George Washington to figure out how to get weapons and supplies to the Colonies. This commitment was arduous and frustrating as supplies were hard to come by and the need was very pressing. He was also asked to help gain the trust of some Indian tribes, in the hope that they would fight on the side of the Colonies against Britain. Because many colonists were linked with officers of the royal government, there was at first strong resistance in New York to independence from the mother country. Morris believed that drafting a document to declare official separation from Britain was a legislative duty to promote patriotism. He signed the Declaration of Independence, thereby risking all his holdings. In fact the British army landed within cannon shot of his home. Soon his estate was almost completely destroyed, and his family was forced into hiding. Morris left Congress in 1777 and rose eventually to the rank of major general. After the war, he resumed work at his plantation. He lived to the age of seventy-one and died at home at Morrisania Manor.

PAUL ROBESON

Born April 9, 1898
Died January 23, 1976

Born at Princeton, New Jersey, Robeson was an acclaimed actor and singer. He attended Rutgers University where he was an All-American football player. He went on to receive a law degree from Columbia University in 1923. After being discovered by Eugene O'Neill in an amateur stage production, Robeson was offered a part in O'Neill's play *The Emperor Jones* with the Provincetown Players. His outstanding performance launched his acting career. Robeson had a fine bass singing voice. He never took a lesson but went on to become a popular singer.

His stage credits included *Show Boat, Porgy and Bess, The Hairy Ape*, and *Othello*, which enjoyed the longest Broadway run of any previously produced Shakespeare play. His film credits included *King Solomon's Mines* and *Songs of Freedom*, among others. Robeson took on leftist causes that at times got him in trouble with the federal government. Like many famous people, during the McCarthy era he was denied a passport by the United States for refusing to sign an affidavit answering the question of whether he was or had ever been a member of the Communist Party (1950). The action was overturned by the Supreme Court in 1958, but Robeson was unable to take jobs in Europe for nearly a decade. Robeson died at Philadelphia, Pennsylvania.

WILLIAM BOOTH

Born April 10, 1829
Died August 20, 1912

"General" William Booth, the founder of the movement that became known in 1878 as the Salvation Army, was born at Nottingham, England. Apprenticed to a pawnbroker at the age of thirteen, Booth experienced firsthand the misery of poverty. He became a Methodist minister but broke with conventional church religion to establish a quasi-military religious organization (complete with uniforms and ranks) at the East End of London in 1865. Recruiting from the ranks of poor people, social outcasts, and even converted criminals, Booth's organization grew rapidly.

The Salvation Army's influence spread from England to the United States and other countries. At revival meetings in slum areas, the itinerant evangelist ministered to the poorest of the poor. Offering more than just food for the soul, Booth created "rescue homes" for abused women and runaway girls, homes for the homeless, sobriety for alcoholics, job training centers, legal aid, and soup kitchens. The Salvation Army is now one of the biggest charitable organizations in the world and is still active in job training and other forms of community outreach. Booth died at London, England.

LIZZIE "LILLIE" BLISS

Born April 11, 1864
Died March 12, 1931

One of the three prominent female art patrons who cofounded New York's Museum of Modern Art (MOMA), Bliss was born at Boston, Massachusetts. At a time when there was much disagreement about what constituted modern art, Lizzie Bliss collected early works by many modern artists that art critics of the time called "gorillas" who made messes that insulted the intelligence of onlookers. Many of these artists of the early part of the twentieth century are now seen as geniuses.

Bliss was a friend and patron to many struggling artists. Abraham Walkowitz, a modern artist of the era, said in a Smithsonian oral history interview: "She was a wonderful person, Lizzie Bliss, a princess; the Lady in Black, we used to call her."

In 1929 Lizzie Bliss, Abby Rockefeller, and Mary Quinn Sullivan gathered support to form the first modern art museum in the United States. Before that time, New York's nod to modern art consisted of nothing more than a few private galleries such as the one owned by photographer Alfred Stieglitz, where artists such as Georgia O'Keeffe had their first shows. But Bliss and Rockefeller donated their extensive modern art holdings to form the nucleus of MOMA's permanent collection. Bliss died at New York City.

HENRY CLAY

Born April 12, 1777
Died June 29, 1852

An American statesman, Clay was a larger-than-life character who was one of the most important pre–Civil War congressional leaders. Born at Hanover County, Virginia, he earned his law license in 1797. He was elected to the U.S. Senate for the first time in 1806 and spent the rest of his life trying to become president. He failed three times. He once said that he ". . . would rather be right than president." President Andrew Jackson and he were enemies—each was the other's greatest critic. Clay was the leader of the newly formed Whig party. He served as senator, member of the U.S. House of Representatives, Speaker of the House from 1809 to 1820, and U.S. secretary of state under President John Quincy Adams. His run as Speaker is the longest on record for the nineteenth century; Clay changed the position from a ceremonial function to one of great influence and power. Dubbed "The Dictator," Clay was a hot-headed, polarizing, partisan politician, yet he was also a statesman perhaps best known for his authorship of important compromise legislation.

As a slaveholder who condemned slavery, he tried to have it outlawed in his home state of Kentucky. He is said to have influenced Lincoln, who often quoted Clay on the subject. He believed slaves should be freed slowly, educated, trained, and sent back to Africa. He was known to treat his slaves well and let most go free before his death. His views on slavery infuriated the emancipationists as well as Southern slave owners and probably cost him the presidency. He authored the Missouri Compromise of 1820 and the Compromise of 1850, both balancing interests of the Northern and Southern states with the intention of avoiding civil war. Clay died at Washington, D.C.

ALFRED M. BUTTS

Born April 13, 1899
Died April 4, 1993

Born at Poughkeepsie, New York, Butts was an unemployed architect when he invented the board game Scrabble, which involves making words out of randomly selected letters. At first the game was a fad among Butts's friends, many of whom, like Butts himself, had plenty of time on their hands. Then in 1952, a Macy's executive saw the game being played at a resort, and he convinced the world's largest store to begin selling it. Soon, Scrabble was flying off the shelves, and thirty-five workers were producing more than 6,000 sets a week. Manufacturing had to be turned over to a bigger company, Selchow and Richter.

Butts received three cents per game for years. He said, "One-third went to taxes, one-third I gave away, and one-third allowed me to have an enjoyable life." Scrabble is now found just about everywhere in the world and is even used in schools to teach language skills. Butts died in his midnineties at Rhinebeck, New York.

ANNE SULLIVAN MACY

Born April 14, 1866
Died October 20, 1936

Born Anne Sullivan at Feeding Hills, Massachusetts, this dedicated teacher became well known for her work with blind and deaf Helen Keller. Sullivan was nearly blind herself. She came to work for the Kellers when Helen was seven years old. What Anne Sullivan found was distressing: a howling, raging, out-of-control child who was allowed to roam the house destroying things and hitting servants and parents alike. Sullivan told the parents that feeling sorry for young Helen had led them to do her a disservice. She began to connect with her young charge, attempting to reach her using a newly invented form of physical, or touch, sign language, where letters are signed into the hand of the recipient by forming shapes with the fingers.

Sullivan and Keller experienced a famous breakthrough when pumping water. Sullivan pumped water over Keller's hand signing W-A-T-E-R. Suddenly Keller discovered that things had names. Her progress from this point was rapid; she eventually learned to read, write, and speak and went on to college at Radcliffe. Sullivan's patience and energy in the face of overwhelming odds made her a heroine of her era and the subject of a popular play and then a movie entitled *The Miracle Worker*. She died at Forest Hills, New York.

JAMES CLARK ROSS

Born April 15, 1800
Died April 3, 1862

Born at London, Ross was a British naval officer who made several discoveries in the Arctic and Antarctic. In 1830, Ross discovered the North
Magnetic Pole. This had been a serious navigational issue for sailors ever
since the invention of the magnetic compass because the geographic pole
and the magnetic pole are about 1,000 miles apart. Having the exact location meant more accurate sailing.

Ross's attempts to reach the South Magnetic Pole were part of a
three-nation race. The French set sail in vessels designed for exploring
the tropics; the Americans headed out in warships and had to deal with
icy water pouring in their large gunports; and England sent Ross, who
wisely chose two small sturdy ships named the *Erebus* and the *Terror*. The
French and Americans sighted the Antarctic landmass on the same day
but Ross sailed on to the discovery in 1841 of a huge area of open water
now called the Ross Sea and a gigantic slab of floating ice, which is now
called the Ross Ice Shelf. He named the area of land he discovered in the
Antarctic Victoria Land in honor of England's young queen. Upon his
return to England in 1843 he was knighted. *A Voyage of Discovery and
Research in the Southern and Antarctic Regions*, Ross's account of his expeditions, was published in 1847. He died at Buckinghamshire, England.

CHARLES SPENCER CHAPLIN

Born April 16, 1889
Died December 25, 1977

The celebrated film comedian who created a beloved character called the Little Tramp was born at London, England, where he experienced a childhood of poverty and Dickensian workhouses. His parents were music hall performers and separated when Charlie and his brother Sydney were young. Both boys aspired to be performers and eventually were hired by the Karno Company where they developed and performed comedy acts. During a tour of the United States, Charlie was hired by the Keystone Film Company and starred in a number of silent movies, including *Making a Living*. After getting a taste of directing on the film *Twenty Minutes of Love*, he decided to make it his main focus.

He became a successful filmmaker jumping from one company to another, each time negotiating a better deal for himself. By 1915 he had thirty-five films under his belt. He moved to the Essanay Company where he encountered Edna Purviance, the leading lady he would feature in many of his most famous works. Most of his films were short comedies, but he also made a full-length masterpiece called *The Kid* (1921). He also helped form United Artists (UA). He made films for UA for a few decades, including his first talkie, in 1940, *The Great Dictator*. In the 1950s, when anticommunist fears created tensions for left-leaning movie stars, Chaplin was forced out of the country. He moved to Switzerland with his wife (Oona O'Neill) and children and didn't return to the United States until 1972, when he was given a special Academy Award. In his later years he made films with such stars as Marlon Brandon and Sophia Loren. He died at Vevey, Switzerland.

JOHN PIERPONT MORGAN

Born April 17, 1837
Died March 31, 1913

The Hartford, Connecticut–born Morgan became one of the world's richest and most influential financiers from the late nineteenth century until his death in 1913. As a young man in 1857, he followed in the steps of his powerful father, Junius Spencer Morgan, by entering the banking business. By 1871 he had formed with partner Anthony Drexel the banking firm of Drexel, Morgan and Company (which became J.P. Morgan and Company in 1895). This bank became the most powerful in the world under his management—two times, in 1893 and 1907, it helped bail out the country during depression and financial panic by shoring up the U.S. Treasury and the federal banking system.

Morgan also consolidated and organized railroad lines of the northeast and Atlantic seaboard, making them more efficient and better able to cooperate among themselves. Through consolidation of companies, he helped create General Electric (by merging Thomas Edison's company with another), United States Steel Corporation (which became the world's largest corporation), and International Harvester. The power he demonstrated by rearranging the face of major industry made him a lightning rod for criticism and suspicion. The U.S. Congress undertook investigations of his influence, which he routinely discounted.

The great businessman was also an active philanthropist, giving much to civic institutions. After his death at Rome, Italy, Morgan's art collection went to the Metropolitan Museum of Art, and his book collection was given to New York City and opened to the public.

CLARENCE SEWARD DARROW

Born April 18, 1857
Died March 13, 1938

A famous American lawyer often associated with unpopular causes, Darrow was born at Kinsman, Ohio. While his early cases were very lucrative and focused on private and corporate law, his defense of the underdog in a case stemming from the Pullman strike of 1894 created the kind of public stir for which he later became well known. Also famous for his opposition to the death penalty, Darrow took on client after client. None of his more than 100 clients was ever sentenced to death.

In 1925 he defended the teaching of evolution in the Scopes trial (also known as the "Monkey Trial"). In this famous court battle he argued against the highly respected and devoutly religious prosecuting attorney William Jennings Bryan. Darrow was quoted as saying: "I do not consider it an insult, but rather a compliment, to be called an agnostic. I do not pretend to know where many ignorant men are sure—that is all that agnosticism means." This trial, which was hotly debated across the United States, changed the way science is taught in U.S. schools. The trial was the subject of *Inherit the Wind*, which was first a play and later a movie starring Gene Kelly with Spencer Tracy as Darrow. Darrow died at Chicago, Illinois.

OLE EVINRUDE

Born April 19, 1877
Died July 12, 1934

Born at Norway, Evinrude moved to the United States at the age of five and settled in Wisconsin. He worked on his father's farm where he developed a keen interest in machines. As a young man he moved to the Chicago area where he worked in factories and read about mechanics. He closely followed developments in the internal combustion engine. In 1900 he returned to Wisconsin to open a pattern-making shop. In his spare time he tinkered with motorcars. In 1904 on a hot summer outing he determined to get the woman he loved an ice cream cone. He had to row across a lake to do so. By the time he returned, the ice cream was, of course, melted. Vowing it would never happen again, he set out to build the world's first outboard motor.

In 1909 he built a plant to produce one-cylinder motors. He patented his motor in 1910, and it was quickly accepted by the boating world. He continued to create new designs and moved his growing plant to Milwaukee. Eventually he produced a two-cylinder, three-horsepower motor in an aluminum casing. He also created a successful lawn mower. When he died at Milwaukee, in 1934, his son Ralph Evinrude took over. Two years later Evinrude merged with Johnson Motor Company to form the Outboard Motor Company. Evinrude's motor remained largely unchanged for almost a century—recently, four-stroke engines have been designed, which are quieter and less polluting than the earlier designs.

ADOLF HITLER

Born April 20, 1889
Died April 30, 1945

A German dictator obsessed with the superiority of the Aryan race and the evils of Marxism, Hitler was responsible for more than 12 million deaths during World War II. Born at Braunau, Austria, a small town just across the Inn River from Germany, Hitler fancied himself an artist but could not gain admission to an academy, nor could he find a steady job. After serving in the military in World War I, Hitler returned to a Germany that was broke, stripped of privileges, and saddled with high debt and war reparations. He joined the National Socialist (Nazi) Party. Hitler and his fellow Nazis attempted to overthrow the government, but the attack failed and he was sentenced to five years in prison. He served only nine months, using his time to write the now infamous manifesto, *Mein Kampf.*

By 1929 the Nazis were an important minority party, and the German economy was failing. As leader of the Nazis and a wily speaker, Hitler promised a weary Germany a return to greatness—while blaming Jews and Communists for Germany's problems. He promised to reunite Germans everywhere and rid the country of everyone who did not fit his description of a true German. By 1932 the Nazis represented the strongest party in Germany, and in 1933 the president appointed Hitler chancellor. Hitler quickly secured power and became a dictator. His new government was called the Third Reich. Other political parties were banned, political opponents were executed, and anti-Semitic policies were instituted. Attempting to unite all German-speaking peoples, he invaded Poland in 1939 and thereby launched another world war. Anti-Semitic policies became genocidal, and his troops set up extermination camps all over Poland, Germany, and Russia. Millions of innocent people were sent to their deaths for Hitler's dream of unification. In 1945, with the Allied countries closing in, Hitler took his own life at a Berlin bunker, where he and his mistress had been hiding out for months.

JOHN MUIR

Born April 21, 1838
Died December 14, 1914

American naturalist, explorer, and author John Muir was born at Dunbar, Scotland, and came to the United States in 1849. Hard labor on the family farm in Wisconsin left him no time for schooling. When he finally convinced his father to let him rise early to have time to read, Muir started getting up at one o'clock in the morning. The five hours he had to himself each day were his happiest. Eventually he escaped the farm life and, despite having almost no formal education, was able to gain admission to the University of Wisconsin. He chose mostly courses in natural science. He left school in 1863 but did not complete a degree. While working in Canada soon after, he lost sight in one eye from an accident. Soon the other eye went blind. Over a period of months, however, his eyesight gradually returned. Muir felt he had been given a new chance at life. He resolved to spend every possible moment in the places he loved—the unspoiled forests, streams, lakes, and mountains of the United States.

He ended up in San Francisco in 1868. From there he asked the way out of town. When asked where he meant to go, Muir replied, "Any place that is wild." He was directed to Yosemite where he spent much of the rest of his life exploring, working, learning, and writing. After marrying, Muir spent more of his time near San Francisco raising his family. His trips to Yosemite presented him with increasing evidence of human encroachment on his beloved landscape. He helped launch the Sierra Club and served as its president. One of the greatest conservationists of all time, he saved innumerable natural places from destruction by highways, dams, and development. His writing and lobbying efforts profoundly affected U.S. policy and led to the establishment of better forestry and conservation practices. Muir's efforts also led to the designation of Yosemite as a National Park. Years after Muir's death in 1914 at Los Angeles, California, two great mountaineers were comparing the Alps to mountains in the western United States. The American asked the European why the Alps are so highly developed with trains, hotels, and highways all crowding the natural beauty. The answer was very simple: "You had Muir."

VLADIMIR ILYICH LENIN

Born April 22, 1870
Died January 21, 1924

Lenin was the Russian revolutionary leader who presided over the first government of Soviet Russia and then led the Union of Soviet Socialist Republics (USSR). Born Vladimir Ilich Ulyanov in the city now known as Ulyanovsk to an educated landowning family, he later took the pseudonym Lenin. His older brother was arrested and executed in 1887 for his involvement in a plot to assassinate Tzar Alexander III. Later that same year Lenin was expelled from university for his involvement in a student demonstration. After becoming a lawyer, he began developing an underground Marxist movement. In 1895 he was arrested and exiled to Siberia for three years.

When his exile was over, he and his wife went abroad and helped start a radical paper *Iskra* (*Spark*). He wrote many influential pamphlets and newspaper articles. The St. Petersburg Massacre of 1905, where Cossacks fired on a peaceful demonstration, led Lenin to advocate violent action to take over the Russian government. It wasn't until 1917 that the pressures of World War I and the tzar's waning power combined to allow real change to occur. Lenin made a deal with Germany: he promised that if they could get him back into Russia, he would end the war. His return led to the October Uprising, a nearly bloodless coup that tossed out the monarchy and instituted the "rule of the masses."

In 1918, Lenin was elected head of the government and spent his final years consolidating sweeping reforms to Russia's society and economy. Land was redistributed; factories, banks, and power companies were taken over; and the Russian Orthodox Church was banned. After serious setbacks, which cost the lives of thousands of people, Lenin modified his stance to allow limited capitalism. When he died in 1922, after a series of strokes, Lenin wanted Trotsky to succeed him but was outmaneuvered by Joseph Stalin, who took over leadership of the country.

GRANVILLE T. WOODS

Born April 23, 1856
Died January 30, 1910

Sometimes referred to as the black Thomas Edison because he invented so many electronic devices and held so many patents, Woods was born at Columbus, Ohio. His 1887 invention of the Synchronous Multiplex Railway Telegraph, which allowed communication between dispatchers and trains while trains were in motion, is credited with greatly improving the safety of rail travel and commerce. Granville left school at the age of ten. When he was sixteen he got a railroad job and also started to study electrical and mechanical engineering. He invented a regulator that made electrical motors run better. Soon demand for his inventions allowed him to dedicate himself to full-time inventing.

In 1884 he invented a steam boiler furnace. Many other inventions followed, such as an automatic air brake, an electric battery, a telephone transmitter, and a number of devices for the telegraph. His 1890 invention of an electronically heated egg incubator allowed growers to hatch fifty thousand eggs at a time. Granville sold many of his creations to Westinghouse, General Electric, Bell Telephone, and other large companies. When Woods died at New York City, he had more than fifty patents to his credit. He had the recognition of the world. His overhead conducting system for electric trolleys and rail cars is still in use today.

ROBERT PENN WARREN

Born April 24, 1905
Died September 15, 1989

An American novelist, three-time Pulitzer winner, and first poet laureate of the United States, Warren was born at Guthrie, Kentucky. He became well known for his writing but his greatest influence was in the field of literary criticism. He was a member of a literary group at Vanderbilt University that was active between the world wars and became known as the New Critics. As writers they were known as the Fugitives; they briefly published a magazine, *The Fugitive*, advocating the literary traditions of the rural South.

After earning a teaching degree from the University of California and fulfilling a stint as a Rhodes scholar at Oxford, Warren went on to teach at Vanderbilt, Louisiana State, the University of Minnesota, and Yale.

Warren and Cleanth Brooks published a series of college-level English literature anthologies that influenced a generation of college students by emphasizing the importance of close reading and textual critique. Widely regarded as one of the best poets of his generation, he nevertheless won his most popular acclaim, and his first Pulitzer Prize, in 1947, for his novel *All the King's Men*. As he lived in the Northeast, his views liberalized somewhat and his style of poetry loosened up, which made him even more popular as a writer. He received two more Pulitzers, one in the 1950s and one in the late 1970s. He was asked to serve the Academy of American Poets, where he was chancellor from 1972 to 1978. Appointed the first poet laureate of the United States in 1985, he died in 1989 at Stratton, Vermont.

MEADOWLARK LEMON

Born April 25, 1932

The beloved "Crown Prince of Basketball" was born Meadow George Lemon at Lexington, South Carolina, and grew up in Wilmington, North Carolina. During his childhood years, the Harlem Globetrotters (formed in 1926) were a traveling basketball phenomenon, touring the United States (and later the world), taking on all comers, and almost always beating them. In the 1930s, the team began to clown around as well as demonstrate dazzling skills, and eventually this sense of fun became their hallmark.

Lemon served briefly in the army before winning a position on the team in 1954. He was twenty-two years old when he began his first season and continued playing for the team for twenty-four years. While with the Globetrotters, he gained the nickname "Meadowlark" and became one of their most popular players because of his amazing athletic abilities as well as his comedy routines. (His most well-known routine was threatening to douse a spectator with a bucket of water, which magically became confetti when thrown.) By 1978, Lemon was named among the top five most popular personalities in America. He was honored with the prestigious John W. Bunn Award in 2000 in recognition of his outstanding lifetime contributions to basketball.

Lemon continues to be a sports ambassador to the world as an inspirational speaker (he received his doctor of divinity degree in 1998) and as the founder of Camp Meadowlark, a co-ed sports camp for youth. His jersey (No. 36) was retired by the Globetrotters in 2001.

JOHN JAMES AUDUBON

Born April 26, 1785
Died January 27, 1851

An ornithologist, naturalist, and artist whose name became inextricably linked to birds and bird watching, Audubon was born at Haiti, the son of a sea captain and his French mistress. Raised mostly by his stepmother in France, he was sent at age eighteen to live on the family's estate near Philadelphia, perhaps to avoid being drafted into Napoleon's army. A life-long fan of bird watching, Audubon possessed a good eye for detail and a fine hand for replicating what he saw. He even banded the legs of Eastern Phoebes to discover that they return to the same nests each year.

After several failed business ventures, marriage to Lucy Bakewell, and the birth of two sons, Audubon left home and journeyed down the Mississippi River painting birds. His wife became a tutor to earn money to feed their children. He returned with a huge mass of drawings and paintings and then sailed to London to see about having them published. There he found his work was an immediate success. His life-size dramatic portrayals of birds, accompanied by his somewhat embellished tales of the wild American continent, played perfectly in Europe at the time. Audubon soon found a printer for his *Birds of America*, which was published in four volumes. *Ornithological Biography* and *A Synopsis of the Birds of North America* followed. These books and his activities in Europe established Audubon as a bird authority. He returned to America and proceeded to publish several more books. The Audubon Society adopted his name, which had become synonymous with both the love of birds and the need to protect them. Audubon died at New York City.

ULYSSES SIMPSON GRANT

Born April 27, 1822
Died July 23, 1885

Born the son of a tanner at Point Pleasant, Ohio, Ulysses S. Grant became the eighteenth president of the United States. He graduated from the United States Military Academy in 1843. During the Civil War he successfully whipped an unruly bunch of volunteers into shape for the governor of Illinois. In 1861 he rose to the rank of brigadier general of volunteers. After a series of bloody battles, a Confederate commander asked Grant for his terms of surrender. When he replied, "No terms except an unconditional surrender can be accepted," his nickname, "Unconditional Surrender" Grant, was born. President Lincoln promoted Grant to lieutenant general in command of all Union armies in the spring of 1864.

Lincoln admired Grant's fighting spirit and defended him against critics when he lost battles. In the spring of 1865 Grant received General Lee's surrender. He went on to become the president of the United States but had a hard time figuring out a course of action for a nation reeling from the aftershock of a brutal and expensive war. Despite his personal honesty, news of financial scandals plagued his administration and his personal business endeavors. His own financial firm went bankrupt after he retired from the presidency. Upon learning that he had cancer of the throat he began a last-ditch effort to write and sell his memoirs in the hope of providing financial security for his family. He died at Mount McGregor, New York, soon after completing his book, which ultimately brought in nearly half a million dollars.

JAMES MONROE

Born April 28, 1758
Died July 4, 1831

The fifth president of the United States was born at Westmoreland County, Virginia, and served two terms. Monroe fought in several campaigns in the Revolutionary War. He studied law with Thomas Jefferson, served in the Virginia legislature, and was a delegate to the Continental Congress (1783–1786), where he opposed the Constitution on the grounds that it made the government too centralized. After serving in the U.S. Senate he served as governor of Virginia. He played a major role in diplomatic missions to Spain, England, and France. As minister to France he helped negotiate the Louisiana Purchase in 1803.

He won the presidential election by a large margin in 1816 and again in 1820. The nation was enjoying a mood of optimism, and his presidency went well: he settled boundary issues with Canada; signed the Missouri Compromise, which involved negotiating the rights of slaveholding and nonslaveholding states; and acquired Florida. In 1823 he issued the Monroe Doctrine, which announced to European nations that they were no longer welcome as colonizers in the Americas and that the United States would not tolerate European intervention. Monroe was one of three U.S. presidents who died on Independence Day (July Fourth). He died at New York, New York.

HIROHITO

Born April 29, 1901
Died January 7, 1989

The world's longest-reigning ruler, Hirohito was born at Tokyo and was number 124 in a line of Japanese monarchs when he ascended the Chrysanthemum Throne in 1926. Hirohito presided over perhaps the most eventful period in the 2,500 years of recorded Japanese history. His reign included the era of attempted military conquest of Asia and the attack on Pearl Harbor that brought the United States into World War II, which ultimately led to Japan's defeat when the United States unleashed the atomic bomb on Hiroshima and Nagasaki. Although he opposed initiating hostilities with the United States, he bowed under the pressure of his militaristic prime minister, Hideki Tojo, and signed a declaration of war. During the war's final days he overruled Tojo and advocated surrender. Hirohito broke tradition to broadcast his message directly to the Japanese people asking them to "endure the unendurable" and stop fighting. This radio message marked the first time the emperor's voice had been heard by anyone outside the royal compound or inner circle of government officials. He also ruled during the era of massive economic recovery following the war, when Japan renounced military aggression and rebuilt itself to a position of preeminent economic strength.

In 1946 he chose to become a symbol of the state in Japan's new parliamentary democracy. Hirohito returned to his first love, marine biology, and became a noted world authority. When he died at Tokyo, in 1989, his son Akihito inherited his throne.

CARL FRIEDRICH GAUSS

Born April 30, 1777
Died February 23, 1855

Gauss is said to have corrected some of his father's mathematical calculations at the remarkable age of two. Later, his teachers noticed his potential when it seemed he could instantly visualize mathematical relationships. Born at Brunswick, Germany, he attended the University of Göttingen and made remarkable discoveries in math while still a teenager. His thesis for a Ph.D. in 1799 gave the first proof of the fundamental theorem of algebra.

For many years Gauss was supported in his endeavors by his patron, the Duke of Brunswick. Despite great personal tragedy, including the loss of his patron, his wife, and an infant son all in the space of a few years, he never stopped researching and writing. He had a lifelong interest in astronomy and made many contributions to the mathematical calculations needed to pinpoint a celestial position. He used his amazing ability to make instant calculations when he was asked to survey the state of Hanover to link it to an already completed Danish grid. To do the survey work he invented a heliotrope that used the sun's rays, mirrors, and a telescope. He also made contributions to applied sciences, including discoveries about electricity and magnetism. He died at Hanover, Germany.

MAY

GEORGE INNESS

Born May 1, 1825
Died August 3, 1894

Born near the middle of the Hudson River Valley at Newburgh, New York, but raised at New York City, Inness started out his career by apprenticing to an engraver. He went on to become one of the greatest American landscape painters of his generation. In his twenties he traveled to Italy and France and became very taken with the paintings of the Barbizon School, especially those by Theodore Rousseau. He observed other painters keenly, and when he returned to the United States he started to paint. At first he stuck to the accepted motifs involving waterfalls, trees, and pastures—in short, he painted all things romantic. By 1860, he felt enough confidence in his own skills to create more expressive and descriptive landscapes.

Inness chose the Delaware Valley, a picturesque area of Pennsylvania, for many of his paintings. He is known for his use of light and shadow. His work often reveals great vistas. He preferred civilized landscapes to those of unfettered wilderness, though nature is present in every scene. Many of his paintings reflect the soft effects of spring and the burnt colors of autumn. Among his most noted works are *Peace and Plenty*, *The Home of the Heron*, and *Niagara Falls*. He died at Bridge of Allen, Stirling, Scotland.

BENJAMIN SPOCK

Born May 2, 1903
Died March 15, 1998

The author of the bestselling book of the twentieth century was born at New Haven, Connecticut. Spock studied literature and history at Yale University, then attended Yale School of Medicine and Columbia University's College of Physicians and Surgeons where he specialized in pediatrics. By the time he received his doctor's degree in 1929, Spock was married and had two children of his own. Early in his career, Spock became interested in child psychology and family dynamics; he considered these elements to be key factors in pediatric medicine. It was a radical view at the time.

After six years of study in psychoanalysis, Spock became one of the first pediatricians to use this kind of background. He strongly believed that the childcare guidance of the day was flawed, and in 1946 he published *The Common Sense Book of Baby and Childcare*. Along with a great deal of sound medical advice and instruction, the book was written in a reassuring tone, which made it stand out among the authoritarian parenting books of the time. It revolutionized childcare by telling parents that, since children (like adults) are all different, effective parenting should be flexible. Over the decades, the book has been translated into thirty-nine languages and has sold more than 50 million copies. Spock revised the book seven times, always incorporating new medical developments and changing social issues such as single parenthood and daycare centers. His is still the most recognized name in childcare. Benjamin Spock died at San Diego, California.

GOLDA MEIR

Born May 3, 1898
Died December 8, 1978

Born Goldie Mabovitch at Kiev, Russia, she moved with her family to Milwaukee, Wisconsin, in 1906. As an adult she worked as a school-teacher and became involved in the Milwaukee Labor Zionist Party, where she began her career in politics. She held an ardent belief that Jews should have a homeland in the Middle East. In 1921 she moved to Palestine with her husband. She was a prime mover throughout the fight for an independent Jewish homeland and then played a role in the area's politics for more than thirty-five years.

In 1936 she became head of the General Federation of Jewish Labor. After Israel received its independence in 1948, she was appointed minister of labor and then foreign minister. In 1966 Meir became secretary general of the Mapai Party. After the death of Prime Minister Levi Eshkol in 1969, she became prime minister of Israel and held that office until she resigned in 1974. At that time, the government was facing charges of military unpreparedness during the Yom Kippur War. A strong leader who had a sense of humor, she is fondly remembered for her question to Egyptian Prime Minister Anwar Sadat when he made his historic trip to Israel: "What took you so long?" Golda Meir died at Jerusalem.

HORACE MANN

Born May 4, 1796
Died August 2, 1859

The American educator, author, and public servant who became known as the father of public education in the United States was born at Franklin, Massachusetts. Like many youngsters in the early days of the country, Mann's schooling consisted of brief periods of only eight to ten weeks a year. However, he spent many hours at his local library where he read great works. This self-education combined with a brief period of study with a tutor gained him admission at the sophomore level at Brown University in 1816. After graduation he went on to become a lawyer and eventually a state senator.

Mann was a person of many interests but chief among them was his desire to make education a reality for every child in the country. He left his Boston law practice in 1837 to take the newly formed post of secretary of the state board of education. During his tenure he published twelve annual reports illuminating the relationship among freedom, democracy, and education. He wanted school to be available to all children, not just the rich, and he aimed to create an environment where the social classes could come together in harmony. He truly believed that education for all would dramatically reduce crime and many other social ills. He helped establish schools to teach teachers and founded Westfield State College (in Massachusetts). He went on to become a U.S. representative in 1848 and then accepted a post as president of Antioch College in 1852. He died at Yellow Springs, Ohio.

NELLIE BLY

Born May 5, 1867
Died January 27, 1922

Journalist and adventurer Nellie Bly was born Elizabeth Cochran at Cochran's Mills, Pennsylvania. She was the first female reporter with star quality, and her exposés instigated needed reforms in many areas. She got her first journalism job at age eighteen, writing for the *Pittsburgh Dispatch*, where her editor suggested her pen name. While there she wrote series on divorce, the conditions of women and children in factories, and the quality of life in Mexico. In 1867 she went to work for the *New York World* and became an immediate sensation when she had herself committed to an insane asylum to investigate conditions there.

Bly set out on November 14, 1889, to break the record of the hero in Jules Verne's *Around the World in Eighty Days*. The *World* published her daily reports of her adventures and held a contest to guess her return time. When Bly completed her trip in 72 days, 6 hours, 11 minutes, and 14 seconds, she received a hero's welcome. She was one of the most exciting women of the era. When she married millionaire Robert Seaman in 1895, many speculated that her writing days were over. In fact, she did take a break from writing and adventuring but joined the *New York Evening Journal* in 1919. Her final major piece was a report of an execution at Sing Sing, which resulted in public opposition to the death penalty.

ROBERT E. PEARY

Born May 6, 1856
Died February 20, 1920

Born at Cresson, Pennsylvania, Peary made his name by discovering the North Pole after many of his predecessors had died in the attempt. He got his start as a cartographic draftsman in the U.S. Coast and Geodetic Survey for two years. He then joined the U.S. Navy Corp of Civil Engineers in 1881. At first he worked in tropical climate exploration, but after reading of the inland ice of Greenland he became more interested in the Arctic. He ended up organizing and leading eight Arctic expeditions and is credited with verifying Greenland's island formation, proving that the polar ice cap extended beyond 82 degrees north latitude, and discovering the Melville meteorite on Melville Bay.

He showed good judgment when he changed the way he organized his expedition. He chose to take on the pole the way mountaineers take on a peak. He hired native Inuit help and tried to travel, eat, dress, and camp as the Inuit did. This trip was difficult, but it was made easier by Peary's assistants. The team made it to the North Pole April 6, 1909. When he returned he found that Frederick Cook, another American explorer, was claiming he had been at the pole a year earlier. Questions about both men's claims persist, but the scientific community eventually hailed Peary the true discoverer. Peary died at Washington, D.C.

JOHANNES BRAHMS

Born May 7, 1833
Died April 3, 1897

Regarded as one of the greatest nineteenth-century composers, Brahms was born at Hamburg, Germany. His works were firmly rooted in traditional classical principles and romantic spirit. At age seventeen, Brahms's talents were discovered and promoted by the Hungarian violinist, Edward Remenyi, who took him on a national concert tour in 1850. During this tour he met composer Robert Schumann and his wife Clara Schumann, who was also a composer and was considered the most brilliant concert pianist of her day. The endorsement and support of the Schumanns quickly established Brahms's musical reputation.

After Robert Schumann's death in 1856, Brahms was devoted to Clara and supported both her and her children. He wrote his first piano concerto in 1859 and completed his most important work, *German Requiem*, in 1868. Its success gave him the confidence to complete his first major symphony in 1876. He went on to complete three more symphonies, a second piano concerto, chamber music, and many songs. During his lifetime, his music was sometimes critiqued as dry or academic, but after his death at Vienna, Austria, his reputation continued to grow. He is now regarded as one of the three great musical B's—along with Bach and Beethoven.

ROBERT JOHNSON

Born May 8, 1911
Died August 16, 1938

Singer, songwriter, and master blues guitarist Johnson was born at Hazelhurst, Mississippi. He developed a unique guitar style and was possessed of such skill that it was said he acquired his ability by selling his soul to the devil. (The film *Crossroads* is based loosely on this popular myth.) Johnson had no supernatural protection when the jealous husband of a lady friend killed him in 1938. Although he lived to be only twenty-seven, his music was more influential than that of many musicians who lived to see old age.

Johnson's only two recording sessions captured the classics "Sweet Home Chicago," "Cross Road Blues," and "Me and the Devil Blues." Because of the influence he has had on the generations of musicians that followed him, many think of him as one of the most important bluesmen ever. It took decades for private opinions to mount into public notice, but he was inducted into the Blues Hall of Fame in 1980 and the Rock and Roll Hall of Fame in 1986.

JOHN BROWN

Born May 6, 1800
Died December 2, 1859

The subject of the song "John Brown's Body," Brown was born at Torrington, Connecticut. During the 1820s and 1830s, when Brown was a young man, his house was an active stop on the underground railroad, a network of emancipation sympathizers who helped runaway slaves make it to safety in states in the North or even Canada. His hatred of slavery was fueled by the horrible stories he heard while living in a black settlement in northern New York. He and five of his sons settled in Kansas and led several raids on proslavery outposts there. After proslavery forces attacked the city of Lawrence in 1856, Brown led a counterattack that killed five men.

Increasingly convinced that violence would be necessary to secure freedom for the thousands of enslaved people in the United States, Brown announced he was setting up antislavery strongholds in the mountains of Virginia and Maryland. He was planning to attack a number of targets in the South. On the night of October 16, 1859, together with two of his sons and nineteen others, he attacked the federal arsenal at Harpers Ferry, Virginia, and rounded up sixty men from the area as hostages. Colonel Robert E. Lee and troops attacked the armory, killing ten men, including Brown's sons. Brown himself survived but was wounded and had to surrender. Brown was tried for treason. He was found guilty and hanged at Charlestown, Virginia. His actions heightened tensions between Northern abolitionists and Southern slaveholders.

FRED ASTAIRE

Born May 10, 1899
Died June 22, 1987

Considered one of the best dancers of his time, Astaire was born into a wealthy family at Omaha, Nebraska. He took dance lessons from fine arts academies and began his professional career while still in his teens. With his sister, Adele, he danced at vaudeville houses and cabarets all over the world. The two Astaires were in one hit after another in New York. They were considered the height of grace and charm. When his sister gave up her career to marry, Fred teamed up with dancer Ginger Rogers, and they debuted as a dancing pair in the movie *Flying Down to Rio* (1933). Their relatively minor roles won them fans who demanded to see more. Astaire's popularity flew in the face of the studio's initial perception of his talents. Legend has it that he failed his first screen test when he was dismissed with the notes: "Can't act. Slightly bald. Can dance a little."

Rogers and Astaire went on to wow audiences; they danced—more than a little—in ten different musicals, including *Top Hat* (1935), *Follow the Fleet* (1936), and *The Barkleys of Broadway* (1949). Astaire tried to go out on his own a number of times, but the studios preferred him to work with Rogers because audiences adored them as a duo. Astaire later worked with just about every glamorous leading lady in Hollywood and was one of the top leading men of his era. A true artist, he insisted camera tricks and the like not be used to "improve" his performances. Even as he aged he always managed to make his dance numbers look easy and spontaneous. He took nondancing roles in his later years and won a number of awards, including an Oscar for his work in *The Towering Inferno* in 1974. He remained active until his death at Los Angeles.

137

MARTHA GRAHAM

Born May 11, 1894
Died April 1, 1991

Martha Graham was born at Allegheny, Pennsylvania, and became one of the giants of the modern dance movement in the United States. She began her dance career at the comparatively late age of twenty-two and joined the Greenwich Village Follies in 1923. Her revolutionary ideas began to surface in the late 1920s, and by the mid-1930s she was incorporating motifs from her studies of southwestern American Indians. At the time Graham began choreography, the idea of dancing in bare feet was quite revolutionary.

Graham brought a new psychological depth and excitement to dance by exploring primal emotions and ancient rituals in her work. She worked closely with composer Aaron Copland to produce uniquely American works. Her dancing and choreography inspired a new generation of modern dancers who were more willing to break molds and explore new territory. She lived to see her concepts accepted and integrated into many forms of dance. Graham remained in great shape throughout her life and performed until the age of seventy-five. She received the Presidential Medal of Freedom in 1976. She died at New York, New York.

FLORENCE NIGHTINGALE

Born May 12, 1820
Died August 13, 1910

This English nurse and public health activist and reformer was born at Florence, Italy, and trained in Europe before taking a job in London. She is credited more than any other single person for the development of modern nursing procedures. Her efforts improved the nursing community by making the field more professional. In 1854, during the Crimean War, she volunteered for duty and organized a unit of thirty-eight women to care for the wounded. Her supervision of nurses at the British hospital at Scutari, Turkey, and her emphasis on hygiene reduced the death rate dramatically. By the war's end she had become a living legend. When she returned to England in 1856, she was rewarded with a fund for training nurses.

In 1860 she established a nursing school at St. Thomas's Hospital in London. Her 1859 book, *Notes on Nursing*, was highly influential. In 1907 she was the first woman ever given the British Order of Merit. Her compassion for wounded men and her support of women trying to make nursing a real profession earned her such a reputation that English-speaking people everywhere call a person who ministers to others in a selfless fashion a "Florence Nightingale." She died at London, England.

MARY WELLS

Born May 13, 1943
Died July 26, 1992

Motown's first big star was born at Detroit, Michigan—otherwise known as the Motor City, which gave Motown its name. At the tender age of seventeen, Mary Wells offered her song "Bye Bye Baby" to rhythm and blues star Jackie Wilson. His producer saw her talent and signed her to the newly formed Motown Records label. Wells's rendition of the song created one of the company's first Top Fifty hits in 1960. Her popularity, along with a that of a few other recording artists, gained Motown crossover airtime on white stations and helped desegregate the country's airwaves.

Wells worked closely with Smokey Robinson, who oversaw all her Motown releases that followed her first big hit. Robinson himself composed her music, using clever lyrics and hard-to-resist melody lines for which Wells's natural talent was perfectly suited. The pair created a number of Top Ten hits in the early 1960s but climbed to the very top with a number one hit in 1964, "My Guy." This song was popular abroad as well as in the United States and even was a Top Five contender in the United Kingdom. An album of duets with Motown's top male star, Marvin Gaye, followed, which produced another hit single, "Once Upon a Time." At the zenith of her career Wells accepted an offer from a film company, but without the assistance of Smokey Robinson to guide her, nothing much came of it. After marrying Cecil Womack of the Valentinos, she recorded for Atco Records, but despite a few popular tunes, her career never blossomed again. After rerecording some of her big hits, she went on the road touring in the early 1980s, even continuing after she was diagnosed with throat cancer. Wells lost the battle at age forty-nine, at Los Angeles, California.

THOMAS GAINSBOROUGH

Born May 14, 1727
Died August 2, 1788

Born the son of a clothier at Sudbury, Suffolk, England, Gainsborough became one of the most versatile portrait and landscape painters of the eighteenth century. He showed an early aptitude for drawing and was encouraged by his mother, a fine painter in her own right who specialized in flowers. When he was thirteen he was sent to London to continue his art studies. He worked in the studios of a number of different artists, including a draughtsman/engraver and a scene painter/illustrator. When he married the daughter of a nobleman, his wife's annuity allowed him to settle into a career as a portrait painter.

At first he had few commissions, which meant more hours to pursue his real love, landscape drawing. He also made many famous paintings of his wife, Margaret, and his daughters. He was inventive and original, always prepared to experiment with new ideas and techniques. Unlike many painters of his day he devoted serious attention to landscapes. He painted many wealthy families in the 1760s when he moved to Bath, where the upper classes often wintered. His drawings used a variety of mediums, including chalk, pen and wash, and watercolor. *The Blue Boy*, probably painted around 1770, is his best-known work in oil. He became a founding member of the Royal Academy, where he exhibited paintings each year until his retirement. He died a well-known and greatly respected painter at London, England.

MADELEINE ALBRIGHT

Born May 15, 1937

The former U.S. secretary of state was born Marie Jana Korbel, at Prague, Czechoslovakia, and later took the name Madeleine from her grandmother. Her father, Joseph, was a diplomat. When the Nazis invaded in 1939 the family had to flee to safety in London. After World War II, they returned to Prague, but they were forced to move again when the Communists took power. This time they settled in Denver, Colorado, and became U.S. citizens. By this time, Albright spoke Czech, French, and English. She was raised as a Roman Catholic, so she was shocked to discover in the late 1990s, at the height of her career, that her parents were born Jewish and that three out of four of her grandparents and most of her other relatives had perished in Nazi concentration camps. Her parents had chosen to hide this information to protect themselves and their children.

Albright attended Wellesley College where she studied journalism and political science. Her first career as a journalist ended with marriage and motherhood. Despite devoting long hours to her three daughters, Albright managed to pursue a Ph.D. at Columbia University over the course of a decade. Her political career started with fundraising for an unsuccessful presidential candidate. Later Jimmy Carter asked her to assist him with congressional relations and national security issues. She served as a professor at Georgetown University and as foreign affairs adviser to the first female candidate for vice president, Geraldine Ferraro. In 1993 President Clinton appointed her to a cabinet post as ambassador to the United Nations, and in 1996 he nominated her for the position of secretary of state. She was approved warmly by a Congress that liked her unflappable, pragmatic style. She promised to "tell it like it is, here and when I go abroad." In her years as the leader of foreign policy she managed to continue to make friends of former enemies abroad even while standing firm for U.S. policy. She remains in high demand as a talk show guest, lecturer, and public speaker.

WILLIAM HENRY SEWARD

Born May 16, 1801
Died October 10, 1872

Born at Florida, New York, William Seward is best remembered for his purchase of Alaska from Russia when he was secretary of state under President Andrew Johnson. At the time of the purchase, in 1867, the price of $7,200,000 was seen as too steep and thus the deal was christened "Seward's Folly." In later years it became clear that this deal was comparable with the Louisiana Purchase in terms of benefit versus cost to the nation. Seward had a long political career, including a stint as governor of New York, from 1839 to 1843, where he established himself as the head of the antislavery faction of the Whig party. After the collapse of the Whig party, Seward assumed the leadership of the Republican party. He also served as a member of the United States Senate from 1848 to 1860.

Seward was President Lincoln's secretary of state. On the evening of Lincoln's assassination, April 14, 1865, he was stabbed in the throat by a coconspirator of John Wilkes Booth. Seward recovered from the stabbing. He kept his position under the new president, Andrew Johnson, until 1869. Seward died at Auburn, New York.

EDWARD JENNER

Born May 17, 1749
Died January 26, 1823

Now seen as the father of immunology and virology, and developer of a vaccine for smallpox, Jenner was born the son of a vicar at Berkeley, Gloucestershire, England. When only twelve he served as a surgeon's apprentice. Many years later he pursued a medical degree from St. Andrew's University and became a successful physician and surgeon. At the time, smallpox was rampant; the disease killed between 10 and 20 percent of those who contracted it. Those who survived often suffered permanent disfigurement. Experimentation with inoculation of small amounts of serum from sick people to healthy people was not fully successful as some people still caught the illness. Jenner used a different method: he used cowpox, a related but less deadly disease, to inoculate against smallpox. His tests were promising, and he wrote a book, *An Inquiry into the Causes and Effects of the Variolae Vaccinae*, which prompted other doctors to adopt the practice of vaccination. The smallpox vaccine is credited with saving millions of lives worldwide.

Jenner is the originator of the term *virus*. The medical field of immunology is based on his experiments and includes allergy treatment, organ transplants, AIDS research, cancer treatments, and the study of autoimmune diseases. Throughout his life Dr. Jenner provided information free of charge to anyone who wished to learn more. He vaccinated the poor, also free of charge, in a thatched hut he called his Temple of Vaccinia. He continued to make detailed observations of birds and animals, write medical articles, and treat patients. Jenner died at Berkeley, and his home is now a museum that reflects his wide-ranging interests— from hydrogen balloons to hedgehogs to cuckoo birds to grapes.

FRANK CAPRA

Born May 18, 1897
Died September 3, 1991

This Academy Award–winning director created movies suffused with affectionate portrayals of the common man and the strengths and foibles of American democracy. Capra was born at Palermo, Sicily, but immigrated with his family to America at age six—and America became his beloved homeland. Starstruck, he bluffed his way into silent movies in 1922 and, despite nearly complete ignorance of moviemaking, directed and produced a profitable one-reeler. During the Depression, he turned out sparkling comedies and dramas about everyday people.

He was the first to win three directorial Oscars—for *It Happened One Night* (1934), *Mr. Deeds Goes to Town* (1936), and *You Can't Take It with You* (1938). The first and third of these were deemed best picture at the Academy Awards of their respective years. *It Happened One Night*, a romantic comedy starring Clark Gable as a wisecracking reporter following a runaway heiress (played by Claudette Colbert), was the first film to sweep the best picture, director, and major actor categories at the Academy Awards. After World War II, Capra made the Christmas classic *It's a Wonderful Life* (1946)—which turned out to be his favorite film. He died at La Quinta, California.

MALCOLM X

Born May 19, 1925
Died February 21, 1965

Black nationalist and civil rights activist Malcolm Little was born at Omaha, Nebraska, and raised in Lansing, Michigan, where the family home was burned by the Ku Klux Klan. In his teens he moved to the East Coast where he became involved in petty crime. While serving a jail sentence for burglary, Little made a major life change when he joined the black Muslim organization Nation of Islam. Upon his release from jail, he became Malcolm X. He chose *X* to stand in for the family name that was lost when his ancestors were sold into slavery in Africa. Malcolm X followed the strict Nation of Islam code of behavior and worked tirelessly to bring the message of African-American separatism and racial pride to a new generation.

He was a very powerful and charismatic speaker. His message of black liberation "by any means necessary" was soon heard all over the United States. However, his support of violence as a means of self-defense, his denunciation of white people, and his rejection of the more moderate approach of Martin Luther King Jr. made him a controversial figure for both black and white Americans. In 1964 Malcolm X split with the Nation of Islam, made a pilgrimage to Mecca, and became an orthodox Muslim. He chose a new name, El-Hajj Malik el Shabazz. He also moderated his antiwhite and separatist views. In 1965, at a rally in Harlem, New York, he was assassinated while making a speech.

JOHN STUART MILL

Born May 20, 1806
Died May 8, 1873

Born at London, England, the son of a Scottish economist, historian, and philosopher who taught him Greek at age three and Latin at age eight, John Stuart Mill was a formidable intellect who is seen as a giant in the field of political economy. Mill was the transitional link between eighteenth- and nineteenth-century economic and philosophical thought. He helped enunciate and refine the ideas of economies of scale, comparative advantage in trade, and opportunity cost. He was willing to research almost any topic and would debate the best minds of his time happily, and effectively, either in person or in writing.

Mill was part of the movement that championed the idea of individual liberty and human reason. Among his noted works is the celebrated essay "On Liberty," in which he said "the sole end for which mankind are warranted, individually or collectively, in interfering with the liberty of action of any other of their number, is self-protection." Mill felt it was fine to be thought of as foolish or even wrong but that no person should impede another. His support of women's equality and his outspoken voice for universal suffrage (including women's right to vote) was shocking to many gentlemen of his era. He held lifelong opinions that were not popular, such as the idea that those with more education should be given more votes. He supported inheritance taxation and trade protectionism. After working thirty-eight years for the East India Company, he died at Avignon, France.

ANDREI DMITRIEVICH SAKHAROV

Born May 21, 1921
Died December 14, 1989

Soviet physicist, human rights activist, and environmentalist Sakharov was born at Moscow, Russia. He attended the Soviet Academy of Sciences, and in the late 1940s to mid-1950s he worked out the theories that led to the development of thermonuclear fusion. His expertise in nuclear physics brought about the Soviet Union's first atomic and later hydrogen bombs. He saw shortcomings in his nation's government and emerged in the late 1960s as an outspoken critic of the arms race. He worked for human rights, founding the Soviet Human Rights Committee in 1970. One of the leading dissidents of his generation, he received the Nobel Peace Prize in 1975.

The government reacted to his demands for civil liberties by exiling him to Gorky, Russia, from 1980 to 1986. This banishment created a huge international response and worldwide protest. Sakharov used his powerful intellect to build the concept that would become known as *perestroika*, a movement of reform and rebuilding. This idea is credited with creating *glasnost*, or freedom, for the people of his nation. He was named to the Congress of People's Deputies eight months before his death at Moscow. As a physicist he helped develop weapons of mass destruction; as a humanitarian he was a courageous advocate of human rights and a fierce opponent of militarism.

MARY CASSATT

Born May 22, 1844
Died June 14, 1926

A leading American painter of the Impressionism school, Cassatt was born in 1844 at Allegheny City, which is now a part of Pittsburgh, Pennsylvania. After studying in Spain, Italy, and Holland, Cassatt settled in Paris where she spent much of her life. In the late 1870s and 1880s her work was shown alongside that by Edgar Degas, Claude Monet, and other Impressionists. Through her influence, the works of these artists became well known in the United States. While she herself never had children, Cassatt's paintings and pastels often depict tender moments between mothers and children.

Today, almost every major American art museum has at least one of Cassatt's paintings on display. One of the most popular American painters of all time, her work is featured on greeting cards, art calendars, and reproductions. After 1900, when she was in her fifties, her eyesight began to fail, and by 1914 she was unable to paint. Cassatt died at Chateau de Beaufresne near Paris, France.

JOHN BARTRAM

Born May 23, 1699
Died September 22, 1777

Talented botanist born at Chester County, near Darby, Pennsylvania, Bartram had little formal education. He began conducting experiments in hybridization on land he bought near the Schuylkill River in Philadelphia. He corresponded with European scientists and exchanged specimens with them, introducing many American plants to Europe and many European plants to the Americas. His circle included Carl Linnaeus, who was studying the changes animals underwent over generations.

Bartram later became botanist in the Colonies to King George III. Bartram traveled the colonies from the Carolinas to the Catskills, and from Florida to the Alleghenies, collecting seeds, bulbs, and plants and recording his findings in journals. His son William Bartram continued his work and was also an ornithologist. Bartram's Gardens is still open to the public in Philadelphia and was the first botanical garden of the United States.

EMANUEL LEUTZE

Born May 24, 1816
Died July 18, 1868

An itinerant painter, Leutze was born at Württemburg, Germany, and came to the United States when he was nine years old. At age fifteen he began painting and soon was creating depictions of favorite American historical events. He is best known for the painting *Washington Crossing the Delaware*. This painting was painted and destroyed more than once. Ironically, Leutze originally painted it while he was in Germany. The featured river was not the Delaware but the Rhine. He had visited a museum to make notes on Washington's uniform and had studied paintings of Washington so that he could make an accurate recounting of the famous voyage.

His paintings were popular in Germany and in the United States, and some sold for exorbitant prices. The U.S. Congress asked Leutze to paint a mural for the Capitol. The painting that resulted is *Westward the Course of Empire Takes Its Way*, but it's more commonly referred to as *Westward Ho* and has become one of Washington's most popular tourist attractions. This is just one example of a work by Leutze that depicts historical events in a romantic and sweeping style. Other famous works include *Washington Rallying the Troops at Monmouth* and *Columbus Before the Queen*. Leutze died at Washington, D.C.

RALPH WALDO EMERSON

Born May 25, 1803
Died April 27, 1882

An absolute giant of his time, Emerson was one of the nineteenth century's most influential thinkers and writers. Born to an educated Boston family, Emerson began keeping a journal to record his observations in 1820. He maintained this habit throughout his long life. After attending Harvard in the early 1820s he continued at Harvard Divinity School and became an ordained minister of the Unitarian Church in 1829. However, he diverged from the thinking of the church, moving toward a study of nature and eventually embracing the new Transcendentalist movement. In an 1837 lecture to some Harvard students, he suggested that they keep journals. One of those students was a young man named Henry David Thoreau, who would become a lifelong follower of Emerson's. Thoreau even moved onto Emerson's property at Walden Pond, near Concord, to live more closely with nature.

Emerson's 1838 address to the Harvard Divinity School made him unwelcome for the next thirty years. He accused the church of acting "as if God were dead" and of squelching the spirit by emphasizing dogma. His words were controversial and painful, but they caused many churchgoers and church leaders to reexamine their practices. *Emerson's Essays: Second Series* sold well and was influential to other thinkers of the day. He called for a new national vision and advocated the use of first-person experience and the idea that there is one cosmic "over-soul." He suggested getting away from the rule of religion to a direct relationship with nature and God. Over the years he published a very long list of essays and poems. He also spoke out against slavery and the Fugitive Slave Law and was once mobbed by angry proslavery activists. In 1866 Harvard took Emerson back by granting him an honorary doctorate. He died at Concord, Massachusetts.

SALLY KRISTEN RIDE

Born May 26, 1951

Born at Encino, California, Ride was a competitive tennis player and an astrophysicist before she became famous as the first female astronaut at NASA. She attended Stanford University, graduated in 1973, earned her master's in science two years later, and earned a Ph.D. in physics just three years after that. She answered a help-wanted ad placed by NASA on a school bulletin board and was one of more than a thousand women who responded. In 1979 she became a mission specialist and four years later flew on the seventh space shuttle mission. It had been twenty years since Russia sent Valentina Tereshkova into space—and the world was watching.

Dr. Ride understood the significance of her presence, but she preferred to focus on doing her job. On her first mission the crew deployed two commercial communications satellites, set up more than twenty scientific experiments, and practiced rendezvous maneuvers. Dr. Ride was credited with securing a German satellite with a robotic arm so that it could be brought back to earth. Her second opportunity to go up in space came in 1984. This time she had another woman on board, Dr. Kathryn Sullivan, who became the first woman to walk in space. By now NASA and the world at large could see that these women were not mere tokens; they were the best-qualified people for the positions. Ride was in training for a third mission when the space shuttle *Challenger* exploded with its crew aboard, in 1986. She was appointed to the commission charged with investigating the accident. She then took a position for NASA developing the Office of Exploration. After leaving NASA in 1987, she taught at Stanford and the University of California, San Diego. She remains interested in sharing her experience and has written several books, including two for children, *To Space and Back* and *Exploring Our Solar System.*

RACHEL CARSON

Born May 27, 1907
Died April 14, 1964

An American biologist and nature writer, born at Springdale, Pennsylvania, Carson is credited with waking Americans to the dangers of widespread spraying of herbicides and pesticides. She detailed the problem in her 1962 book *Silent Spring*. Carson wrote a few other books, including *The Sea Around Us* and *The Sense of Wonder*, and a number of acclaimed magazine articles, each of which showcased her meticulous writing coupled with detailed scientific information. It was her ability to explain the complexities of ecology while voicing her scientific and personal concerns for nature that created lasting change in public awareness and even in governmental policy.

A solitary and serious figure, she was unprepared for the volatile reaction to *Silent Spring*. The idea that songbirds were being poisoned and that water tables were being made toxic by the widespread use of chemical sprays created a widespread sense of urgency. Congress assembled a subcommittee to investigate the dangers of pesticide use and asked Carson to testify. By this time she was suffering from cancer. She had been harshly criticized, and even slandered, by those who supported the chemical industries. Yet she testified calmly and brought evidence to show the committee. She died at Silver Spring, Maryland.

JIM THORPE

Born May 28, 1888
Died March 28, 1953

Declared the greatest male athlete of the first half of the twentieth century, James Francis Thorpe was born to a poor American Indian family
in what is now Oklahoma.

Thorpe won gold medals for both the pentathlon and decathlon at
the 1912 Olympic Games. At that time, the Olympics used strict rules
concerning athletes' amateur status, so when it was discovered that he had
briefly played minor league baseball, officials stripped him of his medals.
From 1913 to 1919 he played professional baseball for the New York
Giants, the Cincinnati Reds, and the Boston Braves. Then from 1919
until 1926 he played professional football. Additionally, Thorpe became
the first president of the American Professional Football Association (now
the NFL). He died at Lomita, California, at the age of sixty-five. In 1950,
American sports writers honored him as the greatest American athlete and
the best football player of the twentieth century. Decades after his death,
the International Olympic Committee agreed to return his Olympic
medals to his family.

PATRICK HENRY

Born May 29, 1736
Died June 6, 1799

An American revolutionary, lawyer, and statesman who became the spokesman for the Southern Colonies during the American Revolution, Henry was born at Studley, Hanover County, Virginia. A brilliant orator, he served first in the Virginia House of Burgesses. While there he opposed the Stamp Act, stating that the British Parliament had no right to tax the American colonies. He was a Virginia delegate to the first Continental Congress and in 1776 became the first governor of Virginia. He was a staunch advocate of the Bill of Rights and opposed the adoption of a new Constitution in 1788.

He was known for his linguistic abilities. The phrases "If this be treason, make the most of it!" and "Give me liberty or give me death!" are attributed to him. He felt the country would be a better place if certain rights were clearly enumerated. He worked very hard to see that the Bill of Rights was eventually added to the Constitution. He died of cancer at Red Hill, near Brookneal, Virginia.

COUNTEE CULLEN

Born May 30, 1903
Died January 9, 1946

Along with Langston Hughes, Countee Cullen was a leading poet of the Harlem Renaissance, the flourishing of African-American art, literature, and culture in the 1920s. Born at Kentucky, Cullen was raised by a grandmother and unofficially adopted by influential Harlem minister F. A. Cullen. In his youth, he won several poetry prizes, and he published his first poetry collection, *Color* (1925), while still in college. A brilliant student, he graduated from New York University Phi Beta Kappa. He went on to Harvard. While there he helped edit *Opportunity* magazine and there his column, "The Dark Tower," increased his literary reputation. In 1926 he earned a master's degree from Harvard.

Cullen published several books of poetry in the 1920s and 1930s, including *The Ballad of the Brown Girl* and *Copper Sun*. As a poet he usually avoided racial themes and was conservative, often writing in traditional sonnet form. He received a Guggenheim Fellowship in 1928, which allowed him to study abroad, mostly in France. He published his only novel, *One Way to Heaven*, in 1932. It was a comedy about lower-class blacks and the bourgeoisie of New York City. From 1934 until the end of his life he taught English, French, and creative writing at Frederick Douglass Junior High in New York City. He also wrote two books for young readers during these years: *The Lost Zoo*, about the animals that did not get onto Noah's ark, and *My Lives and How I Lost Them*, a biography from the point of view of his cat. Cullen died at New York City.

NORMAN VINCENT PEALE

Born May 31, 1898
Died December 24, 1993

This inspirational author and clergyman, the father of positive thinking, was born at Bowersville, Ohio. He grew up supporting his family by doing odd jobs and working long hours. He attended Ohio Wesleyan and Boston University before taking his first job as a reporter. He entered the ministry and went on to author more than forty books. By 1932 he was in charge of the Marble Collegiate Church in New York City, where he became famous for his sermons on how to approach modern living positively. Many of his sermons were broadcast on radio and later TV. In 1937 he established a clinic with Freudian psychologist Dr. Smiley Blanton, and for fifty-four years Peale had a weekly NBC radio broadcast heard by millions. His sermons were mailed to 750,000 people a month.

Peale developed the positive thinking/positive confession philosophy to help himself grow out of an inferiority complex; he is credited with bringing psychology into the church. He said, "through prayer you . . . make use of the great factor within yourself, the deep subconscious mind . . . [which Jesus has called] the kingdom of God within you." He also said, "Positive thinking is just another term for faith." His way of looking at psychology through religious terms eventually became known as Christian Psychology. Peale and his wife, Ruth, started *Guideposts* magazine in 1945, which grew to a circulation of 4.5 million and became the largest religious magazine ever. He also authored several bestselling books, including *The Power of Positive Thinking*, which has been translated into more than forty languages and has sold more than 20 million copies. He died at age ninety-five, at Pawling, New York.

JUNE

BRIGHAM YOUNG

Born June 1, 1801
Died August 29, 1877

Young was the second president of the Mormons, or Church of Jesus Christ of Latter-day Saints. Born at Whittingham, Vermont, Young led Mormons to Nauvoo, Illinois, after they were driven out of Missouri. After the assassination of Mormon founder Joseph Smith in 1844, Young replaced him as head of the Mormons. In 1846, Young led his followers on another long cross-country trip all the way to Salt Lake City, Utah.

Once there, Young established a settlement in which he exercised total control of the group. The Mormons prospered under his command. When the area became part of United States territory, he became territorial governor. When the government sent troops over concerns about church power and the practice of polygamy, he wisely avoided a complete break with the government but had to resign as governor. Despite his reputation for being stern and moralistic, many historians regard him as a brilliant leader. He was said to have had more than twenty wives and fathered forty-seven children by the time of his death at Salt Lake City.

JOHNNY WEISSMULLER

Born June 2, 1904
Died January 20, 1984

Peter John Weissmuller was an Olympic swimmer and a successful actor born at Freidorf, Romania, the son of Austrian parents. The family moved to the United States when he was four years old, and he grew up in Windber, Pennsylvania, where his father was a coalminer. Weissmuller, who had an athletic build, was first introduced to swimming when the family lived in Chicago and the children swam in Lake Michigan. In 1916 Johnny lied about his age and made the YMCA swim team. He caught the eye of William Bachrach, the legendary swim coach of the Illinois Athletic Club. Weissmuller was soon in full-time training. Before long, sportswriters were calling him the "Prince of Waves," the "Human Hydroplane," and the "Chicago Whirlwind."

Weissmuller went on to Olympic competition and blew the competition out of the water. In the 1924 and 1928 games he won five gold medals. Over his lifetime he won fifty-two national championships. He retired from swimming in 1929 and became a spokesman for BVD swimwear. At the Hollywood Athletic Club, a screenwriter noticed Weissmuller's physique and thought he might be good for the role of Tarzan in an upcoming film project. *Tarzan, the Ape Man* came out in 1932 and made Weissmuller a star. In 1934 he became one of the first athletes ever featured on the front of a Wheaties cereal box. A whole series of Tarzan movies, marriages (five), and divorces (four) followed. In 1950, the sportswriters of America voted him the best swimmer of the half-century. His film career came to an end after a short stint on TV in 1956. In the mid-1960s he helped launch an International Swimming Hall of Fame in Florida and became its founding chairman of the board. In 1974 the International Palace of Sports dubbed him the King of Swimming. A stroke laid Weissmuller low in 1976, and he recovered somewhat only to be diagnosed with chronic brain deterioration syndrome. He died at Acapulco, Mexico.

JAMES HUTTON

Born June 3, 1726
Died March 26, 1797

Born at Edinburgh, Scotland, Hutton became an influential geologist. Early in his life he was apprenticed to a lawyer who quickly saw Hutton's love of science and encouraged him to choose a more suitable career. Hutton went into medicine and completed his doctorate in 1749, only to find there were no positions available. He turned to agriculture, as he had inherited a small property in Berkwickshire. After setting the farm in order he moved to Edinburgh, where he spent his life surrounded by literary and scientific friends. He lived comfortably with his three sisters and never married.

At this time there was no field of geology, although there was interest in mineralogy. Hutton wanted to trace the origin of rocks and minerals to arrive at a clear understanding of the history of the earth. After much study he published a paper that is seen today as the foundation of modern geology, the study of rocks and their origins from sea sediment, pressure, or heat. He had a coherent theory based upon careful observation. In 1795 he published two volumes of what was supposed to be a three-volume work, *The Theory of the Earth*. Densely written, it did not find a big market, but it did influence other scientists of the time. His biographer and friend, John Playfair, had access to the manuscript for the third volume and consequently the book, *Illustrations of the Huttonian Theory of the Earth*, illuminated Hutton's theories in a much more accessible way. Hutton was a natural scientific genius who wrote on a wide array of subjects, including physics, metaphysics, rainfall, and climate. He had nearly completed a book on farming, called *Elements of Agriculture*, when he died at Edinburgh.

GEORGE III

Born June 4, 1738
Died January 29, 1820

The English king against whom the American Revolution was directed was born at London, England. His grandfather, George II, was an active king. But he also was greatly influenced by the Whigs and William Pitt (the elder), whose policies led to the Seven Year War. George III wanted to rule personally and had to get Pitt to resign in order to do so. He appointed a new minister, Lord North, whose harsh policies against the colonists in North America led directly to the American Revolution.

During the years of George III's rule (1760–1820) many great changes took place. Britain expanded its empire and trade and soon found a foothold in almost every corner of the earth. The Industrial Revolution, with its accompanying mechanization and changes in how humans labored, brought a surge in leisure time and great energy in the world of arts and letters. Eventually King George III's growing mental illness led to the appointment of a regent in 1811. George III died at Windsor Castle, near London. His son, George IV, who ruled for a decade (1820–1830) through his Tory ministers, was hated for his personal habits and extravagant lifestyle.

ADAM SMITH

Born June 5, 1723
Died July 17, 1790

A social philosopher and political economist, born at Kirkcaldy, Fife, Scotland, Smith is considered one of the founders of the field of economics. Schooled at the University of Glasgow, Smith found himself surrounded by the great thinkers of the day in a period now termed the Scottish Enlightenment. From 1764 to 1766, Smith traveled through Europe as a tutor. He used his off hours to write his most influential work, *An Inquiry into the Nature and Causes of the Wealth of Nations*. Published in 1776, this work had a profound influence on how the young United States set up its economic principles. At the time of Smith's travels, Britain was a wealthy and powerful country but still very much in the control of aristocrats and certain industrial monopolies. Smith felt this system was holding Britain back and proposed instead an open economy where the market itself establishes a price for goods and labor.

This system would be self-balancing as it would be driven by the "invisible hand" of competition based on the self-interest of all parties involved in commerce. Smith argued against government interference in commerce and for the establishment of a free market system. This idea had a profound effect on commerce in the United States and other capitalistic economies worldwide. Smith died at Edinburgh a much honored man.

MARIAN WRIGHT EDELMAN

Born June 6, 1939

A civil rights activist, Edelman was born into a lively and hardworking family at Bennettsville, South Carolina. She was the youngest daughter of a Baptist minister. She experienced a childhood rich in faith, dignity, and ethics. Her father encouraged her to pursue an advanced education. Edelman went on to become the first black woman admitted to the Mississippi bar. From 1963 until 1968 she was the NAACP's legal defense attorney. In 1968 she moved to Washington to serve as counsel to the Poor People's Campaign. She was also involved in the early days of the well-known government early education project, Head Start. She recalls that audiences often turned a deaf ear to pleas for change when a speaker talked of black poverty or civil rights but would remain interested and engaged if the speaker focused on children.

Her desire to make change happen is apparent in this quote: "Service is the rent we pay for living. It is the very purpose of life and not something you do in your spare time." She went on to found the Children's Defense Fund (CDF) in 1973, which brings children's needs to the attention of the nation. Edelman remains active, taking everyone from the president to corporations to task when they forget our nation's youth. *Harper's Bazaar* crowned her "America's Universal Mother." She remains involved by mentoring young leaders, giving speeches, running the CDF, and writing.

PAUL GAUGUIN

Born June 7, 1848
Died May 8, 1903

The post-Impressionist painter was born Eugène-Henri-Paul Gauguin at Paris, France, but raised mostly in Peru. He joined the merchant navy at seventeen and then pursued a successful career as a stockbroker. He collected Impressionist works and began painting in his spare time. In 1883, when he was thirty-five, he left his wife and family to devote himself entirely to painting. Moving to Brittany in 1888, he soon developed a personal style featuring symbolic or primitive subjects with brilliant color and strong, simple forms.

Gauguin's art was influenced deeply by a journey to Tahiti in 1891. He fell in love with the people, the climate, and the physical beauty of the islands. He decided to settle in the South Seas in 1895. He wrote an autobiographical novel, *Noa Noa*, while living there, and his works from this period are some of his best known, including *Manao Tupapau: The Spirit of the Dead Watching* and *Where Do We Come From?* Gauguin died in poverty at age fifty-four at Atuana, Marquesas Islands. He did not live long enough to see his work gain worldwide recognition.

FRANK LLOYD WRIGHT

Born June 8, 1867
Died April 9, 1959

An American architect born at Richland Center, Wisconsin, Wright was encouraged in his architectural leanings by his mother, who reportedly hung drawings of famous buildings on his nursery walls. His idea that a building must be in harmony with its surroundings profoundly influenced twentieth-century design. He was the foremost promulgator of the Prairie School of design. Famous for huge public buildings such as the Price Tower and the Guggenheim Museum, Wright was also responsible for many private homes and smaller buildings across the nation. He often used local building materials (for example, stone or wood) to create a harmonious feel in his projects.

Over the years he experienced many problems with money and with the women in his life, but these distractions did not keep him from designing and teaching. He had many willing disciples, and some of the talented students who flocked to him have become influential architects in their own right. His style, as interpreted by these men and women, is still prominent in American and European architecture today. Wright lived into his nineties. In his autobiography he wrote, "No house should ever be *on* any hill, or on anything. It should be *of* the hill, belonging to it, so hill and house could live together, each the happier for the other." He died at Phoenix, Arizona.

COLE PORTER

Born June 9, 1891
Died October 15, 1964

Porter was born at Peru, Indiana, to a socialite mother and a shy druggist father. His maternal grandfather, J. O. Cole, was the richest man in Indiana; he made sure his daughter had everything she needed to be the height of fashionable society. This included an allowance for clothes, as well as dance and music lessons for her son. Cole practiced for hours every day and showed an early talent for composition. His mother had his piano piece "The Song of the Birds" published when Cole was only ten. In 1905 he enrolled at an academy where he met a teacher who taught him the importance of the meter of words in a song.

Later, as a student at Yale University, he composed numerous songs for elaborate fraternity musical productions. Leaving Yale, Porter left behind a legacy of more than 300 songs, including some full-scale productions. In later years the contacts he had made at Yale helped him in his Broadway career, and he even lived at the Yale Club in New York City. Despite pressure from his grandfather and a short stint in law school, he was drawn to creating music. His younger days were filled with social climbing and elaborate parties. He married a wealthy divorcee who encouraged his musical talents. He proceeded to turn out songs for shows and films, including "The Gay Divorcee," "Kiss Me, Kate," "Let's Do It (Let's Fall in Love)," "Night and Day," and "Silk Stockings." A horseback riding injury left him bedridden and depressed. The injury eventually led to the amputation of one of his legs in 1958. A man who was proud of his physical appearance, he never felt fully himself after the operation and went into a decline until his death at Santa Monica, California. His popular songs are still sung today by a whole new generation of artists. One album that has kept Cole Porter's music in the limelight is the fundraising pop album *Red Hot + Blue*, which features covers of Porter songs by pop musicians of the 1980s and 1990s.

MAURICE SENDAK

Born June 10, 1928

Born at Brooklyn, New York, with a brother who liked to draw and a father who liked to tell stories, Sendak claims he knew he wanted to write and illustrate books by the time he was four years old. He drew through the schoolday and after school worked for All American Comics drawing backgrounds for the characters Mutt and Jeff. He illustrated a book for his high school biology teacher and later went on to art school. His first job was in window display. He got the chance to illustrate a children's book for author Marcel Aymé in 1951. From that point on he illustrated many popular children's books in the 1950s but did not write one of his own until *Kenny's Window* in 1956.

A number of creative children's books followed including the popular *Nutshell Library*, a set of four miniature books that include the stories "Chicken Soup with Rice" and "One Was Johnny." This set eventually was adapted into books on tape and filmstrips. His most acclaimed book, *Where the Wild Things Are*, followed. There had never been a children's book quite like this one. A boy named Max is sent to his room for acting like a "wild thing." He proceeds to have an adventure and become king of the wild things but misses home and returns to find his dinner waiting. The illustrations and text for the book were so original and engaging that it soon became a household favorite for millions of families, though some critics and even a prominent child psychologist thought the book was too frightening. Sendak has earned numerous awards, including the 1996 National Medal of Arts. In the 1980s he contributed to the design of costumes and sets for theatrical productions. Sendak lives on a seven-acre farm near Ridgefield, Connecticut.

JACQUES COUSTEAU

Born June 11, 1910
Died June 25, 1997

French undersea explorer, writer, environmentalist, and filmmaker, Cousteau was born at St. Andre-de-Cubzac. A sickly child, Cousteau nevertheless loved the ocean and learned to swim. School bored him, and he once got expelled for breaking windows. In 1930 he passed a stringent test to enter France's Naval Academy. He went on to serve in the navy and entered naval aviation school. A near-fatal car accident when he was in his twenties meant he could no longer be a pilot. He was transferred to sea duty. Working hard to strengthen his arms, he felt fate had sent him back to his first love, the sea. For his work in the resistance movement in World War II, he was awarded the Legion d'Honneur. In the mid-1940s, while making his first underwater film about sea life, he and engineer Emile Gagnan created a revolutionary piece of equipment, which some dubbed the Aqualung. It later became known as SCUBA (self-contained underwater breathing apparatus).

In 1950 Cousteau purchased a 400-ton ship, the *Calypso*, which had previously been a minesweeper. He modified it to create a floating laboratory and film studio. The books, films, and television series that followed made Cousteau famous and opened up the wonders of the sea to millions of people who otherwise would not have had the chance to see the amazing fish, coral, and other wonders of underwater life. The more than eighty documentaries he made garnered him forty Emmy nominations and won him two Oscars. In the 1970s, appalled by the degradation of the planet's oceans, Cousteau launched an environmental and educational group, the Cousteau Society. When he died at age eighty-seven, at Paris, France, he was still going strong. He was in the process of building the *Calypso II* to replace his first vessel. His society remains an active voice for understanding and protecting our fragile seas.

HARRIET MARTINEAU

Born June 12, 1802
Died June 27, 1876

An early feminist and socialist, Martineau was born the daughter of a textile manufacturer at Norwich, England. Her family members were progressive Unitarians who believed in educating their daughters as well as sons. However, they drew the line at university attendance for the girls. Harriet responded to this unfairness by writing an anonymous article in the Unitarian journal. Her brother praised the article, and when he discovered who'd written it, he encouraged his sister to make a career of her writing. She wrote for the Unitarian *Monthly Repository* and received a small stipend. She also wrote a series of religious books. She then began a very ambitious project, *Illustrations of Political Economy*, a series of twenty-five entertaining short stories meant for the ordinary reader to illustrate principles of political economy. This book sold very well and brought her financial independence.

Despite many health problems, including deafness, Martineau was very well traveled. Wealthy from the sale of her early books, she decided to take a few years to tour the United States from 1834 until 1836. She published her reactions in *Society in America*, published in 1837, which is a blunt, unsparing look at slave ownership and the relationship between owners and slaves. It is for the most part a critique of the United States' failure to live up to its democratic ideals. She was especially critical of the place of women in American society, where they were treated much as slaves and had very few property rights and no voting rights. She continued to write and to ruffle the feathers of those around her, even publishing a book that rejected religious belief. In 1852 she took a job with the *Daily News* and wrote more than 1,600 articles for it over the next decade and a half. She lobbied for women's suffrage in England and for the right for women to become doctors. Though her health was often frail, she continued to write until her death from bronchitis near Ambleside, England.

WILLIAM BUTLER YEATS

Born June 13, 1865
Died January 28, 1939

One of the greatest poets of the English language in the twentieth century was born at Dublin, Ireland. Yeats was also a politician, Irish nationalist, and playwright. Irish legend and his interest in the occult inspired his early works, but later writings focused on the present. He once said, "consciousness is conflict"—and he experienced plenty of conflict. His love married another, his political views were discouraged, and the National Theatre, which he had helped found, began to flounder. Through all these challenges Yeats wrote. His style toughened and grew away from its romantic leanings.

In 1922, at the end of the Anglo-Irish war, Yeats became a senator for the Irish Free State, and in 1923 he won a Nobel Prize for Literature. He continued to write in his later years and managed to complete his life story in *Autobiographies* (1938). His final play, *Death of Cuchulain*, was completed just days before his death in France in 1939. As was his wish, his body was returned after the end of World War II to be reburied in Sligo, the region where he had spent his happiest days. His tombstone is inscribed with the last words from his book *Collected Poems*: "Cast a cold eye/On life, on death./Horseman, pass by!"

HARRIET BEECHER STOWE

Born June 14, 1811
Died July 1, 1896

The daughter of Reverend Lyman Beecher and sister to Henry Ward Beecher, Harriet Beecher Stowe was born at Litchfield, Connecticut. This influential journalist and novelist had a strict religious upbringing and grew to see the evils of slavery—especially after the Fugitive Slave Act of 1850. She wrote *Uncle Tom's Cabin* (1852) to make "the whole nation feel what an accursed thing slavery is." The book took the nation by storm. It sold 300,000 copies in the first year alone and provoked a storm of protest from Southern slaveholders. However, the book convinced many people who had never taken a stand on slavery to come out against it in the years leading up to the Civil War. Two of the characters in the book took on such importance that their names have a place in the English language: the villainous slaveholder, Simon Legree, and the slave Uncle Tom.

The reaction to this novel had a profound impact on politics. It is said that during the Civil War when Harriet Beecher Stowe was introduced to President Abraham Lincoln, his words to her were, "So you're the little woman who wrote the book that made this great war." Stowe wrote a second book dealing with slavery, *Dred* (1856), and a number of much loved books about life in New England. She died at Hartford, Connecticut.

EDVARD GRIEG

Born June 15, 1843
Died September 4, 1907

A pianist, composer, conductor, teacher, and the first Scandinavian to compose nationalistic music, Grieg was born at Bergen, Norway. His mother was a professional pianist who started teaching him when he was just six years old. At thirteen he enrolled at the Leipzig Conservatory. As a young adult he traveled to Italy where he worked on his first major compositions. By 1866 he was appointed to conduct the Harmonic Society in Oslo. Soon after he married his cousin, a gifted singer. On a second visit to Italy in 1870, Grieg met Franz Liszt, the Hungarian nationalist composer. Liszt encouraged Grieg to compose music inspired by Norway.

Taking Liszt's encouragement to heart, Grieg went home to advocate a school of music inspired by and rooted in Norwegian folk music. His favorite pieces were the smaller piano pieces, songs or chamber compositions, as opposed to sweeping symphonies or concertos. Grieg was loved by his countrymen and honored by other countries. He was elected to the French Academy of Arts in 1889, and he was given an honorary doctorate from Cambridge University in 1894. He died at home in Bergen.

JOHN HOWARD GRIFFIN

Born June 16, 1920
Died September 9, 1980

An American author and photographer who was deeply concerned about racial inequities in the United States, Griffin was born at Dallas, Texas. Reared in Texas in the 1920s and 1930s Griffin was exposed to the widespread racism of his day but did not recognize it fully until he was older. He attended school in France and ended up in the French resistance during World War II. Due to his firsthand experience of the Nazi-created Holocaust, he came to equate the mistreatment of blacks at home with that of the Jews abroad. His understanding of racism was deepened when he was blinded. He could not tell people's race when interacting with them.

Back in the United States his years as a blind man were very frustrating; people automatically treated him as if he were mentally slow and a second-class citizen. He knew that blacks in the South had similar problems. He regained his eyesight in 1957, but the experience of blindness had changed the way he perceived race forever. In the late 1950s he underwent medical procedures using chemicals and ultraviolet light to darken his skin. He shaved his head and went on a journey, often by foot, through the South, recording his experiences in a journal. He experienced firsthand the hardships blacks faced: unequal facilities and poor treatment by whites. Poor blacks nonetheless took him in off the street, often giving him food and a place to sleep. His first-person narrative, *Black Like Me*, was a wakeup call for people in the United States. A devout Catholic, after the publication of the book, Griffin admitted he had left out how poorly he was treated by churches in the South, which often turned him away and would not allow him to worship. Later in life he wrote an essay on this topic, but he always regretted its omission from his book. He died at Fort Worth, Texas.

JOHN WESLEY

Born June 17, 1703
Died March 2, 1791

John Wesley was born at Epworth, England. He was educated at Oxford and was ordained in the Church of England in 1728. He found the spiritual leadership of the church uninspiring. He and his brother Charles laid the foundations for Methodism at Oxford, starting the Holy Club in 1729 and earning the title of their movement from their methodical approach to spiritual improvement. After a brief and troubled stint as a missionary in the Georgia colony, Wesley returned to England.

In 1738 he was at a religious meeting when he received an assurance of salvation through faith in Christ alone. This was his evangelical message from that day forth. Forbidden to preach in churches, he took his message directly to the people. Often he rode into the country on horseback to preach to people in their fields. Despite church disapproval, the Methodist movement grew enthusiastically, publishing *Rules* in 1743 and ordaining preachers in 1784. He traveled to North America, where his teachings became very popular. Wesley's views were unpopular to the orthodox church, but by the time of his death he was a revered figure in Britain, especially among the poor. He is said to have preached more than 40,000 sermons. Wesley continued to preach up until his late eighties. He died at London.

PAUL MCCARTNEY

Born June 18, 1942

British rock singer-songwriter McCartney was knighted in 1997. He was born at Liverpool, England, and as a teenager he played in the Quarrymen, a band that morphed into the most popular musical group in the world, the Beatles.

McCartney's post-Beatles life has been very productive. It has included a long and loving marriage, three children, a stepdaughter, the band Wings, and fifty Top Ten singles. He has managed to release an average of one album per year. His music is eclectic: pop, rock, and even classical. Using Top Forty statistics, and combining Beatles and post-Beatles efforts, McCartney is the most successful pop music composer of all time and the second biggest maker of hits (right behind the legendary Elvis Presley).

McCartney has always refused to play the superstar. He moved away from the glamour and stress of life as a Beatle and remade himself in the eyes of the world. He is at heart a family man with a serious music career.

He carefully promoted Wings as a *band*, not just as his show. Their album *Band on the Run* (1973) created three Top Ten hits. Later, five albums in a row topped the charts. Wings included his wife, Linda Eastman-McCartney, who sang and played keyboards, and the band survived a number of personnel changes to last a whole decade. In the 1980s he sang with Stevie Wonder ("Ebony and Ivory") and Michael Jackson ("The Girl Is Mine" and "Say Say Say"). Since the mid-1980s McCartney has been involved in solo albums, acoustic MTV sessions, classical forms such as the *Liverpool Oratorio*, and even a few albums he recorded under an alias. He recorded an album called *Wide Prairie* with his late wife, Linda, who was a highly regarded photographer and animal rights activist. She died of breast cancer in 1998. In 2000 McCartney was in the news for his original paintings, and in 2001 he released a book of poetry. McCartney recently toured in support of his album *Driving Rain*. In June of 2002, McCartney married anti-landmine activist Heather Mills.

BLAISE PASCAL

Born June 19, 1623
Died August 19, 1662

Considered one of the greatest minds of the seventeenth century, French mathematician, physicist, and religious philosopher Pascal was born at Clermont-Ferrand. He is credited as the founder of the modern theory of probabilities. Pascal astounded society when he published a theory on conics—the physics governing shapes—when he was only sixteen. In fact, the French philosopher René Descartes refused to believe a teenager was capable of that level of writing. Working with his father, Pascal performed experiments with mercury that led to the invention of the barometer. He also made other discoveries about pressure, which led to the first hydraulic press and the syringe.

In 1647 Pascal invented a calculating machine, the precursor of modern digital calculators. But while only in his early thirties, he put his mind to work on something he found even more fascinating than scientific research and invention, the religious teachings of Cornelius Jansen. In 1646 Pascal embraced Jansenism, and from about 1654, after a mystical vision, until his death in 1662, Pascal focused his powerful intellect on religious studies. He went to live at the Jansenist Port-Royal convent, to reflect and write on philosophy and religion. His notes on Christianity were not discovered until after his death. Published under the title *Pensées* (*Thoughts*), they became quite famous. Pascal died in his late thirties at Paris.

CHARLES WADDELL CHESNUTT

Born June 20, 1858
Died November 15, 1932

Born at Cleveland, Ohio, the grandson of a white man and the son of free blacks, Chesnutt was a pioneering novelist whose works used realism, moral complexity, and black dialect in an era marked by romanticism and a lack of true black voices. He spent his whole life working for the betterment of his race. His family returned to the South after the Civil War, and Chesnutt helped in the family grocery while attending a school founded by the Freedmen's Bureau. He became a teacher and eventually a school principal in Fayetteville, continuing his private studies of English literature, music, stenography, and foreign languages. Despite his personal success, he resented the climate of racial oppression and moved his family to Cleveland, Ohio, in the early 1880s, where he became a court reporter and eventually passed the state bar examination and founded his own court reporting firm.

A prosperous and prominent man in Cleveland, he remained there for the rest of his life. His story "The Goophered Grapevine" marked the first time an African-American writer was published in the *Atlantic Monthly* magazine. Other tales of blacks in the South followed and were published in other magazines. Chesnutt approached a publisher with a collection of these stories that became his first book, *The Conjure Woman* (1899). *The Wife of His Youth and Other Stories of the Color Line* (1899), which took on a broader range of racial issues than any other author had yet attempted, followed soon after. The popularity of these first two books convinced Houghton Mifflin to publish his first novel, *The House Behind the Cedars* (1900), which told the story of two blacks who passed as white in the postwar South. This and his later works of fiction met with less public approval, though they are now seen as classics. In later years he concentrated on writing powerful essays and on his work with the NAACP. He is viewed as a pioneer in his treatment of color issues in American literature. He died at Cleveland, Ohio.

INCREASE MATHER

Born June 21, 1639
Died August 23, 1723

Mather was born at Dorchester, Massachusetts, to a minister father and a mother who prayed he would be a scholar and a good Christian. Her prayers were answered as Mather went on to be the pastor of the famed and prestigious North Church in Boston for more than fifty years. He was president of Harvard from 1685 to 1701. Mather is also remembered for his role in trying to retain the Puritan ethic in the Colonies' second generation. His life was marked by his efforts to keep the colonists on the narrow path of godliness—and his sorrow as they backslid and sinned. He pinned many hopes for redeeming the younger generations on his son Cotton Mather (a minister who became famous during the Salem Witch Trials).

He is best known for his effort to bring back the Massachusetts Charter. He traveled to England to plead for it to be restored after its revocation by King Charles II. He spent years lobbying royals but did not get the charter for which he had worked. He returned and continued to preach a special form of sermon: the jeremiad, which involved publicly exhorting specific groups and even individuals. The third generation of settlers was focusing more on their economic welfare than on their spiritual well-being, and leaders were alarmed. Despite his concern for moral behavior, the elder Mather was often opposed to the witch-hunt mentality of his time, even saying that it was better to let ten witches go than to condemn one innocent person. He wrote convincingly and denounced "spectral" (intangible) evidence in witch trials. After speaking with several condemned witches, he later expressed concern that they were in fact innocent. It was even rumored at one point that his wife was to be investigated on charges of witchcraft. Mather preached until he was too ill to stand and died after almost a year in bed, in the arms of his son Cotton, at Boston.

ANNE MORROW LINDBERGH

Born June 22, 1906
Died February 7, 2001

Born at Englewood, New Jersey, Lindbergh served as her husband Charles's copilot and navigator on the famous transatlantic speed flight in 1930. She was a prolific writer and a poet as well. Her books *North to the Orient* (1935) and *Listen! The Wind* (1938) tell the stories of flights she made with Charles. As a couple, the Lindberghs were among their time's most famed celebrities. Being in the limelight was not an easy job; the Lindberghs suffered terribly when their infant son was kidnapped and murdered in 1932. Feeling under siege from the public and the press, they moved to England to get away from the chaos.

Their troubles increased in the days leading up to World War II, when Charles Lindbergh's speeches supporting U.S. neutrality were viewed as pro-Nazi. He changed his stance after the bombing of Pearl Harbor and even flew combat missions during the war, but public sentiment remained dubious. Anne Lindbergh continued to write and published a poetic study of women's issues in 1955 called *Gift from the Sea*. She wrote: "By and large, mothers and housewives are the only workers who do not have regular time off. They are the great vacationless class." She died in her mid-nineties at Passumpsic, Vermont.

WILMA RUDOLPH

Born June 23, 1940
Died November 12, 1994

Wilma Rudolph was born at St. Bethlehem, Tennessee, and reared in Clarksville, the twentieth of her father's twenty-two children from two marriages. As a child she endured severe health problems: scarlet fever, whooping cough, pneumonia, and polio that left her left leg useless and both legs in braces. She counted the loving ministrations of her large family as part of the reason she overcame these illnesses. With daily leg massages and hospital therapy, Rudolph was able to discontinue her braces at nine years old and went on to become the fastest woman in the world at the 1960 Rome Olympics.

She was a basketball star in high school then a star sprinter at Tennessee State University. In the 1956 Melbourne Olympics, she won a bronze medal as a member of the 400-meter relay team. At the Rome Olympics, she won the 100-meter and 200-meter sprints and anchored the winning U.S. 400-meter relay team, thus becoming the first American woman to win three gold medals at one Olympics. An instant hero worldwide, Rudolph was declared the Associated Press U.S. Female Athlete of the Year 1960. When she returned to Clarksville, she insisted that any celebrations be integrated, and they were—for the first time in that city's history.

Rudolph went on to become a track coach , speaker, broadcaster, and creator of the Wilma Rudolph Foundation for underprivileged youth. She was inducted into the U.S. Olympic Hall of Fame in 1983. Her inspiring life was cut short by brain cancer, and she died at home at Nashville.

JEDEDIAH STRONG SMITH

Born June 24, 1798
Died May 27, 1831

An American hero of early exploration, Smith was born at Bainbridge, New York, and only lived to the age of thirty-three before he was killed by Comanches on the Santa Fe Trail. He started his short and exciting life as a fur trapper. Setting out to find trade routes, he ended up a noted explorer and trailblazer of the new Western frontier. From Salt Lake City he headed west and became perhaps the first white man to arrive in California from the east.

He was the first non–American Indian to cross the Sierra Nevada. He was also the first non–American Indian to survive crossing the Great Salt Lake Desert. He finally ended up at Fort Vancouver, which is now Vancouver, Washington, where he recounted his journeys. He kept traveling and died in a battle on the Santa Fe Trail in the southwestern part of the country.

GEORGE ORWELL

Born June 25, 1903
Died January 21, 1950

"Big Brother is watching you," "thought police," "doublethink"—these now familiar catchwords were born out of George Orwell's brilliant Cold War dystopian masterwork *1984*. The journalist, essayist, and novelist was born Eric Arthur Blair in Motihari, India, where his father served in the British colonial government. He was educated at Eton but returned to Asia in 1922 to serve with the Indian Imperial Police. Concerned by his role in what he saw as an oppressive colonialist system, he resigned from the police in 1928 and decided to pursue writing. His first works, the autobiographical *Down and Out in Paris and London* (1933) and the novel *Burmese Days* (1934), are drawn from his experiences in Asia and as an impoverished vagabond in Europe following his resignation.

He adopted the pen name George Orwell for the publication of *Down and Out*. Orwell participated briefly in the Spanish Civil War, and from 1941 to 1943 he worked at the BBC. He came to mistrust most forms of government. In 1945 he published his political allegory *Animal Farm* (1945), which featured animals (specifically, pigs) playing the parts of Stalin and Trotsky, complete with horrendous communist purges. It contained the damning totalitarian line: "All animals are equal, but some animals are more equal than others." Fighting a losing battle with tuberculosis, Orwell was able to finish his frightening futuristic novel of total dictatorship, *1984*, during 1948 (it was published in 1949). With *1984* and *Animal Farm* Orwell created thought-provoking classics that have remained remarkably apt as well as popular through the decades. Orwell died in his late forties, at London, England.

LORD KELVIN

Born June 26, 1824
Died December 17, 1907

Born William Thomson at Belfast, Ireland, the man that would become physicist, engineer, and mathematician Lord Kelvin made his mark on science and industry in many ways—from the invention of the absolute temperature scale, which we now refer to as the Kelvin, to founding the first physics laboratory in a British university. Kelvin was influential in the study of thermodynamics and developed the law of the conservation of energy. His work in physical science, mostly in electricity, led to the development of wireless telegraphy and submarine telegraphy.

Kelvin was chief consultant on the first transatlantic underwater telegraph cable, a project which had many detractors. He believed in the modern advances of science and disparaged those who feared technological advances. His was the first house in Glasgow to switch from gas to electric lights. In 1857 he hit the big time by inventing and patenting a device that made telegraph transmissions faster. This single patent made him a wealthy man, though he invented many other devices, such as a more effective ship's compass, a tide gauge, and dozens of electric instruments. He died at Largs, Scotland.

JUAN T. TRIPPE

Born June 27, 1899
Died April 3, 1981

World War I pilot and airline founder Trippe was born into a prominent family at Seabright, New Jersey. He attended Yale University and flew in World War I. After the war, commercial air travel boomed in Europe but was quiet through most of the decade of the 1920s, until Trippe formed Eastern Air Transport with some of his former Yale flying buddies. Eastern later merged into a small Caribbean transport company known as Pan American, which grew to be Pan American World Airways, one of the giants of air travel. What began as a little mail route from the Florida Keys to Cuba, soon grew. Pan Am developed and ordered larger and larger planes and eventually became the first airline to offer round-the-world flights. Pan Am was the first in everything: the first to use radio communications, the first to use flight attendants, and the first to serve in-flight meals. It was all driven by Trippe's vision.

The company grew into a huge corporation with interests in hotels, airlines, business jet travel, helicopter service, real estate, and even guided missiles. The company had spectacular success and changed the face of world travel. Trippe was honored many times for his achievements; he was given an honorary doctorate by the University of Miami and a Boeing 747 was named for him—the *Clipper Juan T. Trippe*. After years of success, Pan Am suffered financial setbacks in its last two decades and ceased operations ten years after its founder's death at New York City in 1981.

JEAN-JACQUES ROUSSEAU

Born June 28, 1712
Died July 2, 1778

In 1728, as a teenager, Rousseau left his home in Geneva, Switzerland, and traveled to Italy. There he converted to Catholicism, then moved on to France and worked as a musician. In France he began to develop his philosophy, and he became one of the leading members of the French Enlightenment. His influence profoundly shaped nineteenth-century Romanticism, which in turn influenced such thinkers as Kant, Goethe, Tolstoy, Robespierre, and the American and French Revolutionists.

Rousseau's most celebrated theory was that of "natural man." In two of his important works, *Discourse on the Inequalities of Men* (1754) and *Social Contract* (1762), he puts forth the idea that people are essentially good and equal but become corrupted by property, science, agriculture, and commerce. He proposed that by using a social contract among themselves people could correct inequalities for the betterment of all. He also believed that education should not give children facts but should instead draw out what they innately know. His book *Émile* (1762) expounded on these educational theories. From the 1760s on, he was troubled by feelings of persecution that became so strong he went into hiding. His *Confessions* (1781) created a sensation due to its highly personal and intense reflections on his life. He died at France.

JULIA C. LATHROP

Born June 29, 1858
Died April 15, 1932

A social reformer and advocate for child-labor laws, Lathrop was born at Rockford, Illinois, and remained a lifelong Illinois resident. She was the first woman to serve as a member of the Illinois State Board of Charities and in 1900 was instrumental in the creation of the first juvenile court in the United States. Her efforts on behalf of children, especially her work exposing the dangers of child labor in Illinois, came to the attention of President Taft, who named Lathrop chief of the Children's Bureau, which was a part of the United States Department of Commerce and Labor. This bureau was formed expressly to focus on the needs of children in the United States.

At a time when children were used as labor from about age six on, conditions in factories and on the streets of the nation were appalling. Lathrop took the nation to task, asking whether this treatment of children was what could be expected of a great and civilized nation. In 1925 she broadened her scope, when she was appointed to the Child Welfare Committee of the League of Nations. Her work there was highly respected, and politicians and businessmen alike sought her opinions on issues affecting women and children until her death at Rockford, Illinois.

LENA HORNE

Born June 30, 1917

Born at Brooklyn, New York, Lena Horne was left in the care of her paternal grandmother for much of her early life. Her father left home and her mother took off to pursue an acting career. Horne's grandmother was a civil rights activist and suffragist. When Horne's mother returned she took Lena on tour with her, eventually moving to New York City, where Horne attended high school until finances forced her to take a dancing job at the famed Cotton Club in Harlem. Though hired for her looks, she worked hard to improve her voice. She took a number of roles on Broadway and launched a successful acting and singing career and helped transform the image of black women everywhere.

She moved to California in the 1940s and signed a movie contract with MGM. She insisted in her contract that she would not be cast in stereotypical black roles, which at the time was a gutsy and revolutionary move. Though at first she only got small roles, her grace and elegance began to transform the movie industry's portrayal of black women. The film *Stormy Weather* (1943) gave her her trademark song of the same name and her second husband, Lennie Hayton. Their interracial marriage in 1947 was so controversial that it was not publicly announced until 1950. She made many films, appeared on Broadway and television, and won a Grammy for her long-running show *Lena Horne: The Lady and Her Music*. She has received the Kennedy Center for the Arts Lifetime Achievement Award, an honorary doctorate from Howard University, and two special awards from the NAACP. Today, she remains the epitome of style and grace with a lovely smoky voice.

JULY

THOMAS A. DORSEY

Born July 1, 1899
Died January 23, 1993

Known to the world as the father of gospel music, Dorsey was born at Villa Rica, Georgia. Musical from his early days of making church music, he actually got his professional start as a blues composer. Eventually he combined his early experience of inspirational music with his love of the blues to create a new and uniquely American musical form: gospel. His songs tell of redemption and of loss, of freedom and of sin, of sorrow and of true happiness. A talented all-around musician as well as composer, Dorsey sang and played with such gospel legends as Ma Rainey and Bessie Smith.

Dorsey was a prolific writer whose works have been sung by generations of churchgoers and music lovers alike. He wrote more than a thousand gospel songs and hundreds of blues songs during his long life. His songs remain standards among both gospel choirs and blues bands. It was Dorsey's composition "Take My Hand, Precious Lord" that Dr. Martin Luther King Jr. requested just moments before his assassination. Among his best-known compositions are "This Little Light of Mine," "There Will Be Peace in the Valley," and "The Angels Keep Watching Over Me."

Thomas Dorsey died at Chicago, Illinois. Attend almost any church where gospel music is a part of the service next Sunday and you will hear his works, which are as lively and inspirational as they were when he first wrote them.

THURGOOD MARSHALL

Born July 2, 1908
Died January 24, 1993

Thurgood Marshall, the first African American on the U.S. Supreme Court, was born at Baltimore, Maryland. A talented and analytical youth, he graduated from Lincoln University in 1930 and then graduated magna cum laude from Harvard University, in 1933. In an era when blacks were seldom seen at Ivy League schools, Marshall was something of a pioneer. He practiced law and became a legal director of the NAACP. To bring the possibility of a good education to all people, regardless of race, he and his mentor, Charles Hamilton, created a long-term strategy for desegregating schools in the United States. They began lawsuits over admissions policies at graduate and professional schools, figuring they would be more likely to gain the sympathies of the court at this level. As they won cases, they moved on to the high school and elementary school levels.

Marshall had many years of winning cases before the Supreme Court when he landed his biggest victory, *Brown v. Board of Education*, in 1954. This victory meant an end to the "separate but equal" system of racial segregation in the public school systems of twenty-one states. Marshall argued thirty-two cases before the Supreme Court, winning twenty-nine of them before becoming a member of the high court himself. Nominated by President Lyndon Johnson, who said that it was "the right thing to do, the right time to do it, the right man and the right place." Marshall began his twenty-four-year Supreme Court career in 1967. He served until his retirement in 1991. Marshall became a voice of dissent in an increasingly conservative court. He was known for remaining very quiet on the bench except for the occasional outburst of sarcasm and biting wit. He died at Washington, D.C., just a few years after stepping down from the high court. His two sons have also pursued careers related to law: Thurgood Jr. is a lawyer and John is a police officer.

JOHN HURT

Born July 3, 1893
Died November 2, 1966

"Mississippi" John Hurt, as he became known later, was born at Teoc, Mississippi, but his family soon moved to Avalon, Mississippi, which is where Hurt lived for the rest of his life. One of ten children, Hurt dropped out of school at age nine to begin working as a farmer. About the same time he began playing the guitar his mother had bought him for $1.50. He was soon proficient on both harmonica and guitar. He was offered work with a traveling medicine show but didn't want to leave home. He played parties and gained a local reputation for his fluid and syncopated style of guitar strumming. In 1912 he began to play at Jackson, Mississippi, and in the 1920s he came to the attention of two country musicians who recommended him to their record producer. Two successful recordings followed for the Okeh label, "Nobody's Dirty Business" and "Frankie." When record sales fell off during the Depression, Hurt kept on farming, doing odd jobs, and playing music locally.

Decades passed and blues folklorists had given him up for dead when someone figured out his location from the title of his song "Avalon Blues." He was living a quiet life when he was rediscovered during the blues revival of the 1960s. Soon after, he began recording albums again and playing at big venues such as the Newport Folk Festival and on television (though he himself didn't own one). His isolation in rural Mississippi may have helped him develop and preserve what came to be known as his pure Delta blues sound. Once, a landlord asked him how he made his melodies. He replied, "Well, sir, I just make it sound like it ought to." His style is seen as the common source of blues and country in the United States. Hurt was modest, kind, and well loved. He enjoyed three years of fame before his death in 1966. He is buried near Avalon, Mississippi.

STEPHEN FOSTER

Born July 4, 1826
Died January 13, 1864

An American songwriter and composer with little formal training, Foster was born at Lawrenceville, Pennsylvania. He was influenced by his sisters, black church services, minstrel shows, and black laborers in Philadelphia. Foster wrote more than 200 songs and ended up taking a job with the Edwin P. Christy minstrel troupe. He acquired some knowledge of what was then known as Negro dialect, and using simple words and melody he wrote songs that eventually became American folk song classics. Because he sensed prejudice against such songs, at the time he was reluctant to be acknowledged as the writer.

His most famous work, "Old Folks at Home" (or "Swanee River"), was written for the minstrel show in 1851. He also wrote "Camptown Races," "My Old Kentucky Home," "Beautiful Dreamer," "Jeannie with the Light Brown Hair," and "Oh! Susanna." Foster was the most beloved American songwriter from the mid-1800s until World War I. Adventurous journalist Nellie Bly took her pen name from a Foster song, and cartoon character Bugs Bunny crooned Foster's songs in Warner Brothers cartoons of the 1940s. Since 1952 U.S. presidents have proclaimed Foster's birthday Stephen Foster Memorial Day. Foster never became rich from his talent: he sold the rights to all his songs for a one-time sum before he actually wrote them. He died in debt at New York City.

CECIL JOHN RHODES

Born July 5, 1853
Died March 26, 1902

Born at Bishop's Stortford, England, Rhodes went to South Africa in 1869 in search of diamonds. He found them at Kimberley, where he became wealthy and powerful as a result of successfully exploiting the mines. By 1888 he was the richest man in the world. His British South Africa Company, which he formed in 1889, allowed English settlers to seize the land north of South Africa. These lands were then named Rhodesia, in Rhodes's honor. (Today they comprise Zimbabwe.) The political turmoil of the region got its start under the auspices of his mining company and other British interests that took over the rule of many tribal groups. Early policies also led to the removal of resources from the continent for more than 100 years.

Rhodes was prime minister of the Cape Colony from 1890 to 1896. When he died he left his vast wealth to a number of philanthropic projects. The most famous of these is the Rhodes Scholarship, which enables outstanding students from around the world to attend Oxford University in England. The scholarship is among the most prestigious in the world. Recipients of the Rhodes Scholarship often go on to become academic, community, and political leaders.

JOHN PAUL JONES

Born July 6, 1747
Died July 18, 1792

Born John Paul (he added Jones later) at Kirkcudbrightshire, Scotland, Jones was the son of a gardener for the estate of Arbigland. He showed an early interest in ships and naval warfare. In his early teens he signed up for a seven-year seaman's apprenticeship and proceeded to learn about life on the open sea. He was released early and at age seventeen went into the slave trade. After a few horrid years as mate on a slaving ship, he quit in disgust and was given a ride home on another ship. During the voyage, the captain and first mate died of fever, and John Paul brought the ship safely to port. The owners promptly made him the master in charge of buying and selling on a ship. By age twenty-one he was captain of his own ship. A small, wiry, handsome man, he dressed well and could be charming. However, his temper on board was legendary, and rumors of his violent beatings of his men eventually got him hauled into court in Tobago on charges of murder. He was not convicted, but afterward he changed his name to avoid notoriety.

In Philadelphia at the time of the American Revolution, he advised the Congress on naval matters and became a senior lieutenant in the Continental navy. He proved very successful in capturing enemy ships and was much admired for his bravado and tactics. In a legendary battle off the coast of England, while aboard the ship *Bonhomme Richard*, he was asked to surrender. Instead he uttered the famous refusal: "I have not yet begun to fight!" After the war he served in the Russian navy before returning to Paris in 1790. He died at forty-five of pneumonia on the same day he dictated his will. He was buried in an unmarked grave at Paris. Years later, President Teddy Roosevelt mounted a search for Jones's grave. In 1905 it was rediscovered, and Jones's remains were brought to the United States by a convoy of four naval cruisers. They were met by seven American battleships, and a naval parade escorted the cruisers into Chesapeake Bay. Seen by the British as a pirate and the Americans as a hero, Jones was laid to rest in a marble sarcophagus at the Annapolis Naval Academy.

LEROY "SATCHEL" PAIGE

Born July 7, 1906
Died June 8, 1982

Born Leroy Robert Paige at Mobile, Alabama, Paige was one of eleven children in a poor family. Sent out to work early in life, he got his famous nickname at the tender age of seven due to his ability to lug lots of baggage for a railroad. Known both for his incredible pitching ability and for being one of the first black men to integrate professional baseball, Paige was also admired for his wit. Paige was the greatest attraction in the Negro Leagues, playing perhaps 2,500 games and pitching as many as fifty no-hitters, before moving to the American League at age forty-two.

The Brooklyn Dodgers signed Jackie Robinson in 1947, and the Cleveland Indians signed Paige in 1948. Even in his forties, his pitching amazed fans and baffled hitters. His race made his six seasons of travel with the team difficult. Despite his status and popularity, he often had to sleep in a different hotel and eat separately from his teammates. A man of great integrity and grit, he has been called the greatest arm in baseball. In 1971 Paige was the first Negro League player to be inducted into the Baseball Hall of Fame. He died at Kansas City, Missouri.

RAFFI CAVOUKIAN

Born July 8, 1948

Born at Cairo, Egypt, to an Armenian family, Cavoukian used his first name as a stage name and became the preschool set's superstar music-maker. When he was ten, the family moved to Canada to settle in Toronto. Raffi continued to play the accordion and sing in an Armenian church choir. As a teenager he added guitar and was influenced by favorite singer-songwriters Bob Dylan and Joni Mitchell. In 1970 he began performing in local music joints. A few years later, he started performing for schoolchildren and was rewarded with enthusiastic response. In 1976 he recorded *Singable Songs for the Very Young*, which is now seen as a classic and is still his bestselling recording.

Raffi went on to make another twelve albums, perform hundreds of sold-out concerts, and record original songs that have become perennial favorites: "Baby Beluga," "Bananaphone," "Five Little Ducks," and his version of "Down by the Bay." In 2000 he founded the Troubadour Institute to help provide a catalyst to move society in the direction of honoring the world of children. His autobiography, *The Life of a Children's Troubadour*, recounts his efforts to honor children and the environment. Raffi lives in Vancouver, Canada, and serves on the boards of a number of child- and environment-focused advocacy groups.

TOM HANKS

Born July 9, 1956

Thomas J. Hanks was born at Concord, California, into a home that didn't fit the standard 1950s image of the suburban nuclear family. His father moved around a lot; Tom had three moms, attended five schools, and lived in ten houses by the time he was ten years old. After attending high school in Oakland, California, he went off to Chabot College in Hayward, California, and then California State at Sacramento. Because money was tight, Hanks preferred paying work as an actor and took roles in a community theatre instead of spending time on college drama. His first big break was a role in *Bosom Buddies*, a television comedy series (1980–1982). His first film break happened when director Ron Howard saw him perform.

Howard asked Hanks to audition for a role in the movie *Splash* (1984). To Hanks's surprise, he was cast in the lead role. The film was a hit at the box office and made Hanks a star. Many top-selling films followed. He won back-to-back Oscars for *Philadelphia* (1994) and *Forest Gump* (1995) and has been nominated for Best Actor three times since. He's won three Golden Globe awards. Hanks has also been the voice of "Woody" in the *Toy Story* films. Branching out from acting, Hanks has directed, produced, and written screenplays—he even wrote the song at the center of the film *That Thing You Do*. His documentaries on the U.S. Space Program and his miniseries on U.S. soldiers in World War II have earned him further acclaim.

MARY MCLEOD BETHUNE

Born July 10, 1875
Died May 18, 1955

Born one of seventeen children (some of whom were sold away from the family during slavery) at Mayesville, South Carolina, Bethune became an award-winning activist for women and African Americans. She won a scholarship to a seminary and in 1895 graduated from the Moody Bible Institute, where she was the only African-American student. She taught at a series of southern mission schools, until 1904 when she founded the Daytona Normal and Industrial Institution for Negro Girls, later called Bethune-Cookman College, and served as the school's president until 1942.

Although black men were granted the right to vote in 1869, American women of all races were denied voting rights until 1920. Once the laws changed, blacks still faced discriminatory Southern voting stipulations. Bethune offered night classes to help blacks of both genders learn to read well enough to pass the literacy test. She went door to door on her bicycle to raise money to cover the poll tax. Soon she had more than 100 qualified first-time voters. The night before the election, eighty members of the Ku Klux Klan tried to intimidate her. She stood her ground, and they left without harming her. The next day she led her group of voters to the polls. Her educational work and her activism on behalf of black people caught the attention of presidents from Coolidge to Roosevelt who appointed her to government positions. She developed a close relationship with Eleanor Roosevelt and was instrumental in the creation of legislation that allowed black women to become officers in the Women's Auxiliary Corp during World War II. Ninety-nine years to the day of her birth the nation erected a statue of her in Lincoln Park in Washington, D.C.

E. B. WHITE

Born July 11, 1899
Died October 1, 1985

Born Elwyn Brooks White, the youngest child of a loving family, at Mount Vernon, New York, E. B. White went on to become the leading essayist and literary stylist of his time. His writing was elegant, fluid, relaxed, and clear. James Thurber once said, "No one can write a sentence like White." He wrote hundreds of very popular essays for *Harper's Weekly* and the *New Yorker* under the heading "One Man's Meat." Friends with many of the best writers of his day, White told the *New Yorker* (May 23, 1953): "*Walden* [by Henry David Thoreau; see the entry for July 12] is the only book I own, although there are some others unclaimed on my shelves. Every man, I think, reads one book in his life, and this one is mine. It is not the best book I ever encountered, perhaps, but it is for me the handiest, and I keep it about me in much the same way one carries a handkerchief—for relief in moments of defluxion or despair."

White wrote several bestselling children's books including *Stuart Little* (1945) and *Charlotte's Web* (1952), both of which have since been made into animated feature films. His manual for writing, *The Elements of Style* (1959), combined notes from Professor William Strunk and White's own knowledge of the art of good writing. This text was required reading for generations of students and is still used today by many a budding writer. In it, White states, "A sentence should contain no unnecessary words, a paragraph no unnecessary sentences, for the same reason that a drawing should contain no unnecessary lines and a machine no unnecessary part." White died at North Brooklin, Maine.

HENRY DAVID THOREAU

Born July 12, 1817
Died May 6, 1862

Influential transcendentalist and nature writer Thoreau was born at Concord, Massachusetts, to the struggling family of a Huguenot businessman. His Scotch mother was fond of nature and took him for long walks when he was a child. His passion for nature turned into a lifetime of reflection and writing after his attempts at teaching failed due to his unwillingness to use corporal punishment on the children. Ralph Waldo Emerson persuaded the twenty-year-old Thoreau to keep a daily journal. Thoreau took to the task well—he eventually compiled enough daily writing to make up thirty volumes. When his brother died of lockjaw, Thoreau decided to write a book about a canoe trip they had taken together. Emerson offered him a quiet place to write. It was located on a piece of property at Walden Pond. Thoreau started working on a cabin there in 1845.

He wrote the memorial to his brother *A Week on the Concord and Merrimac Rivers* (1849), built the small rustic cabin, talked with neighbors and visitors, and read—but mostly he took long walks and thought. His writings on the importance and beauty of nature have become classics. His experiment in living in an intentional way influenced generations of thinkers and writers. He was actively involved in supporting the abolitionist cause, and by way of protesting, refused to pay taxes. This civil disobedience landed him in jail for one night. He gave a lecture, "Resistance to Civil Government," which became a blueprint for later struggles for civil rights by Gandhi and Martin Luther King Jr. He is best known for *Walden* (1854), which Ralph Waldo Emerson revised many times after Thoreau's untimely death from tuberculosis at Concord, Massachusetts.

WOLE SOYINKA

Born July 13, 1934

Nobel Prize–winning writer Soyinka was born at Abeokuta, near Ibadan in western Nigeria, to a close and encouraging family. After attending school in Nigeria he went on to the University of Leeds, where he later received a doctorate. He became involved with the Royal Court Theatre in London before he returned to Nigeria to study African drama and to teach drama and literature. He founded a number of theaters and produced and acted in his own plays. In addition to being a prolific writer, Soyinka has often served as a visiting professor in England. A man who seems to have complete facility for the rich and varied English language, his words have at times gotten him in trouble. A plea for a ceasefire during the Nigerian civil war in 1967 landed him in jail for twenty-two months.

As a dramatist he uses a winning combination of dance, music, and action, often drawing on the mythology of his native Yoruba tribe. He has written dozens of plays and poetry collections. His two novels are *The Interpreters* (1965), a complicated work that has been compared to James Joyce's and William Faulkner's longer works, and *Season of Anomy* (1973), a compendium of his thoughts during imprisonment. He has written two autobiographical accounts and many essays. He won the 1986 Nobel Prize for Literature and is considered by many to be Africa's finest writer. He is a professor of comparative literature at the University at Ife. He recently published a personal narrative about Nigeria.

FLORENCE BASCOM

Born July 14, 1862
Died June 18, 1945

Born at Williamstown, Massachusetts, the youngest of six children, Bascom went on to become a woman of firsts, especially in the area of geology. Because her father was a professor there, she was able to attend the University of Wisconsin. She was an able student with a broad range of interests. She earned a number of bachelor's degrees in the 1880s before aiming for a Ph.D. in geology. She attended John Hopkins University, where she had to sit behind a screen during lectures so as to not disturb the male students. In 1893 she earned her doctorate. She was one of the first women in the world to hold a Ph.D. in geology.

Bascom taught while she was in school and after graduation. She held positions at Hampton University (then called Hampton Institute for Negroes and American Indians), Rockford College, and Ohio State University. She founded the geology department at Bryn Mawr College where she was a professor. In 1896 she became the first female member of the U.S. Geological Survey. She was also the first woman to present her own paper before the Geological Society, and when she became the vice president of the Geological Survey, she was the first woman to hold any office in the organization. She was an expert on petrography, crystallography, and mineralogy. She served as the associate editor of a newspaper called the *American Geologist* from 1896 until 1905. She died at Northampton, Massachusetts.

REMBRANDT VAN RIJN

Born July 15, 1606
Died October 4, 1669

The artist who became known simply as Rembrandt was born at Leiden, Holland. One of the undisputed geniuses of western art, he studied with master painter Pieter Lastman before becoming an independent master himself in 1625. Rembrandt moved to Amsterdam and soon attracted an eager following. Starting mainly with religious subjects, he moved on to paint many portraits and group portraits such as *The Anatomy Lesson of Dr. Tulp* (1632). Over the years Rembrandt grew to be more and more fashionable, and his paintings earned him an excellent living.

Then, in 1642, he painted *The Night Watch*, which is today his most celebrated work but was received badly at the time. His fortunes began to diminish, and he was forced to declare bankruptcy in 1656. Despite his financial problems, Rembrandt continued to paint and created some of his finest works, including *St. Matthew and the Angel* (1661) and *The Return of the Prodigal Son* (around 1669). Rembrandt's use of light and shadow and his ability to show the character of the people he painted made him one of history's greatest artists. He painted many self-portraits, each of which show a thoughtful man engaged in the activity that made him who he was. He died at Amsterdam, Holland.

ROALD AMUNDSEN

Born July 16, 1872
Died June 18, 1928

Arguably the greatest of the polar explorers, Amundsen was born near Oslo, Norway. After leaving a career in medicine, he became a sailor and first participated in an Antarctic expedition in 1899. In 1906 Amundsen became the first to travel through the Northwest Passage. He hoped to make a similar claim at the North Pole, but Robert E. Peary beat him to it (in 1909). Undeterred, and with a fully prepared expedition, Amundsen decided to tackle the South Pole, but he planned it secretly.

The world thought he was traveling to the North Pole. An organized and experienced leader, he was the first to set foot on the South Pole on December 14, 1911. British explorer Robert Falcon Scott, little dreaming he had competition, arrived there one month later. (Scott and his companions died during their return journey.) Amundsen went on to establish a successful shipping company, but still he hungered for adventure. In 1926 he flew across the North Pole in a dirigible with Lincoln Ellsworth and Umberto Nobile, three days after Richard Byrd flew the same path. There is ongoing dispute over which party can claim credit for the first transatlantic Arctic flight. Amundsen ended his life as dramatically as he'd lived it: he disappeared in the Arctic while on a rescue mission to find survivors of the crash of the airship *Italia*.

BERENICE ABBOTT

Born July 17, 1898
Died December 11, 1991

Born at Springfield, Ohio, Abbott became a pioneer of American photography. After an unhappy childhood she left the Midwest at the age of twenty. Aware of the restrictions on women, she resisted tradition and chose not to marry. She spent a decade in Paris in the 1920s but is best remembered for her black-and-white photos of New York City in the 1930s, which were published in the book *Changing New York*. Her love affair with New York City is reflected in the hundreds of documentary photos she made contrasting old parts of New York with the growing building of skyscrapers.

Attitudes of the day made being a small woman with a huge camera difficult, and finances were tight when she received funding from the Federal Arts Project during the Depression. The salary meant she could hire a driver and an assistant to continue her work documenting New York. She was a woman with wide interests, which are reflected in her photographs: portraiture, modernist experimentation, documentary, and scientific. One of her books, *Guide to Better Photography* (1941), became one of the most influential works of the period on photography. Her interest in science led to four patents for photographic and other devices. She continued to take photographs during her final years in rural Maine. She lived to the age of ninety-three and died at Monson, Maine.

NELSON MANDELA

Born July 18, 1918

Mandela was born at the Transkei region of South Africa, the son of a tribal chief. His middle name, Rolihlahla, which means "stirring up trouble," turned out to be prophetic. Mandela gave up his hereditary rights and established the first black legal practice in South Africa. He joined the African National Congress (ANC) in 1944, eventually becoming deputy national president in 1952. His involvement in the movement to overthrow the system of strict segregation, called apartheid, in which blacks and whites were kept apart and nonwhites were not allowed to vote or move freely, got him in trouble with the government.

After the Sharpeville massacre, in 1960, when sixty-nine protesters were shot down by police, the government banned the ANC. Mandela moved away from a policy of peaceful demonstration because he felt more aggressive opposition might be needed. In 1964 he was found guilty of sabotage and sentenced to life in prison. During the twenty-nine years Mandela spent in prison, he remained a symbol of hope to the nonwhite majority of South Africa. Human rights activists from around the world demanded his release. In 1990, as pressure mounted and word of his physical frailty spread, President F. W. de Klerk lifted the ban on the ANC and released Mandela, as millions watched via satellite TV. President de Klerk had already begun the process of dismantling apartheid. He and Mandela won a joint Nobel Peace Prize in 1993, and in 1994 the country held its first all-race election. The ANC won, and Mandela became the first black president of South Africa. He retired from office after one term at age eighty-one.

ROSALYN YALLOW

Born July 19, 1921

Nobel Prize–winner Rosalyn Yallow was born at New York City. She went on to become a medical physicist and once said, "Before I got the Nobel Prize, I was just as smart as I am now. But nobody listened. . . ." In 1977, along with Andrew Schally and Roger Guillemin, she was awarded the Nobel Prize for Medicine for her research on medical applications of radioactive isotopes. Yallow developed RIA, radioimmunoassay, which is a simple and highly sensitive technique used to measure minute concentrations of hormones and other substances in the blood.

RIA was first used to measure insulin in the blood of diabetics, which led to safer and more effective treatments. The RIA methodology could be used for other tests and soon was a normal part of procedure for thyroid and other medical problems. Yallow made a point of urging the public to help improve opportunities for female scientists. In her Nobel acceptance speech she said, "The world cannot afford the loss of the talents of half its people if we are to solve the many problems which beset us."

EDMUND HILLARY

Born July 20, 1919

Born at Auckland, New Zealand, this onetime beekeeper became a famous explorer and mountain climber. He learned mountain climbing in the New Zealand Alps before moving on to the challenges of the Himalayas in Asia. He was part of the British expedition, led by Colonel John Hunt, to climb the summit between Nepal and Tibet. Hillary was chosen to make the final ascent. He and Nepali Sherpa guide Tenzing Norgay became the first men to reach the summit of Everest, the world's highest mountain, on May 29, 1953. When asked why he wanted to do something like that he replied, "We climbed because nobody climbed it before." Hillary was knighted later the same year.

He went on to explore the South Pole by tractor in 1958, leading the first successful overland trek since 1912. He continued to climb and explore, concentrating on the Nepali and Alaskan highlands. In 1977 Hillary led the first expedition up the Ganges River by jet boat. The Ganges expedition went all the way to the source of the river in the Himalayas.

As climbing in Nepal became more popular, that nation saw an increase in tourism, which led to a negative environmental impact on the mountainous region. Since the 1980s, Hillary has been working to stop the environmental degradation of the Nepali highlands, paying special attention to the need for better forestry.

ERNEST HEMINGWAY

Born July 21, 1899
Died July 2, 1961

An American novelist and short-story writer, born at Oak Park, Illinois, Hemingway was one of the great figures of twentieth-century literature. Hemingway knew how to live life large and then write about it in an intriguing way. Notorious for wild parties, feats of daring, awful periods of writer's block, and a depressive streak, he was hard on those that loved him. Major themes in his books reflect his love of adventure: war, big-game hunting, and bullfighting. His writing style was intense and masculine; his social life was passionate.

Hemingway won the Nobel Prize for Literature in 1954. Among noted works: *In Our Time, The Sun Also Rises, A Farewell to Arms*, and *For Whom the Bell Tolls*. In his later years, he dealt with health issues related to lifestyle and aging and was increasingly hard to handle for the team of family members and medical personnel who tried to keep him healthy. Because he frequently threatened to commit suicide, his family locked up his guns; he then attempted suicide by walking into a plane propeller on a trip to the Mayo Clinic. He was stopped in time, and after a hospital stay and medical treatment he convinced everyone he was feeling much better. He died of a self-inflicted gunshot wound upon returning home to Ketchum, Idaho.

EMMA LAZARUS

Born July 22, 1849
Died November 19, 1887

Born at New York City into a prominent fourth-generation Jewish family, Lazarus received a good education and became a published poet and author by the age of twenty-five. She wrote articles for both Jewish and Christian readers and became a spokeswoman for Judaism in the United States. The population of New York had recently doubled to more than a million people—many of the new arrivals had come to the United States to escape anti-Jewish pogroms in Eastern Europe. They found themselves in an overcrowded city with little available housing. Lazarus opened her home to immigrants from all over the world. She moved in high-society circles, yet she took the time to work with these newly arrived people and publicized their plight to the upper classes. She also became an outspoken supporter of the idea of resettlement of Jews to Palestine.

In 1883 Lazarus wrote what was to become her most famous poem, "The New Colossus," to raise funds for the pedestal of the Statue of Liberty. Her poem, which includes the lines "Give me your tired, your poor, your huddled masses yearning to breathe free . . . ," was eventually carved into the pedestal of Lady Liberty. Emma Lazarus died in 1887; she didn't live long enough to know how powerfully her poem would affect millions of people around the world. It was added to the bronze plaque at the base of the statue in 1901, when Lady Liberty, an immigrant herself, was erected and began welcoming newcomers to the shores of the United States of America.

JUDIT POLGAR

Born July 23, 1976

Polgar was born at Hungary to a family of chess-playing sisters and a father who wanted to create geniuses of his girls. Both older sisters Zazusa and Sofia were good at chess, but Judit began beating everyone in the family at a very early age and showed a fierce devotion to the game at age four. The family kept the girls at home from school and concentrated on chess to the exclusion of almost everything else. The Hungarian government even tried to intervene at one point, but the Polgars' unorthodox methods produced three talented and bright chess players.

Judit has been called a "chess goddess" by her fans who love to watch her aggressive yet thoughtful playing style. In 1986, at the age of nine, she won the unrated section of the New York Open—and the hearts of the chess world. She unseated Bobby Fischer as the youngest-ever grandmaster when she won the title at age fifteen years, four months, and twenty-seven days (a record that has since been broken). At age eleven she earned an International Master title; she was younger than either Fischer or Gary Kasparov. Preferring to play in open games or against men, she has challenged the way the chess world works, and she has won game after game. Polgar's sisters married and moved away—one to New York and one to Israel. Polgar herself has married, but she has elected to stay in Hungary. She has played less often since winning the Najdorf Tournament and scoring 10/13 at the thirty-fourth Olympiad (where she played as a member of the Hungarian Men's Team) in the year 2000.

AMELIA EARHART

Born July 24, 1897
Died early July 1937

American aviator Earhart, whose death is still something of a mystery, was born at Atchison, Kansas. She took an early interest in flying and worked to earn money to take lessons. In 1928 she became the first woman to fly across the Atlantic as a passenger. In 1932 she flew it again, this time solo, in just over fifteen hours, becoming the first woman to make a solo crossing. In her lifetime Earhart broke many records and set the standard for adventurous women. Gracious and earnest, she was loved by the public. Many young women imitated her simple and practical wardrobe—and envied her unusual career path. She wrote a number of books, including *Twenty Hours, Forty Minutes* and *The Fun of It*.

The world was watching when she and navigator Frederick Noonan took off for an around-the-world air trip. She transmitted reports to her husband, giving information he would later publish as the book *Last Flight*. The trip was more than two-thirds complete when she and Noonan disappeared somewhere over the South Pacific. A massive search was mounted, but until recently no trace of them was found. Evidence from a remote Pacific Island suggests they may have crashed and camped for a time, perhaps dying of dehydration. Earhart wrote in her last letter home: "Women must try to do things as men have tried. If they fail, their failure must be but a challenge to others."

MAXFIELD PARRISH

Born July 25, 1870
Died March 10, 1966

Born at Philadelphia, Pennsylvania, Frederick Maxfield Parrish became one of the most beloved and popular illustrators of the first half of the twentieth century, creating fantastical dreamscapes for children's books, calendars, magazine covers, and bestselling prints and posters.

He was born into an artistic family and trained at the Pennsylvania Academy of the Arts and the Drexel Institute of Art in his hometown. After illustrating Kenneth Grahame's stories in *Scribner's Magazine*, he began to offer lovely color paintings and covers to the top magazines of the day. His ethereally cyan blue skies would win such notice that "Maxfield Parrish blue" became a universally recognized color. He illustrated such books as *Poems of Childhood* (1904), *The Arabian Nights* (1909), *The Knave of Hearts* (1925), and many more. In the 1920s, his prints and calendar art (not to mention his hotel lobby murals) made him the bestselling artist of the day. His painting *Daybreak* (1922) sold more than 200,000 prints and became his most popular work. Parrish was a careful craftsman—he often photographed himself in the positions his painting subjects took so that he could re-create them in exact detail—and the resulting paintings were mesmerizing because of the realistic quality of what was obviously a fantasy scene. In his later years, Parrish almost exclusively painted quiet landscapes. He died at Plainfield, New Hampshire.

GEORGE CATLIN

Born July 26, 1796
Died December 23, 1872

Catlin was born at Wilkes-Barre, Pennsylvania, in the early years of the United States. He studied law at Litchfield, Connecticut, and practiced there for several years before moving to Philadelphia, where he turned his attention to painting and drawing. In the 1830s Catlin had the opportunity to travel west. He spent eight years among the American Indians of Yellowstone River territory, Arkansas, and Florida. The amazing series of portraits and pictures he created were well-received upon his return to the cities of the east. His pictures showed details of tribal cultures at that historic time, when pressures from settlers and industrialists were forcing much cultural change. Many of his paintings went on to be exhibited in Europe where they attracted a great deal of attention.

Not content to rest on his laurels, Catlin mounted a trip to South and Central America, where he painted and took notes on cultural details from 1852 until 1857. After that he moved to Europe until 1871, which resulted in the book *Notes of Eight Years Travels and Residence in Europe*. More than 100 of his drawings and illustrations on Indian life were exhibited at the Philadelphia Exposition of 1876. Catlin took detailed notes when he traveled, and he wrote a number of books on native conditions, customs, and ceremonies. Hundreds of his pictures hang in the Catlin Gallery of the National Museum in Washington, D.C. His paintings are a lasting testimony to the end of an era in U.S. history. Catlin died at Jersey City, New Jersey.

GEORGE BIDDELL AIRY

Born July 27, 1801
Died January 2, 1892

Born at Northumberland, England, Airy was an all-around scholar and, arguably, something of a genius. He graduated from Trinity College, Cambridge, in 1823 and worked at first as a mathematics tutor. He possessed skills in diverse areas such at Latin, ancient Greek, poetry, history, theology, architecture, engineering, and geology. His idea that education and religion should be kept separate was highly controversial in his day. Bothered by poor eyesight, he manufactured the first corrective lenses for astigmatism; his cylindrical design is still in use.

By 1826, when he was a professor of mathematics at Cambridge University, his love of astronomy rose to the fore. He published a scholarly treatise that concerned mathematics and astronomy, and by 1828 he became director of the Cambridge Observatory. He went on to direct the Royal Greenwich Observatory for more than forty-five years, a time of great growth for the observatory and for astronomy. However, Airy could be caustic, and he was notorious for his fights with his contemporaries. Sometimes he dismissed other scientists' theories out of hand only to be proved wrong later. His water telescope disproved an antiquated theory and laid the groundwork for Einstein's theory of relativity. He measured gravity and by using a pendulum calculated the density of the earth. The queen had to offer four times before he finally agreed to become Sir George in 1872. He died at London, England.

BEATRIX POTTER

Born July 28, 1866
Died December 22, 1943

Born at London, England, Potter's famous Peter Rabbit stories grew out of a letter she sent to entertain a sick child. The only daughter of a wealthy property owner, Potter spent her early years at home. She never attended school and was taught by a governess. Potter enjoyed sketching and painting, especially when at her holiday home in the Lake District. From the age of fifteen until her thirties, Potter kept a daily journal in which she recorded the details of her life in code. She did not marry at the usual age and lived at home until she was past thirty. The letter containing the first version and illustrations of *The Tale of Peter Rabbit* found its way to a publisher. After a romance and engagement with one of the publishers ended with his untimely death from leukemia, Potter turned her energies to creating books for children. By the time of her own death she had written and illustrated more than forty books, most in a small format that proved just right for little hands.

From 1905 on, she spent her time at a little farm in her beloved Lake District, painting and writing works based on her observations of nature and farm creatures. She found great success with her books, which featured interesting animal characters and lovely watercolor illustrations. Soon a whole industry arose to satisfy the demand for her creations, and the resulting monies made her quite wealthy. When she married at age forty-seven, she bought a larger farm and a large herd of sheep, which occupied her time when failing eyesight put an end to her painting and writing. She spent her final years living quietly with her second husband on their land. By the time of her death, at Sawrey, Lancashire, England, she owned several thousand acres. She left her property to the National Trust, and her home is currently open to the public.

BENITO MUSSOLINI

Born July 29, 1883
Died April 28, 1945

This notorious Italian leader was born at Dovia, Italy, the son of a blacksmith. He became a journalist, and his political philosophy—extreme nationalism expressed through an all-powerful state—became known as fascism. His ideas gained prominence during the years following World War I. In 1922 he seized power with the help of supporters known as blackshirts and proclaimed himself il Duce ("the leader"). He promised to return Italy to the glories of the days of the Roman Empire by creating huge public works and conquering neighboring countries. He ended parliamentary government in 1928; those who disagreed with him or his policies were often beaten, killed, or imprisoned. Photographers were only allowed to take his photo from below (to make him appear taller), and newspapers were required to flatter him in every article. It is said that the one good thing he did in Italy was to make the trains run on time.

His imperialistic designs on other countries resulted in much bloodshed for the Italians and those they fought. Italy conquered Ethiopia (1935–1936), occupied Albania (1939), and assisted Franco's forces in the Spanish Civil War. Mussolini joined forces with Nazi Germany in 1939; the resulting Rome-Berlin Axis proved disastrous for Italy. Its military failed in Greece and in Africa, and by 1945 the Allies invaded Italy and Mussolini faced a rebellion in his Fascist party. When Germany collapsed, Italian partisans captured him near Lake Como, Italy. They tried him, found him guilty, and executed him.

HENRY FORD

Born July 30, 1863
Died April 7, 1947

Industrialist and carmaker Henry Ford was born on his family's farm at Wayne County, Michigan. From an early age he showed mechanical aptitude. As a teenager he moved to Detroit, where he eventually was put in charge of the city's power-generating company. In the early 1890s Ford built a gasoline-powered automobile, which had its first successful run in 1895. In 1903 he and his investors launched the Ford Motor Company. By 1908, the company introduced its first car, the Model T, which it sold until 1927. Ford may be most famous for introducing the assembly line into manufacturing. He claimed to have gotten the idea from watching meat butchery at a plant in Chicago, a process in which each person did just one or two tasks repeatedly.

In 1913 he switched his plant over to mass production, and the resulting efficiency reduced assembly time from twelve and a half hours per car to one and a half hours. This enabled Ford to sell his cars for about $500, which meant many more people could afford to buy them. This earned him the moniker "the man who put America on wheels." He was famous for saying you could have a Model T in any color you wanted—as long as it was black. He paid his workers the then princely salary of five dollars per day, but he demanded a lot of those who were fortunate enough to be hired. For all his success, Ford was controversial. He stated that "History is bunk," published an anti-Semitic newspaper, and fought bitterly against the unionization of his factories in the 1930s. Henry Ford died at age eighty-three at Dearborn, Michigan, the home of his manufacturing complex.

MILTON FRIEDMAN

Born July 31, 1912

A Nobel Prize–winning economist and journalist, Friedman was born at Brooklyn, New York. After some time working at Columbia University and for government agencies at Washington, D.C., Friedman moved to Chicago. In 1946 he became a professor of economics at the University of Chicago, where he did much of his best-known work. The group of scholars with whom he associated believed in the power of the free market; they became known as the Chicago School. Friedman became something of an evangelist for this cause. He even made a series of television shows in the 1980s called *Free to Choose*.

His work is controversial but also influential. Margaret Thatcher followed his ideas in setting up her Tory government's Monetarist policies in 1979. Friedman's achievements in the fields of consumption analysis, monetary history, and theory—and his ability to demonstrate the complexity of government stabilization policies—earned him the 1976 Nobel Prize for economics. He has remained a champion of the Federal Reserve's using slow movements in money supply to promote economic stability. He has written many books on capitalism, including *Free to Choose* (1980), which he wrote with his wife, Rose Friedman.

AUGUST

MARIA MITCHELL

Born August 1, 1818
Died June 28, 1889

Born at Nantucket, Massachusetts, to a Quaker family of ten children, Maria Mitchell was encouraged by her father's hobby and by her mother's admonition to seek her independence. She became the first female professional astronomer. In 1847, while assisting her father in a survey of the sky for the U.S. Coast Guard, Mitchell discovered a new comet and determined its orbit.

The discovery made her a celebrity in the Western world. The king of Denmark awarded her a gold medal, and in 1848 she was elected to the American Academy of Arts and Sciences, its first and, until 1943, its *only* woman. Mitchell joined the staff at Vassar Female College in 1865—the first U.S. female professor of astronomy—and in 1873 was a cofounder of the Association for the Advancement of Women.

Mitchell believed that students learn best when participating in their own actual research, a process that she encouraged. In 1878, when North America was abuzz over the coming total solar eclipse, Mitchell and a party of women traveled two thousand miles to Denver, Colorado, to watch the event. In her journal she wrote: "[W]e have a hunger of the mind which asks for knowledge of all around us, and the more we gain, the more is our desire; the more we see, the more we are capable of seeing." The Maria Mitchell Women in Science Award, created in her honor, annually recognizes those individuals or organizations that encourage girls' and women's efforts in the sciences, mathematics, and technology. Mitchell died at Lynn, Massachusetts.

PIERRE CHARLES L'ENFANT

Born August 2, 1754
Died June 14, 1825

Born at Paris, France, to a family of artists, L'Enfant arrived in America in 1777, just in time to serve in the American Revolution as an engineer. His work designing Federal Hall in New York City got the attention of George Washington and other leaders. When the war was won and a capital city was needed, young L'Enfant was ready with a grand and glorious design. He wrote to Washington, "No nation perhaps had ever before the opportunity offered them of deliberately deciding on the spot where their capital city should be fixed. . . ." His plans were deliberately elaborate, making open spaces for public use. He planned for the monuments to future heroes that were bound to be a part of the nation's legacy.

It turned out that he was too hot-tempered and arrogant for a great undertaking that required compromise and communication. In the early days of laying out Washington, D.C., L'Enfant managed to infuriate nearly everyone, especially the three commissioners involved with the process. After hearing many complaints against him, President Washington reluctantly fired him. In the end, the nation's capital proceeded mostly according to L'Enfant's plans, but he was not allowed to be involved. Furious, and running out of money, L'Enfant made a career of lobbying Congress for redress. He died almost penniless on Digges Farm, in Prince Georges County, Maryland. Years later, in the early 1900s, the capital needed improving, and no plans could be found that were better than the originals by L'Enfant. His reputation improved to the point that his remains were moved from his almost unmarked grave to a place of honor at Arlington National Cemetery overlooking the graceful radiating avenues and parks that he designed.

JOHN T. SCOPES

Born August 3, 1900
Died October 21, 1970

When their son was born at Paducah, Kentucky, Scopes's parents could scarcely have imagined the furor he would cause when he grew up and became a high school teacher. Scopes was a science teacher who taught what he felt was the most current and reasonable approach to understanding species in his biology class in Dayton, Tennessee. In 1925 he ended up on trial in one of the most highly publicized and most influential court cases in U.S. history. Two of America's best-known lawyers at that time, William Jennings Bryan and Clarence Darrow, argued the case, and every paper in the country reported the proceedings. It was nicknamed the "Monkey Trial" because of the theory (taught by Scopes) that humans and apes descended from a common ancestor.

The country at the time was divided over the issue of evolution. Darwin's theory was considered just that: a theory. Churches mostly set themselves against the notion that animals and plants evolved, as many Christians believed in a literal translation of the Bible's explanation. Scientists, on the other hand, had taken Darwin at his word and gone out to make their own discoveries through the fossil record, each one adding to the evidence for evolution. As teaching evolution was against state law, Scopes was first convicted and fined a hundred dollars. Then he was acquitted on the technicality that his fine was too high. Scopes lived long enough to witness the overturning of the law, but the change didn't come until 1967. He died at Shreveport, Louisiana.

LOUIS ARMSTRONG

Born August 4, 1900
Died July 6, 1971

The jazz musician extraordinaire who became known as Satchel Mouth (or Satchmo for short) for his huge infectious grin was born at New Orleans, Louisiana, in 1900 (some sources say 1901). His father left the family when Armstrong was young, and they lived in poverty in one of the toughest sections of town. Armstrong began to play trumpet and cornet at age thirteen after a brief time in a boys home where the music director introduced him to singing and percussion. After being released he worked odd jobs and sang on corners to get money to eat. At night he hung out at bars listening to the jazz bands that were just starting to appear. Joe "King" Oliver took a liking to him and helped him launch his career.

By the mid-1920s, Armstrong's career was sizzling. He formed his own band called the Hot Five and cut a few records for the Okeh label. He appeared on Broadway in 1929 in *Hot Chocolates*, where he introduced his first hit, "Ain't Misbehavin'," a song written by Fats Waller. In the 1930s he gathered a bigger band, Louis Armstrong and the New Cotton Club Orchestra. He hit the road in the United States and Europe and earned rave reviews wherever he played. His popular favorites included "What a Wonderful World" and "Hello, Dolly," which he performed with Barbra Streisand. He played with many famous musicians in his life and made a number of films including *When the Boys Meet the Girls*, *A Man Called Adam*, and *Paris Blues*. Asked to define the word *jazz*, Armstrong reportedly replied, "Man, if you gotta ask, you'll never know." He played and recorded until his death at his home at Queens, New York.

MARY RITTER BEARD

Born August 5, 1876
Died August 14, 1958

A historian, writer, and women's rights advocate, born at Indianapolis, Indiana, Mary Ritter attended DePauw University, where she met her future husband, Charles Beard. They married in 1900 and moved to Britain and became involved with the suffrage movement there. In 1907, after returning to New York, she began working for the Women's Trade Union League. From 1910 to 1912 she edited a suffragist periodical, *The Woman Voter*, and then worked with the Wage Earner's League. She helped organize the women textile workers in New York City and lobbied hard for women to get the vote. When that finally occurred in 1920, with the passage of the Nineteenth Amendment, she dropped out of the movement over a disagreement concerning the Equal Rights Amendment (ERA). She felt the ERA would invalidate protective legislation for women.

She spent the next few decades writing books about women and work, including *Woman's Work in Municipalities* and *Women as a Force in History*, in which she claimed that women had in fact powerfully influenced the course of history, despite male dominance. She wrote, "The dogma of women's complete historical subjection to men must be rated as one of the most fantastic myths ever created by the human mind." She also collaborated with her husband on a four-volume work, *The Rise of American Civilization*. Her last work, *The Force of Women in Japanese History*, was published in 1953. She died at Phoenix, Arizona.

ALEXANDER FLEMING

Born August 6, 1881
Died March 11, 1955

Alexander Fleming was born at Lochfield, Scotland. He was a distinguished student, researcher, and instructor at St. Mary's Medical School at London University—a stint interrupted by service in World War I. As a research scientist he focused on immunology and bacteriology—seeking to discover antibacterial agents. In 1928 he noticed a mold growing in a research culture. Through the microscope he could see that the mold repelled and killed bacteria. Further experiments proved the powerful antibacterial qualities of the mold, which Fleming called penicillin. The agent was developed into a drug and brought to production in the mid-1940s.

Fleming's discovery revolutionized the treatment of infectious illnesses such as pneumonia, gangrene, blood poisoning, and meningitis—many of which were conquered by antibiotics. He received many honors, including being elected to the Royal Society. In 1944 he was honored with a knighthood. In Spain, the grateful Bullfighting Association (bullfighters were plagued by gangrenous infections) erected a statue in his honor outside a popular stadium. He died at London, England, and, fittingly for someone who had so aided human welfare, was buried in St. Paul's Cathedral.

RUDOLF C. ISING

Born August 7, 1903
Died July 18, 1992

One of the early pioneers of animation, Rudolf C. Ising was born at Kansas City, Missouri. He began his career at Disney in the mid-1920s but left with fellow animator Hugh Harman to form his own cartoon studio in 1929. Harman-Ising created "Bosko the Talk-Ink Kid" (for Warner Brothers), which featured a clear precursor to Mickey Mouse. This was the first synchronized talkie cartoon, which was a revolutionary concept at the time, only two years after the first talking picture was created. (Because the Bosko character appears in blackface, many people consider these early cartoons insensitive today.)

In the early 1930s Ising and Harman developed both the Looney Tunes and Merrie Melodies series, featuring favorites Porky Pig and Daffy Duck and laying the groundwork for the later success of the Warner Brothers cartoon studio. As a major during World War II, Ising headed the animation division for the Army Air Corps to make training films. His "Milky Way" won the 1940 Oscar for best-animated short film. Ising died at Newport Beach, California.

MATTHEW A. HENSON

Born August 8, 1866
Died March 9, 1955

African-American explorer and author Matthew Henson was born at Charles County, Maryland. A strong, bright youth, he was working at a store in Washington, D.C., in 1888, when he met explorer Robert E. Peary, who took a liking to him and offered him a position as his personal valet. Henson was a quick learner and soon became an invaluable aide to Peary as well as a friend. He accompanied Peary on his next seven Arctic expeditions. Unlike most European and American explorers, Peary and Henson learned from the natives of the regions they traveled through and used native dress and food when exploring. Many believe that this willingness to adapt to the region led Henson and two native guides to be the first to make it to the North Pole in the spring of 1909. A few minutes later Peary arrived and confirmed Henson's readings.

Upon their return, the expedition members received a congressional medal for their accomplishments. However, Henson was not welcomed into the clubby world of gentlemen explorers until he was eighty-one years old. It was then that he finally was invited to become a member of the Explorer's Club in New York. He also was honored with the Gold Medal of the Geographical Society of Chicago. His personal account of the expedition, *A Negro Explorer at the North Pole*, was published in 1912 and gives an insider's view of the Peary expedition. One of his descendants, Ussarquk Henson, now serves as a guide for dogsledding trips in northwestern Greenland.

JEAN PIAGET

Born August 9, 1896
Died September 16, 1980

Piaget is one of the founders of developmental psychology. Born the oldest child of a medieval literature professor at Neuchâtel, Switzerland, Piaget had an aptitude for scientific analysis from an early age. He wrote a brilliant short paper on an albino sparrow when he was only eleven. He studied natural sciences in college and went on for his Ph.D. at the University of Neuchâtel. During a semester at the University of Zurich, he developed an interest in psychoanalysis and went on to work for a year at a special school for boys created by Alfred Binet. At the school, he standardized a test of intelligence and had his first opportunity to study the growing mind. In 1923 he married and had three children, whose development he studied closely.

He was employed over the years by many institutions, wrote many books, and was given more than thirty honorary doctorates for his work in history, psychology, sociology, history of science, history of scientific thinking, genetic epistemology, and experimental psychology. His research in these many fields was aimed at answering an important question: How does knowledge grow? His answer has had an impact on many fields of study: Knowledge is a progressive construction of logically embedded structures, which supersede each other as knowledge grows, changing from a simple, less powerful childhood logic to a more complex higher-order thinking in adulthood. He died at Geneva, Switzerland.

HERBERT HOOVER

Born August 10, 1874
Died October 20, 1964

The thirty-first president of the United States, Hoover was born at West Branch, Iowa, the son of a Quaker blacksmith. He was one of the first students to attend Stanford University in Palo Alto, California, when it opened its doors in 1891. He graduated with a mining degree and married his college sweetheart. The Hoovers were working in China when the Boxer Rebellion caught them in Tientsin. For a month they were barricaded in the settlement; they worked at hospitals and tried to maintain order. Later, while they were in London, Germany declared war on France, and the American consul general asked Hoover to help stranded Americans get home. He and his committee helped 120,000 Americans return home in a mere six weeks. He then received an appointment to help feed Belgium, which had been overrun by the German army.

After the United States entered the war, President Wilson appointed him to head the Food Administration. During the war years, Hoover managed to cut down on the food needed overseas while avoiding rationing at home and still supplying the Allies. After the war, he helped organize food for the millions of central Europeans facing starvation. When a critic worried he might be feeding Bolsheviks, he responded, "Twenty million people are starving. Whatever their politics, they shall be fed!" Much of the country viewed his election to president in 1928 as ensuring the country's continued prosperity. He had barely taken the reins, however, when the stock market crashed and the Depression began. The government created loan programs and attempted to help businesses, but Hoover encouraged local communities to care for their own people and not expect sweeping government programs. Painted as cold and callous, he was not reelected. Hoover was an outspoken critic of Roosevelt's New Deal. He was writing a book when he died at age ninety at New York City.

ALEX HALEY

Born August 11, 1921
Died February 10, 1992

Born at Ithaca, New York, and raised by his grandmother at Henning, Tennessee, Haley went on to win the Pulitzer Prize. He joined the U.S. Coast Guard in 1939 and served as a cook before attending college. After college he became a writer and college professor. He ghostwrote *The Autobiography of Malcolm X*, which went on to become an amazing success. It sold six million copies and was translated into eight languages. In 1976 his book about an African-American man searching for his ancestral history, *Roots*, also sold millions and was translated into thirty-seven languages.

Haley hoped to make the successful book into a film for television. He managed to persuade a skeptical television broadcasting company that they should make a miniseries of the book. Haley made the movie, wisely casting well-known and beloved white actors in the roles of slave traders, slave masters, and other cruel white folk to make the series more acceptable to a mostly white TV audience. He cast mostly unknown actors in the black roles, including now-famous LeVar Burton in the lead role as Kunte Kinte. The film ran as an eight-part miniseries; it shocked TV executives by grabbing one of the largest viewerships in television history. The story was the first of many historical TV docudramas and sparked a huge upswing in interest in family ancestry in the United States. Haley died at Seattle, Washington.

THOMAS BEWICK

Born August 12, 1753
Died November 8, 1828

English artist, wood engraver, and author Bewick was born into a farm family at Cherryburn, Northumberland, England. He was best known for his illustrations in such books as *Aesop's Fables*, *General History of Quadrupeds*, and *A History of British Birds* and for reviving the art of original wood engraving.

Bewick was apprenticed to an engraver in Newcastle in 1767. In 1768 he did his first engravings on wood. By 1776 he had been paid for engravings used to illustrate a book of fables. He spent a summer walking to and all around Scotland. He returned to Newcastle and joined his original master—this time as a partner. His brother John also was apprenticed in the shop and helped illustrate some of the company's many fable books. The engravings used in the books had complex decorative borders, many of which featured intricate details of animals and birds. This level of detail can be attributed to the long hours Bewick spent in museums and in nature. Many of his books, especially those on birds, had to be reprinted many times. *General History of Quadrupeds* and his *Land Birds* books went into eight original editions to satisfy demand. It was Bewick's *British Birds* that young Jane Eyre read for solace in the novel by Charlotte Brontë. Bewick died at Gateshead, Durham, England.

ANNIE OAKLEY

Born August 13, 1860
Died November 3, 1926

Legendary sharpshooter and star of Buffalo Bill's Wild West Show, Oakley was born Phoebe Anne Mozee at Darke County, Ohio. Oakley was a small woman—less than five feet tall and under a hundred pounds. She possessed an uncanny ability to hit a target, which earned her the nickname "Little Sure Shot." She was soon performing feats of sharpshooting for amazed crowds. She would blast a dime tossed into the air and riddle a playing card with holes before it touched the ground. Riding sidesaddle on a galloping horse, she could shoot out a candle as she raced past.

As a rider in the legendary Buffalo Bill's show, she demanded to be treated as a professional and refused to wear scanty costumes. As her fame spread it became clear she didn't need any extra flash. In fact, while performing in Berlin, Germany, the Crown Prince William allowed her to shoot a cigarette out of his mouth. A tragic train crash left her partially paralyzed in 1901, but she retained her shooting ability and kept on performing until her death in 1926. Her fame spread when, in 1946, composer Irving Berlin wrote a fictionalized account of her life in the musical *Annie Get Your Gun.*

ERNEST JUST

Born August 14, 1883
Died October 27, 1941

American marine biologist Just was born at Charleston, South Carolina. His father and grandfather were dock builders who both died when Just was only four, leaving his mother alone to support him and his younger siblings. She taught school to provide for the family. Because schools at the time were so clearly inferior for blacks in the South, he and his mother decided when he was in his early teens that he would have to go north for his education. Just worked his way north, until he finally landed in New Hampshire and became the only African American at a college-preparatory academy. He distinguished himself right from the start; he became editor of the school paper and president of the debate team. Just graduated in 1903 and went on to Dartmouth College. At graduation four years later he faced a problem that would trail him the rest of his life. No matter how well prepared, brilliant, or deserving, a black person was not considered an acceptable candidate for a faculty position at a white college or university.

Just made the best of the situation and was hired by Howard University, a Washington, D.C., college for African Americans. He spent most of his career there. He took courses at Woods Hole Oceanographic Institute every summer and earned a Ph.D. in 1916. He was the chair of the department of zoology until his death. His efforts to better medical school education for blacks earned him the first NAACP Spingarn Medal. He also was given grants by many prestigious organizations and companies. Feeling stifled at Howard, in 1929 he took a visiting professorship in Germany. He had to leave the country when the Nazi party started to gain control. Just was in Paris when it fell to Germany, and he was captured and held as a prisoner of war, until his release in 1940. He returned to Howard, but he was too ill to teach. He died of cancer at Washington, D.C.

SIR WALTER SCOTT

Born August 15, 1771
Died September 21, 1832

Scottish poet and author Scott was born at Edinburgh, Scotland. He started out in law enforcement. He wrote to supplement the income he made from serving as a deputy of the Selkirkshire sheriff and as a clerk of the Court in Session—both positions he held until the end of his life. He translated a collection of ballads by Goethe in 1799, and a book of poetry followed in the early 1800s. Then, using regional speech, local settings, and realism, he created a new literary form, the historical novel. His Waverly novels, Scottish romances that revealed his gift for distinct characterization and vivid storytelling, sold well and made Walter Scott a household name. In the introduction to *The Fortunes of Nigel*, he wrote, "But no one will find me rowing upstream. . . . I care not who know it— I write for the general amusement." His popularity extended to America, where fans actually waited on the docks for ships bearing copies of his novels.

In 1820, at the height of his popularity, he was made a baronet. It was the same year his novel *Ivanhoe* was published. Many other works followed. In 1813 Scott took on the financial obligations of a printing firm, Ballantyne's, meeting its expenses from his publisher's advances. In 1825 economic depression caused both firms to fail. Instead of declaring bankruptcy, Scott chose to work to repay both the printer's and the publisher's debts. In the process of working to meet all the obligations, the author's health was compromised. After his death at age sixty-one, at Abbottsford, Scotland, the rest of the debts were paid from the earnings on his books.

MENACHEM BEGIN

Born August 16, 1913
Died March 9, 1992

Born at Brest-Litovsk in what is now Belarus, Begin was a militant Zionist and anticommunist who fled to Russia to evade the advancing Nazis,
only to be arrested and sent to Siberia. Freed in 1941, he moved to Palestine and became a leader in the Jewish underground movement, fighting
for an Israeli independent state. By 1943 he was the head of the national
military organization. After the formation of Israel he became a member
of the governing body, the Knesset, in 1949. He formed a right-wing
coalition government and was elected prime minister in 1977. At Camp
David in 1979, Begin signed a historic peace accord with President
Jimmy Carter and Egyptian leader Anwar Sadat. Begin and Sadat were
honored with a shared Nobel Peace Prize for their efforts to avoid violence in the region.

However, it wasn't long before violence in Israel continued. Begin
authorized a massive Israeli invasion of Lebanon in 1982 in an attempt
to destroy Palestine Liberation Organization military bases located there.
Israeli soldiers occupied West Beirut, and Begin's government came under
intense criticism due to its Lebanese Christian allies' slaughter of hundreds of Palestinian civilians. Begin died at Tel Aviv, Israel.

DAVY CROCKETT

Born August 17, 1786
Died March 6, 1836

Davy Crockett was born at Greene County, Tennessee. His father ran a tavern after the family moved to Jefferson County. For years, Crockett worked as an Army scout and fought in the Creek Indian War, in the area that is now Florida and Alabama. He went on to a political career. He held several elected positions, including a term in the Tennessee legislature (1821–1824) and three terms in the U.S. House of Representatives.

In 1835, after losing a reelection bid for Congress, Crockett headed to Texas, which at that time was part of Mexico. In February of the following year, he joined forces with men fighting for independence from Mexico at the Alamo, a mission fort in San Antonio. (Some sources claimed that he played the bagpipes atop the fort during the siege.) When the Alamo was overrun by Mexican troops, on March 6, 1836, Crockett was killed in the fighting.

Davy Crockett and his many wilderness exploits became the starting point of some of America's best-loved tall tales. Everything Crockett did, from hunting to swimming to talking, became larger than life each time the stories were retold. His motto was "Be always sure you're right—then go ahead!"

MERIWETHER LEWIS

Born August 18, 1774
Died October 11, 1809

An American explorer and governor, the Lewis of Lewis and Clark fame was born at Charlottesville, Virginia. He served in the army before becoming President Thomas Jefferson's secretary and aide. In 1803 the French sold the lands west of the Mississippi to the United States in what became known as the Louisiana Purchase. Not much was known of these lands, and the government was eager to know about Indian tribes, hunting, farming, timber, and land and water routes to the West. Jefferson chose Lewis and William Clark, a former army officer and friend of Lewis's, to undertake the first overland expedition to the Pacific Northwest in 1804.

Lewis kept a magnificently detailed journal of the two-year expedition, which turned out to be both a scientific and intellectual achievement. The expedition traveled up the Missouri River; along the way it trashed a number of newly built boats. Reaching the land of the Mandan tribe, the Indians welcomed them and the explorers wintered near the Indians. There they hired a hunter and his Shoshone wife/slave, Sacagawea, to accompany them. She turned out to be invaluable in finding edible and medicinal plants, guiding the party west, and translating when they met other Indian tribes. After traversing the Rocky Mountains, they reached the Columbia River, and in December of 1805 they saw the Pacific Ocean. Jefferson rewarded Lewis by making him the governor of Louisiana. In 1809, near Nashville, Tennessee, Lewis died of an apparently self-inflicted gunshot wound. Only in his midthirties at the time of his death, he left many wondering what a man of so many talents could have made of a longer life.

OGDEN NASH

Born August 19, 1902
Died May 19, 1971

A poet and humorist born at Rye, New York, Nash was the son of an importer-exporter whose business kept the family on the move up and down the eastern seaboard. Education was important to the family, but finances were too tight to keep Nash at Harvard University. He dropped out and took a number of jobs, including teaching, selling bonds, and writing ads. He wrote a children's book in 1925, *The Cricket of Carador*. Nash contributed humorous verse to the *New Yorker*, publishing his first funny poem in 1930. Known for outrageous rhymes, he published many collections of poetry over a thirty-year period, including *I'm a Stranger Here Myself* and *You Can't Get There from Here*.

Some of his most beloved poems are only one or two lines long. Nash wrote and published hundreds of poems, but because he himself did not keep track, and because he didn't care where he published his poems, no one knows just how many are out there. His aim was to be a decent provider to his wife and daughters, and he worried that each poem published would be the last, so despite hating travel and speaking, he went on the lecture circuit and appeared on radio and TV. Working at home on lined yellow tablets, he made little notes about words that sometimes would not come together in a poem for years. He wrote the libretto with S. J. Perelman for the Broadway musical *One Touch of Venus* (1943), which was a huge success. Nash died at Baltimore, Maryland.

BERNARDO O'HIGGINS

Born August 20, 1778
Died October 24, 1842

The "Liberator of Chile" was born at Chillán, Chile (some sources place his birth in 1776). He was the illegitimate son of a successful Irish immigrant named Ambrosio O'Higgins (who later became governor of Chile). After pursuing an education in Peru and Spain, O'Higgins returned to Chile in 1802 and shortly thereafter joined revolutionaries fighting for Chilean independence from Spain. During the Napoleonic invasion of Spain, Chile was able to establish its own congress, of which O'Higgins was a member.

Starting in 1814, Spanish forces successfully battled to reassert control. O'Higgins and his freedom fighters regrouped and defeated the loyalists in the Battle of Chacabuco on February 12, 1817. The revolution for Chilean independence was over. O'Higgins was elected director of Chile. For the next five years, he did what he could to build the new nation. He created a military and a navy; established hospitals, libraries, courts, and colleges; and instituted various social and economic reforms. Conflicts with conservative groups grew to the extent that he was forced to resign in 1823. O'Higgins moved with his family to Lima, Peru, where he spent the rest of his life.

WILT CHAMBERLAIN

Born August 21, 1936
Died October 12, 1999

A larger-than-life basketball star, Chamberlain was raised in an Italian-Jewish neighborhood in Philadelphia, Pennsylvania. He grew to be seven feet and one inch tall and weighed 275 pounds at the time when he was playing professional basketball. He claimed the color of his skin wasn't an issue in the area where he played his early games. However, by the time he got to high school and was playing YMCA ball outside his neighborhood, racial discrimination denied him access to some gyms. He took a chance when he and a buddy drove out to the University of Kansas, in 1955, at the invitation of Kansas coach Phog Allen, to get an education and play college ball. At first, there were restaurants that wouldn't serve him even though he was the star center on the Jayhawks team, but that quickly changed. Dr. Allen's son Mit told him that anyplace he wanted to eat, he should eat. He also said, "If they don't serve you, we'll close them up."

Chamberlain's first varsity game against Northwestern is legendary—he scored fifty-two points in an outstanding performance. He also was a winning high jumper. He studied and played at Kansas until after his junior year, when he left to become a member of the Harlem Globetrotters. Chamberlain then moved to the NBA and became a top scorer for the Philadelphia Warriors, the San Francisco Warriors, the Philadelphia 76ers, and the Los Angeles Lakers. On March 2, 1962, Chamberlain scored an astounding 100 points in a game against the New York Knicks. He once said, "Whatever you do, large or small, do it well or don't do it at all." He was elected to the Basketball Hall of Fame in 1979. He died at Los Angeles, California. Basketball legend Kareem Abdul-Jabbar said, "Wilt was one of the greatest ever, and we will never see another one like him."

GEORGE HERRIMAN

Born August 22, 1880
Died April 25, 1944

Comic strip artist George Herriman was born at New Orleans, Louisiana. His family moved to Los Angeles in 1886, where Herriman later became a newspaper gofer and artist at the *Los Angeles Herald*. He made his way to New York around 1901 and produced several comic strips in the early 1900s. In 1910, when he introduced a cat and mouse as subplot characters to his comic strip "The Dingbat Family," their non sequiturs gained enough attention to result in a 1913 spin-off strip for publishing magnate William Randolph Hearst's *New York Journal*.

The superbly drafted "Krazy Kat and Ignatz," which ran from 1913 until Herriman's death in 1944, is considered one of the all-time greatest comic strips. It had as its central theme unrequited love: Kat loved Ignatz, but the malevolent mouse took every opportunity to throw bricks at his devoted suitor. "Krazy Kat" was at first unpopular with local editors and everyday readers because of its offbeat world, but Hearst loved and championed it. Eventually—after a 1925 Broadway show based on the comic strip—it became popular with a mass audience as well as with artists and intellectuals (including Pablo Picasso and Charlie Chaplin). It remained enormously popular after Herriman's death—influencing many of today's comic strips. Herriman died at Hollywood, California.

OLIVER HAZARD PERRY

Born August 23, 1785
Died August 23, 1819

The son of a Quaker naval commander, Perry was born on his family's homestead at South Kingston, Rhode Island. His younger brother, Matthew, became Commodore Perry, who used his military might and his diplomatic skills to get Japan to sign a treaty with the United States, leading to trade and important naval bases in the Pacific. It was a natural decision for young Oliver to go into the navy. His first assignment, at the age of thirteen, was in the Caribbean. Oliver Perry had many adventures fighting pirates and slavers all over the world and was given the rank of lieutenant and command of a small schooner when he was only twenty-one. After many successful missions, in May of 1812 he was promoted to master-commandant. One month later war with Great Britain began as a dispute over naval trade and freedom.

Perry soon asked for a more active post and was given command of the Great Lakes. After building a fleet of ships, and faced with a lack of men, Perry fought the British squadron at the Battle of Lake Erie on September 10, 1813. It was during this battle that Perry's uncanny luck was fully documented. Many times during this intense battle, Perry narrowly escaped being killed by gunfire, cannonballs, and sinking ships; it was as if he had a protective force field around him. His ship, the *Lawrence*, was incapacitated early in the battle and lost 80 percent of the men on board. Perry took the ship's flag, which was crudely emblazoned with Perry's recently deceased friend and colleague Captain Lawrence's famous last words, "Don't give up the ship," to another boat and battled on with the help of a perfect breeze that came just when needed. Fifteen minutes later the British fleet surrendered, and Perry penned his famous line "We have met the enemy and they are ours." He was the first in history to defeat an entire British squadron and successfully bring back every ship as a prize of war; he accomplished all this at the age of twenty-eight. On his thirty-fourth birthday, during a diplomatic mission to Venezuela, he died at sea of yellow fever.

CAL RIPKEN JR.

Born August 24, 1960

The baseball player who broke Lou Gehrig's major league endurance record, Cal Ripken Jr. was born at Havre de Grace, Maryland. He was the son of famed baseball father Cal Ripken Sr. Cal Junior spent a lot of time playing baseball with his athletic brother and sister and hanging out with his father at baseball stadiums all over the United States. He grew up to be a serious player. The Ripkens have stayed loyal to the city of Baltimore and to that city's team, the Orioles. Despite offers of more money, Cal stayed put for most of his career.

A sellout crowd of more than 46,000 fans showed up at Oriole Park on September 6, 1995, to see Ripken break Lou Gehrig's record of 2,130 consecutive games played. President Bill Clinton was there, as was the whole Ripken family. Ripken's children—Rachel, then age five, and Ryan, then age two—tossed him the first ceremonial pitches. When the game began the crowd went nuts, and the celebration delayed the game. His team finally forced Cal out onto the field where he shook hands with police officers, grounds crew, and the players on the other team, the California Angels. Standing ovations, sparklers, and fireworks followed. At a ceremony after the game Cal praised his father, his wife, and former teammate Eddie Murray for their help. His gruff father, who was never a media darling but was well respected for his work ethic, told Cal Junior, "Do the job right; if you're going to hoe the garden, hoe it right." But he also said he hoped Cal would be remembered for all his accomplishments and his contributions to his team and not just for the streak. The right-handed player, known for his abilities as a two-time Golden Glove short-stop and frequent MVP, will probably be best remembered for his ability to play game after game despite illness, injury, and fatigue. Ripken ended his streak September 20, 1998, at 2,632 consecutive games played since May 30, 1982. He retired in 2001, with a total of 3,001 games played.

August 25

HANS ADOLF KREBS

Born August 25, 1900
Died November 22, 1981

Born at Hildesheim, Germany, to a father who was an ear, nose, and throat surgeon, Hans Krebs went on to become a Nobel Prize–winning scientist noted for his explanation of how the body turns food into physical energy. He was educated at the local school and went on to study medicine at several German universities, achieving a medical degree in 1925. He worked in universities and hospitals in Germany and in England, eventually working in the new field of biochemistry. In 1938 he married, and he and his wife had three children. They moved many times to accommodate his research and career needs.

Krebs's work focused on cell metabolism. In 1953 he shared the Nobel Prize for Medicine with fellow biochemist Fritz Lipmann. Among his many scholarly publications is a remarkable survey of how energy transforms in living matter, which he published in 1957 in collaboration with H. L. Kornberg. This research explained a process now known as the Krebs Cycle, or citric acid cycle, where the body uses a complex chemical process to fuel the cells with high-energy phosphate. He was elected a fellow in the Royal Society of London and received that organization's Royal Medal. A Gold Medal from the Netherlands Society for Physics, Medical Science, and Surgery followed in 1954. He was knighted in 1958. He held honorary degrees from many of the world's most prestigious universities. He died at Oxford, England.

LEE DE FOREST

Born August 26, 1873
Died June 30, 1961

American inventor of the electron tube, the surgical radio knife, the photoelectric cell, and the system used to synchronize sound with film, De Forest was born at Council Bluffs, Iowa. His minister father moved the family to Alabama to become the president of Talladega College, a small black institution. De Forest's education was formal and upper class; he attended a private boys school in Massachusetts before pursuing a Ph.D. at Yale. His 1899 dissertation was entitled "The Reflection of Hertzial Waves at the End of Parallel Wires." He worked briefly for a number of companies, including General Electric, but spent most of his life as an independent inventor, receiving more than 180 patents in his lifetime.

De Forest was an undeniably brilliant inventor, but he seemed to have trouble with business ethics and business partners. He spent a lot of time in court, sometimes for misleading the public in stock selling schemes, sometimes for stealing other inventors' ideas. Usually he won, and his name was legally cleared, but each case tarnished his image and played havoc on his finances. After one particularly bad stretch, he was forced to sell his beloved home Riverlure on the banks of the Hudson River in New York to cover court costs. He also had trouble with the women he married. He started in 1906 with a marriage that ended in divorce the same year. Two more marriages followed, one to an engineer who bore him his first child but didn't want to live in De Forest's shadow, and then to a singer who had several children with him. His fourth, final, and most happy marriage, in 1930, was to Hollywood actress Marie Mosquini.

He loved tinkering with devices, and he created the Phonofilm system—in which a film's sound is decoded from a series of black-and-white strips that run along the edge of the film. For this 1920 invention he received an honorary Oscar award in 1959. The Phonofilm system is still used today. He wrote an autobiography, *Father of Radio*, in 1950. He died at Hollywood, California.

MOTHER THERESA

Born August 27, 1910
Died September 5, 1997

This remarkable woman, who felt called upon to help the poorest of the poor, was born Gonxha Agnes Bojaxhiu in Skopje, Macedonia, to Albanian parents. At eighteen she resolved to do missionary work and dedicate herself to God. She joined the Sisters of Loreto, an Irish Catholic order serving Calcutta, India. She was renamed Theresa after the Spanish saint Theresa of Avila. For twenty years she was a teacher at St. Mary's High School, but in 1946 she decided to help the poor in Calcutta slums.

Through her Missionaries of Charity order (which she founded in 1950), she schooled destitute children, created mobile health clinics, established orphanages, provided aid to lepers and relief to the dying in hospices, set up food kitchens, and much more. Her order expanded beyond India to more than twenty other countries and includes today more than 4,000 nuns and brothers—plus many times more volunteers. She was awarded the Nobel Peace Prize in 1979, and the committee noted in their presentation (quoting then-president of the World Bank, Robert MacNamara), "Mother Theresa deserves Nobel's Peace Prize because she promotes peace in the most fundamental manner: by her confirmation of the inviolability of human dignity." In accepting the prize, she stated, "Love begins at home, and it is not how much we do, but how much love we put in that action." Mother Theresa died of a heart attack at Calcutta.

JOHANN WOLFGANG VON GOETHE

Born August 28, 1749
Died March 22, 1832

Noted as one of the greatest figures of German literature, Goethe was a poet, novelist, playwright, scientist, and natural philosopher. He was born at Frankfurt-am-Main, Germany, and studied law in Leipzig, where he started to write poetry and plays. Back at Frankfurt in 1771, he wrote *Sturm und Drang* (*Storm and Stress*), which captured the spirit of German nationalism at that time. In 1775, still in his twenties, he went to work at the court of Charles Augustus, Duke of Saxe-Weimar-Eisenach, where he first set eyes on Charlotte von Stein. This lady provided him with the inspiration to write some of the greatest romantic poetry of all time.

Goethe began his masterpiece, a version of *Faust*, a dramatic poem about the legendary sixteenth-century scholar who sold his soul to the devil in return for magical power and knowledge, in 1775. Volume one was published in 1808 and completed before he died in 1832. Goethe also developed a new literary form, the *Bildungsroman*, which was a novel based on the development of a character through experience over time. Along with his many acclaimed literary works, Goethe wrote fourteen volumes on science. Goethe died at Weimar, Germany, in his early eighties.

CHARLIE PARKER

Born August 29, 1920
Died March 12, 1955

Jazz saxophonist Charlie Parker was born at Kansas City, Kansas. He earned the nickname "Yardbird" from his habit of sitting in the backyard of speakeasies fingering his saxophone. The man who later became known simply as "Bird" was mostly self-taught. His mother gave him a saxophone when he was eleven. When he left school he played with local jazz groups and in a big band with Dizzy Gillespie. He moved to New York and began freelancing, then moved on to lead smaller groups that played the bebop style of jazz. He won gradual recognition for his unique style and talent.

By the time Parker was twenty-five, his ability to create ornate off-the-cuff improvisations was legendary. His compositions include such works as "Ornithology" and "Now's the Time," which are still played today by jazz greats. Parker, like many musicians of his time, had problems with alcohol and heroin, among other drugs. He also struggled with schizophrenia throughout his life. The drug addiction proved his downfall, and he died at Rochester, New York, in his midthirties.

ROY WILKINS

Born August 30, 1901
Died September 8, 1981

Wilkins, a noted African-American leader sometimes known as "Mr. Civil Rights," was born at St. Louis, Missouri, the grandson of a slave. He graduated from the University of Minnesota and worked for a black newspaper, the *Kansas City Call,* before joining the NAACP, in 1931, succeeding W. E. B. Du Bois as editor of the organization's magazine *The Crisis* from 1934 to 1949. He served as the NAACP executive secretary from 1955 until 1977. Asked what he did for a living he said, "I work for Negroes." He couldn't bring himself to use the term *black* when it came into vogue in the 1960s, and that along with his careful, deliberate manner at times made him seem out of step with younger African Americans. He helped organize the famous March on Washington in 1963. He later earned the Spingarn Medal for his efforts.

As head of the NAACP, Wilkins was an eloquent spokesman for the civil rights movement. He was called on countless times to confer with presidents, testify before congressional hearings, and write articles for publications. In the 1970s he and the NAACP came under fire from more militant activist groups, but he never wavered in his belief in nonviolence, nor did he shy away from efforts to use any and all constitutional means to help African Americans achieve the rights of full citizenship due them. He was a trustee of many important foundations, and he sat on the board of directors of many humanitarian organizations. His awards are too numerous to list, but his greatest compliment may have come as younger African Americans began to reevaluate his contributions and came to see him as the great leader he was. When he died at New York City, President Reagan ordered American flags flown at half-mast on all government buildings and installations.

MARIA MONTESSORI

Born August 31, 1870
Died May 6, 1952

This Italian physician and educator was born at Chiaravalle, Italy. In 1894 Montessori became the first Italian woman in the modern era to get a medical degree. Her areas of specialty were psychiatry and the treatment of children. While working with mentally disabled children at the Orthophrenic School in Rome, she experimented with ways of engaging the children and developed what became the Montessori method. She believed that children should work at tasks that interest them, and if they are given the right materials and tasks, they learn best through self-motivation; therefore, teachers should only interfere if a child needs help.

Her method provided a system for educating all children because it allowed children to learn and develop skills at their own pace. She set up a special school in Rome for ordinary preschoolers; her methods again proved very successful. Her classroom environment was rich with learning materials, and it also featured her specially designed child-size furniture. She gained the attention of many leading educators in Italy and abroad. Her books, *The Montessori Method* (1912) and *The Secret of Childhood* (1936), made her famous. Montessori schools are now operating all over the world. They have proved an effective way of educating children from preschool through secondary school. Montessori died at Noordwijk, Holland.

SEPTEMBER

EDGAR RICE BURROUGHS

Born September 1, 1875
Died March 19, 1950

An American novelist and creator of the world-famous character Tarzan, Burroughs was one of the most widely recognized pop culture icons in America. He was born at Chicago, Illinois, into a prosperous family. He attended private academies, including the Michigan Military Academy. He served in the cavalry in Arizona Territory and then in the Illinois Reserve. After his military service, Burroughs bounced from job to job, exploring a number of different and less-than-successful careers. He married in 1900, had children, and spent the next decade near poverty. The turning point for Burroughs came when he sold some early science fiction stories to a pulp magazine. The adventures of an invincible hero named Carter, who finds himself on Mars, and a Martian princess named Dejah, were serialized in 1912 and eventually became a series of eleven books. Many of Burroughs's other pulp writings also became popular series, numbering over sixty titles.

A few short months after his first success, he hit pay dirt with a story about an ape man. He said later, "If I had striven for long years of privation and effort to fit myself to become a writer, I might be warranted in patting myself on the back, but God knows I did not work and still do not understand how I happened to succeed." In 1913 he founded his own publishing house and in 1918 launched himself into the movie business, creating the world's first multimedia empire—complete with merchandising tie-ins. When swimming champion Johnny Weissmuller took the lead role in the 1930s, the Tarzan films became incredibly popular and were dubbed into other languages and shown all over the world. Burroughs himself enjoyed increasing popularity, and his many adventure books continued to sell well. He was even elected mayor of California Beach in 1933. Not content simply to retire, he served as a war correspondent in World War II at the age of sixty-six. Burroughs died of a heart ailment at home in Encino, California, while reading a comic book.

ALBERT SPAULDING

Born September 2, 1850
Died September 9, 1915

Baseball Hall of Fame pitcher and sports executive Albert Spaulding founded the Spaulding sports equipment company and was a major promoter of the early game of baseball in the United States. He was born at Byron, Illinois, and had an outstanding career as a pitcher. He helped found the National League and retired from playing in 1877 to promote the game. He started the Spaulding company to make baseballs, then gloves, and finally hats and uniforms. His fancier uniforms were especially popular with teams funded by wealthy investors in the western part of the country, where even small mining towns came to have competitive teams. Later he branched out to make equipment for other sports.

His deepest mark on baseball came in 1905 when he worked to appoint a commission to investigate the game. He hoped to prove that baseball had been invented in America, by Americans, for Americans. His attitude meshed well with the spirit of the times, as the country tried to heal the wounds of the Civil War and to break away from regionalism to a more united culture. For two years the commission came up with little in the way of evidence. Then on the basis of an elderly gentleman's recollections of schoolmate Abner Doubleday's involvement in creating the game, the commission reconsidered the question. With Spaulding's continual urgings motivating them, they conferred the honor of baseball's creation on retired Union general Abner Doubleday. The official declaration was conveniently timed to go with Spaulding's plans for a great centennial celebration for baseball in 1939. Spaulding died at Point Loma, California, before seeing that centennial. He was inducted into the Baseball Hall of Fame in 1939.

FERDINAND PORSCHE

Born September 3, 1875
Died January 30, 1951

Born at Maffersdorf, Austria, Porsche was fascinated by all things mechanical and electrical. When he was just fifteen, he succeeded in making his family home the second structure in town to be electrically lighted. He built everything needed—including a generator and the light-bulbs themselves. He went on to design motors and vehicles of all types, working for and then walking away from a number of car manufacturers over disagreements often due to his difficult personality. In his lifetime he was a controversial figure as a result of his close ties to Adolf Hitler. He eventually designed successful tanks, all-terrain vehicles, gun cars, electric and diesel trains, and of course the famous "people's car," the Volkswagen, for the Nazis.

His creative genius was diverse and flexible. In his lifetime he worked on air- and water-cooled engines, windmills, huge electric/diesel tanks, aircraft engines, and race cars. After the war, Porsche spent almost two years in a French prison. His son Ferry and a number of associates carried on work during the postwar period of rebuilding. Stalin invited Porsche to Russia with the hope of making him the Russian minister of technology, but, as Russia had no racing, Porsche returned to Germany where he designed the P-wagon of 1932. This car bore striking similarities to the racing cars that would evolve during the 1960s and '70s. The company he created is still in Porsche family hands and continues to make the world's favorite racing cars. The Volkswagen, which Porsche designed in close cooperation with Hitler, became the backbone car of the auto company of the same name that still thrives today. Porsche suffered a stroke and died at Stuttgart, Germany. Cars bearing his name are considered to be among the finest high-performance machines in the world.

DANIEL HUDSON BURNHAM

Born September 4, 1846
Died June 1, 1912

An American architect and city planner, Burnham was born at Henderson, New York. He gained his early experience in architecture with William Le Baron Jenney, who has been called the father of the skyscraper. In 1873 Burnham teamed up with John Wellborn Root; their collaborations would become world famous. Some of their best-known commissions include the Masonic Temple, Monadnock Building, Reliance, Rookery, St. Gabriel's Church, and the Union Stock Yard Gate. The twenty-story Masonic Temple (1892) was one of the first skyscrapers to use a metal skeleton as part of its building method. After Root's death, in 1891, Burnham's firm continued its amazing output, which included many fine public buildings such as railway stations, park field house, and city halls. Burnham's reputation grew even more when he was asked to supervise the layout and construction of the 1893 World's Colombian Exposition, which was to be held in Chicago. The white city he devised for the exhibition favored a neoclassical style, which greatly influenced the designs of many architects in the coming decades.

Perhaps even more important than the great buildings he designed are the great cities he planned. If it were not for a city plan he and assistant Edward Bennett created for Chicago, that city would have ended up with the same crowded waterfront that clutters so many other cities. Burnham's plan featured a policy of "forever open, clear, and free" and is considered to be the first example of comprehensive city planning. He also created plans for Cleveland, San Francisco, Washington, D.C., and Manila (in the Philippines). He once said, "Make no little plans, they have no magic to stir men's blood." He died while touring Heidelberg, Germany.

DARRYL F. ZANUCK

Born September 5, 1902
Died December 22, 1979

Born at Wahoo, Nebraska, this motion-picture executive began his Hollywood career as a screenwriter for Warner Brothers. His first film as a producer was *The Jazz Singer* (1927), the first film ever to use audible dialogue. Of the original Hollywood giants, he is the only one that worked his way up through the ranks in the industry. In 1933 he left Warner Brothers over a salary dispute and the desire for more creative control. He cofounded Twentieth Century Pictures, which was specifically set up to feature Zanuck's talents as a producer. A few years later, Twentieth Century merged with the Fox studios. William Fox had set up his studio as an independent in opposition to Thomas Edison's motion-picture patent monopoly.

The two independents became Twentieth Century Fox Film Corporation, which grew to be a powerhouse in the fledgling industry, and Zanuck, who was only in his early thirties, became head of production. He produced such films as *The Grapes of Wrath* (1940), *Snows of Kilimanjaro* (1952), *The Robe*, which was the first CinemaScope film (1953), and *The Longest Day* (1962). Even though Twentieth Century hadn't lasted long as an independent, Zanuck's initial step of leaving Warner Brothers to form his own company served as a model for other talented producers who struck out on their own seeking more creative freedom and control. Zanuck was also seen as ahead of his time in hiring Jane White, daughter of Walter White of the NAACP, to doctor the script on the 1949 film *Pinky*, the story of an African American passing for white, and in the casting of Sidney Poitier in the 1950 film *No Way Out*. Zanuck died at Palm Springs, California.

MARQUIS DE LAFAYETTE

Born September 6, 1757
Died May 20, 1834

A French general and aristocrat born at Chavaniac, Lafayette's full name was Marie-Joseph-Paul-Yves-Roch-Gilbert du Motier. He came to the American continent to assist in the colonists' struggle for independence and was given a major-generalship. He became a lifelong friend with George Washington, the American commander in chief. After an alliance was signed with France, Lafayette returned to his native country and persuaded King Louis XVI to send troops to assist the American revolutionaries. On his return, he was given command of an army at Virginia. Lafayette fought with Washington at Valley Forge and was a critical force at Yorktown, a victory that led to the end of the war and to American independence.

Popular on both sides of the Atlantic, he was hailed as the "Hero of Two Worlds" and was appointed brigadier general upon his return to France in 1782. His experiences at the birth of the American democracy influenced him greatly. He became a leader of the liberal aristocrats in the early days of the French Revolution, and his "Declaration of the Rights of Man and of the Citizen" was adopted by the National Assembly. As the commander of the newly formed national guard of Paris, he rescued King Louis XVI and his family from a murderous mob that stormed Versailles on October 6, 1789, and brought them to Paris. Lafayette's popularity waned after his guards opened fire on angry demonstrators demanding that the king abdicate his throne. He fled to Austria after the overthrow of the monarchy in 1792, returning when Napoleon Bonaparte came to power. He died in his late seventies at Paris, France.

On July 24, 2002, Lafayette was declared an honorary citizen of the United States by the U.S. Congress and President George W. Bush. He was only the sixth person ever to receive this honor.

BUDDY HOLLY

Born September 7, 1936
Died February 3, 1959

Born Charles Hardin Holley at Lubbock, Texas, Holly became one of the most influential early rock-and-roll singers and bandleaders. He wrote his own songs, which was unusual for the era. He was the first rock artist to record music with a string orchestra. With his group, the Crickets, he was the first to use a bass, two guitars, and drums. This particular combination has become the standard rock-band format.

Holly's musical interests were diverse and reflected the part of the country in which he was raised. It featured country and western, African-American, and Mexican influences. He penned a number of classic tunes in the late 1950s, including "That'll Be the Day," "Rave On," "It Doesn't Matter Any More," and "Peggy Sue." He had split from the Crickets and was on tour with a number of other stars when his plane crashed near Mason, Iowa. There were no survivors. Holly's tragic death at the age of twenty-two sent the nation's teens into mourning. His popularity only increased after his death, and he became a national pop icon. His music has been imitated and recorded by many of the nation's biggest rock artists.

CLAUDE DENSON PEPPER

Born September 8, 1900
Died May 30, 1989

A U.S. representative and senator, Pepper was born near Dudleyville, Alabama. His career spanned a remarkable fifty-three years. He served during the administrations of ten different presidents, and as he aged he became a champion for America's senior citizens. His impact on the nation goes deep; he was the principal architect of some of this country's most important social programs (including Social Security). He also penned legislation for the minimum wage, medical assistance for the elderly, and aid for handicapped children.

Not following the usual career path for politicians, after fourteen years in the Senate, he returned to Congress in the House of Representatives, where he settled in to serve fourteen terms. He was active on a number of fronts and served as the chairman of the House Select Committee on Aging (a subject that remained one of his passionate interests throughout his career). His efforts on behalf of older Americans included drafting legislation that banned forced retirements. He was popular with older Americans for his continued battle against cutting Social Security benefits. Pepper was almost ninety when he died at Washington, D.C.

LEO TOLSTOY

Born September 9, 1828
Died November 20, 1910

The great novelist and philosopher Leo Tolstoy was born Count Leo Nikolayevich Tolstoy to an aristocratic family in Tula Province, Russia. In his youth, he struggled to manage the family estate, then studied law before serving in the Crimean War. Tolstoy began his literary career in the 1850s when he published the autobiographical trilogy that included *Childhood* (1852), *Boyhood* (1854), and *Youth* (1857). Tolstoy's fiction was largely inspired by his diaries, in which he wrestled with understanding his feelings and actions. He is best known for two novels, *War and Peace* (1869), which contains vivid descriptions of battles and shows people as mere victims of chance, and *Anna Karenina* (1877), the story of a married woman's love for an army officer and the tragic results of her passion. However, he was also a prolific writer of short stories, plays, and essays.

In his later years, Tolstoy turned to religious issues and writing, but his ideas were so radical that he was excommunicated by the Orthodox Church. His increasingly odd and austere beliefs alienated his family. Tolstoy came to believe that through simplicity can one find truth, and he renounced his earlier writings as too stylized. His wife and children (other than his youngest daughter) more or less disowned him. Leo Tolstoy died at Astapovo, Russia. Many regard his novels as masterpieces of psychological drama.

ARNOLD PALMER

Born September 10, 1929

Credited with transforming golf from a sport of the rich upper classes to a popular pastime, world champion golfer Palmer was born at Latrobe, Pennsylvania. Years before Tiger Woods was born, Palmer already had a huge following of fans, a factor that turned many people on to the game. He is considered to be one of the greatest golf champions in the postwar period. In the United States and abroad Palmer's style and performance have given him a faithful following of fans who call themselves Arnie's Army.

He won his first championship in 1954, when he became U.S. Amateur Champion. Only one year later he went pro and won the Canadian Open. In 1960 Palmer won the U.S. Open, and in the following two years he went on to take the champion spot again. Palmer was the captain of the United States Ryder Cup team twice. Starting in 1958, and three times in the early 1960s, his fans supported him as he took the U.S. Masters competition. In 1968 he astounded the world of professional sports by being the first golfer to earn a million dollars playing golf. Now a senior citizen, Palmer continues to play competitive golf and charity events on a regular basis. He has been involved with golf course and club designs. The Palmer signature is a well-known trademark.

O. HENRY

Born September 11, 1862
Died June 5, 1910

Born William Sydney Porter, at Greensboro, North Carolina, the American short story writer known for twists of plot, coincidences, and surprise endings was left at age three in the care of his father and an aunt after his mother's death. He attended his aunt's private school and worked for his uncle. Eventually he became a pharmacist. He found life in his hometown boring and was eager to explore the world. When friends invited him to a ranch in Texas he went. He married and settled in Austin, where he and his wife had a daughter. How his downfall came about has never been clear, but while he was working at a bank some cash went missing. He fled to Honduras to avoid being arrested but returned when he found out that his wife was dying. He was convicted for embezzlement in 1897 and sent to prison.

He spent three years in prison, and it was there that he began writing under the pen name of O. Henry. He sold stories to magazines to support his daughter. After his release his short stories of adventure in Central America and the American Southwest gained him an enthusiastic following. In 1902 he moved to New York City, and from December of 1903 until January 1906 he managed to create and write a new story every single week for the *New York World*. He also found time to write stories that were published in other magazines. Soon he was the most widely read author in the nation. His first collection, *Cabbages and Kings*, came out in 1904; the next collection, *The Four Million*, was published just two years later and contained his best-known stories, "The Gift of the Magi" and "The Furnished Room." His stories were often funny, touching, and exciting. In all, he published ten collections and more than 600 short stories before he died of cirrhosis of the liver in New York, the city he sometimes referred to as "Baghdad-on-the-Subway."

JESSE OWENS

Born September 12, 1913
Died March 31, 1980

Born James Cleveland Owens, this American athlete was born at Oakville, Alabama. While competing at Ohio State University in 1935, Owens was hurled into the track and field spotlight when in a little more than an hour he set three world records and equaled yet another. Owens became one of seven African-American athletes to take medals at the 1936 Olympics in Berlin, Germany. Interestingly, Hitler had chosen to host the event as a way of showcasing Aryan (white) supremacy. Despite an icy reception for Owens and his black teammates from some of the crowd, Owens took four gold medals in four events: the 100 meters, the 200 meters, the long jump, and the 400-meter team relay.

Hitler was infuriated by Owens's obvious athletic prowess and left the stadium rather than congratulate a nonwhite athlete. Sadly, the U.S. attitude toward nonwhite talent was not all that different, and Owens's achievements went largely unrecognized upon his return to the United States. Twenty years later, he was finally seen for what he was, the greatest sprinter of his generation. He was elected to the Illinois Athletics Commission, and he returned to the Olympics in 1956, this time as President Eisenhower's personal representative. Finally, at the age of sixty-three, Owens was awarded the prestigious Presidential Medal of Freedom. He served as an important role model to many talented athletes who followed after racial barriers starting coming down. Owens died at Tucson, Arizona.

WALTER REED

Born September 13, 1851
Died November 22, 1902

An American Army surgeon, Reed was born at Gloucester County, Virginia. The military had been experiencing a serious outbreak of yellow fever, especially among the men stationed in Cuba. The illness left thousands sick and many dead. Yellow fever can cause fever, chills, prostration, jaundice, and even internal hemorrhage, coma, and death. A pathologist and bacteriologist, Reed had begun experiments during the Spanish-American War in 1898. The military asked him to lead a commission to investigate the outbreak in 1900. His controversial study, using volunteers, proved Cuban doctor Carlos Juan Finlay's theory that mosquitoes transmit the disease.

Until this time, yellow fever was thought to have been spread by patient-to-patient contact. In 1901, the published findings showed that a mosquito now called *Aëdes aegypti* was to blame. Mosquito eradication campaigns ensued, and the incidence of yellow fever dropped. W. C. Gorgas, the U.S. surgeon general, led sanitation and eradication programs in Panama to control the disease before construction of the Panama Canal began.

Today yellow fever occurs in sporadic and smaller outbreaks, and a vaccine is available for treatment. Reed became a hero to many working in tropical climates and to the medical staff responsible for treatment of yellow fever. The Walter Reed Hospital in Washington, D.C., is named for him. He died at Washington, D.C.

IVAN PETROVICH PAVLOV

Born September 14, 1849
Died February 27, 1936

Born at Ryazan, Russia, Pavlov studied to be a priest, but he left biblical studies because of his interest in science and medicine. He became director of the Institute of Experimental Medicine in St. Petersburg, where he dedicated himself to learning about the processes of circulation and digestion. While researching the digestive processes of dogs, the role of enzymes and the nervous control of saliva, he trained a dog to salivate at the sound of a bell. He called this phenomenon conditioned reflex; he published a book about it in 1926.

This type of conditioned response is now known to occur in many situations and is still a favorite topic for research among psychologists and other behavioral investigators. Many psychological disorders involve such responses, so Pavlov's work laid the foundation for better understanding of human and animal behavior. He received a Nobel Prize for Medicine in 1904. After a long and successful career in science, Pavlov died at St. Petersburg, Russia, in his late eighties.

FRANK GANNETT

Born September 15, 1876
Died December 3, 1957

This American publisher, born at Bristol, New York, to struggling parents farming the hardscrabble land of upstate New York, developed a publishing empire in newspapers and other news outlets. Known for buying up newspapers in U.S. cities and merging them, he set up the Gannett Company in 1906, at Rochester, New York. His first merger came in New York City in 1907 when he bought and merged the *Elmira Star* and the *Gazette*. He was a controversial figure in the newspaper world because he was said to put profit before any other considerations. He had a reputation for salary penny-pinching, yet he also was an early supporter of profit sharing and pensions.

His angle was to pursue the advertising and circulation possibilities of a one-newspaper town, while eliminating competition. He left editorial decisions to his editors, a practice he believed to be an important tenet of good journalism. His system was highly successful and made him very wealthy. A Unitarian who made an unsuccessful bid for the U.S. presidency in 1939 and in 1940, he suggested the cabinet include a secretary of peace. He was a generous contributor to research efforts—especially in the areas of journalism, aviation, health, and medicine. Gannett was honored by many institutions and given a number of honorary doctorates. By 1954 his corporation included twenty-two newspapers, four radio stations, and three television stations. Today the Gannett Co., Inc., publishes seventy-four newspapers—including *USA Today*, an extremely popular nationwide newspaper—and operates twenty-two television stations. He died at Rochester, New York.

MARVIN MIDDLEMARK

Born September 16, 1919
Died September 14, 1989

Middlemark was an inventor born at Long Island, New York. His passion for inventing and tinkering led to many inventions, such as the water-driven automatic potato peeler. However, like the potato peeler, most enjoyed little commercial success. His big success came during the early days of television, when reception was fuzzy. He reduced the fuzz on screens by adding "rabbit ears," or V-shaped antennae. It was just one of his many patents, but this one paid off.

When he died in 1989, at Old Westbury, New York, he was a self-made millionaire. He left behind intriguing evidence of his wide-ranging interests and eccentricities. His Long Island mansion was surrounded by vinyl tube fencing that was stuffed with used tennis balls (he invented a self-renewing tennis ball); eighteen Chinese tractors; dozens of cement statues of Greek gods; and housing for his eight dogs, nine miniature horses, and eight miniature donkeys. Inside there were stained-glass windows featuring both Marilyn Monroe and Albert Einstein—and a mysterious collection of a thousand one-size-fits-all woolen gloves.

HANK WILLIAMS

Born September 17, 1923
Died January 1, 1953

One of the all-time greatest singer-songwriters of country and western music—as well as a major influence on rock 'n' roll—Hank Williams was born at Mount Olive, Alabama. He was small and fragile and suffered from spina bifida. When he was eight, his mother gave him his first guitar. Williams claimed he learned everything he knew about music from his friend Rufas Payne, a black street bluesman. This early blues influence is reflected in his music. Williams quit school at the age of sixteen and began to appear on WFSA radio, in Montgomery, in 1937. His radio performances soon became the station's most popular act. He also started a band, the Drifting Cowboys, and they performed at roadhouses and regional shows. Williams had come to the attention of several Nashville artists and music businessmen, but his fame as a singer was equaled by his reputation for drinking and being generally unreliable.

After recording a couple of regionally successful singles, Williams signed with MGM in 1947, recording his first billboard chart entry, "Move It on Over." Despite the urging of the members of his circle who told him not to waste his time on a "piece of fluff," he felt drawn to record the song "Lovesick Blues." Released in February 1949, it was number one by May. Williams suddenly found himself a star in the United States and abroad. Other hits were "Your Cheatin' Heart," "Hey, Good Lookin'," and "Honky Tonkin'." Williams started performing regularly at Nashville's Grand Ole Opry in 1949. His success was tempered by his habit of showing up drunk or late for performances. Drinking and drug addictions, injuries, and a turbulent domestic life took their toll. Hank Williams died in the backseat of a car en route to a concert in Ohio on New Year's Day. He was twenty-nine years old. He was inducted into the Country Music Hall of Fame in 1961. In 1983 he was honored with a Grammy for the 1952 recording "Your Cheatin' Heart." As his legacy became clear, he continued to receive awards in the decades that followed his death, including induction in 1987 into the Rock and Roll Hall of Fame as a forefather of rock music.

LANCE ARMSTRONG

Born September 18, 1971

National and world champion cyclist, Olympian, humanitarian, cancer survivor, and Tour de France winner Lance Armstrong was born at Plano, Texas. He credits his mother, Linda, with encouraging his natural athleticism and fostering his intensely competitive nature. Armstrong won the Kids Triathlon at age thirteen and became a professional triathlete at age sixteen. By the time he was in high school, he focused on cycling and had a host of interested sponsors. Sometimes his Saturday rides would take him to the Oklahoma border, and his mother would have to drive to pick him up. By 1991 he was the United States amateur champion. He competed in the 1992 Olympics in Barcelona, Spain. He credits his mother with giving him the ethic to keep going no matter what the odds. It turned out that 1993 was a better year for Armstrong: he gained an amazing ten titles, including the United States Pro Championship and his first-stage victory in what was to become his competitive focus, the Tour de France. His abilities led to a U.S. team being ranked in the top five for the first time in history. Armstrong made history again when he won the 1993 Thrift Drug Triple Crown (and a million dollars).

His victories from that point on become too numerous to list, but his biggest personal challenge came with a diagnosis of cancer in 1996. Tests showed testicular cancer that had already spread to the lungs and brain. Things looked pretty bleak, but Armstrong underwent surgeries and chemotherapy. Five months later, weakened but thrilled to be alive, Armstrong started training again. Because his illness was such an enormous challenge and helped him to see the more important things in life, Armstrong claims that getting cancer was actually a gift. Armstrong had a brief struggle after one particularly bad event, but in 1999 he went on to win the first of four consecutive Tour de France races—making him the most successful American Tour cyclist in history. His triumph made for one of the most stunning comebacks in athletic history. He rode more than two thousand miles at an average speed of twenty-five miles per hour.

September 19

WILLIAM GERALD GOLDING

Born September 19, 1911
Died June 19, 1993

Novelist and Nobel Prize–winner Golding was born at the village of Saint Columb Minor in Cornwall, England. His father was a schoolmaster with a strong belief in science. Golding showed an early interest in writing, but he followed his parents' wishes and enrolled in natural science courses at college. He published his first book, a collection of poetry, before he graduated. His early work was in a settlement house in London, where he wrote plays on the side. After teaching English he found himself on active duty during World War II, where he participated in the sinking of the German battleship *Bismarck* and the invasion at Normandy. When he later returned to writing and teaching it was with a darker view of humanity.

His first and most popular novel, *The Lord of the Flies*, was turned down by more than twenty publishers. It has since been translated into many languages and was made into movies in 1963 and 1990. The nightmarish story concerns a group of British boys who become shipwrecked and then create their own society, which degenerates to cruelty, torment, and violence. In his Nobel lecture in 1983, he commented on how people see his writing as pessimistic. He disagreed: "[C]ritics have dug into my books until they could come up with something that looked hopeless. I can't think why. I don't feel hopeless myself." He wrote many books over the years—science fiction, tales of the sea, and historical fiction. His last work, *The Double Tongue*, was in draft form at the time of his death. It was published in 1995. It is the tale of a Delphic oracle in ancient Greece who sees the decline of Hellenistic culture and the rise of Roman power. Golding died near Truro, Cornwall, England.

UPTON SINCLAIR

Born September 20, 1878
Died November 25, 1968

A politically and socially conscious author, Sinclair was born into poverty at Baltimore, Maryland. He attended the City College of New York and Columbia University, and he supported himself with journalistic work. After writing a series of unsuccessful novels, Sinclair had success in 1906 with his self-published *The Jungle*, an exposé on the meatpacking industry in Chicago. "I aimed at the public's heart and by accident I hit it in the stomach," said Sinclair. He intended to illuminate the plight of the workers, but the book generated more alarm and anger over the unsanitary treatment of meat. The outcry led to federal legislation (which was passed June 30, 1906) on meat inspection.

An ardent socialist, Sinclair followed *The Jungle* with more than eighty other politically charged and socially conscious works, including *King Coal* (1917), *Oil!* (1927), and *Little Steel* (1938). None of his later works received the full attention of the nation as his brutally graphic depiction of the Chicago stockyards had. He also wrote a cycle of twelve novels focusing on world events. The third of these, *Dragon's Teeth* (1942), won the Pulitzer Prize. Sinclair remained an activist and advocate for social change all his life, and his works resulted in industrial and social reforms. He died at Bound Brook, New Jersey.

H. G. WELLS

Born September 21, 1866
Died August 13, 1946

An author best remembered for his prophetic works of science fiction, Herbert George Wells was born at Bromley, Kent, England. His father's business skills were poor, and the family never had much money. A voracious reader from a young age, H.G. was forced to leave school while he was still a teenager when he and his brothers were apprenticed to a draper. Later, through scholarships and grants, he was able to complete his education at the University of London. He taught biology for several years, but his interest in the subject soon waned and he became a full-time writer. His early works criticized Victorian society and urged social change.

The Time Machine, published in 1895, was Wells's first work of science fiction. The story—about a dreamer who travels back and forth through time—was both a parody of the British social classes of the day and an extraordinarily accurate scientific work. The huge success of this novel allowed him to continue writing. He followed it up with well over a hundred books; about fifty of them were novels. His other popular works of science fiction included *The Island of Dr. Moreau* (1896), *The Invisible Man* (1897), and *The War of the Worlds* (1898). He also wrote many volumes of political and social commentary, which became increasingly pessimistic over the years. He married twice, although the love of his life was a much younger author named Rebecca West, with whom he had a relationship for many years. He died at London.

JUNKO TABEI

Born September 22, 1939

Tabei was the first woman to climb the world's highest mountain, Mount Everest. She was also the first woman to climb the Seven Summits, which are the tallest mountains on each of the seven continents: Everest in Asia, Aconcagua in South America, McKinley in North America, Kilimanjaro in Africa, Elbrus in Europe, Vinson Massif in Antarctica, and Kosciusko in Australia.

She was born at a small town in North Japan. She began climbing at the age of ten while on a school field trip to Mount Nasu. In 1962 she began climbing in earnest and in 1969 formed a women's climbing club. In May 1975 she led an all-woman expedition to Everest, the summit of which is 29,035 feet high. Despite an avalanche that delayed the final climb to the summit, Tabei (who stands four feet, nine inches tall) climbed to the top on May 16. "Even after reaching the peak," she later remembered, "instead of shouting with excitement . . . I was simply happy that I didn't have to go any higher!" Her feat won her international acclaim and honors from the Japanese government and the king of Nepal.

Tabei still climbs, and her goal is to climb the highest peak in every country of the world. In 2001 alone, at the age of sixty-two, she climbed eight major mountains. Her interest in ecological issues led her to help create the Himalayan Adventure Trust, an organization dedicated to preserving mountain environments, which sponsors annual cross-cultural mountain conservation youth projects that allow youths to climb and clean up mountainsides.

WILLIAM HOLMES MCGUFFEY

Born September 23, 1800
Died May 4, 1873

Despite having no formal schooling during his childhood, William Holmes McGuffey went on to become one of the most significant influences in nineteenth-century American education. Born near Claysville, Pennsylvania, and raised in rural Ohio, his mother taught him to read and a local minister taught him Hebrew, Greek, and Latin. He started his own school and began teaching other area children at age thirteen. At eighteen, he entered the Old Stone Academy in Darlington, Pennsylvania, and then went on to Pennsylvania's Washington College, where he graduated with honors. He became a professor at Miami University in Oxford, Ohio, in 1826, and had a distinguished academic career. He was the president of three colleges: Cincinnati College at Cincinnati, Ohio University at Athens, and Woodward College at Cincinnati. He was also an ordained Presbyterian minister. He became professor of moral philosophy at the University of Virginia in 1845 and remained there in Charlotteville, Virginia, until his death.

During his years at Miami University, he began work on the most influential textbooks in the history of modern education. *McGuffey's Eclectic Readers* were groundbreaking; they provided simple monosyllabic words in the *First Reader*, advanced to more difficult instruction in the *Second Reader*, and so on. Between the years 1836 and 1853 he published six readers, a primer, and a speller. By 1890 these books had been adopted as the basic textbooks of thirty-seven of the forty-four states. An estimated 130 million copies have been printed—that's more than any other book other than the Bible. Today, although no longer used in public school programs, McGuffey's books are still widely used in private schools and literacy programs nationwide.

JIM HENSON

Born September 24, 1936
Died May 16, 1990

Puppeteer Jim Henson created a unique family of puppets known as the Muppets. Kermit the Frog, Big Bird, Bert and Ernie, Gonzo, Miss Piggy, and Oscar the Grouch are just a few of the enduring characters he created.

Henson was born at Greensville, Mississippi. He worked as a television puppeteer beginning in 1954 at Washington, D.C., and introduced the Muppets (a name he made up) in 1956. Basically, the bright, fuzzy Muppets are hand puppets whose limbs are moved by wires that the puppeteer manipulates. Because most of the puppeteers are right-handed, the Muppets tend to be left-handed. Henson's creations captured the hearts of children and adults alike in television appearances and then on PBS's *Sesame Street*, which premiered in 1969. The Muppets branched off into their own TV series with *The Muppet Show* (1976), and into film in *The Muppet Movie* (1979), *The Great Muppet Caper* (1981), *The Muppets Take Manhattan* (1984), and others. Henson created different kinds of creatures for *The Dark Crystal* (1982).

Henson's creativity was rewarded with eighteen Emmy Awards, seven Grammy Awards, four Peabody Awards, and five ACE Awards from the National Cable Television Association. Henson died unexpectedly at New York City.

September 25

CHRISTOPHER REEVE

Born September 25, 1952

Born at New York City, actor Christopher Reeve grew up in New Jersey. Although his parents divorced when he was very young, he remained close to both of them. He grew up in a very intellectual environment. His mother was a journalist, and his father was a novelist whose closest friends included Robert Frost and Robert Penn Warren. He was educated at private schools and attended Cornell University before transferring to New York's famous Juilliard School of Performing Arts. There he studied under renowned acting teacher John Houseman while working in theaters around the city.

His love for acting began at an early age. His first professional performance was in Gilbert and Sullivan's *Yeoman of the Guard* at age nine. He continued to do stage acting throughout his career. He dropped out of Juilliard in his final year to appear with Katharine Hepburn in *A Matter of Gravity* on Broadway. That same year, 1976, he began appearing in small film roles. His big break came when he was cast in 1978's *Superman*, in the lead role. He went on to appear in seventeen feature films, a dozen TV movies, and more than 150 plays. His acting career was cut short when he was severely injured in a horseback riding accident in 1995. Instantly paralyzed from the neck down, Reeve just barely survived his injuries, but he has since made an inspirational, if only partial, recovery.

Since that time, Reeve has become a spokesperson to increase public awareness of spinal cord injuries. In his wheelchair, with a ventilator that controls his ability to breathe, he makes hundreds of public appearances each year to raise money for a cure. He has gone through intense physical therapy and rehabilitation, and in 2001 he regained some of the feeling in his paralyzed limbs. He also returned to his creative work, directing 1996's *In the Gloaming* and taking small acting parts.

LEWIS HINE

Born September 26, 1874
Died November 3, 1940

Lewis Hine earned a place in American history as a crusading photographer. He used his camera to bring social injustices—especially child labor—to public attention. Born at Oshkosh, Wisconsin, Hine traveled to New York City in 1901 where he worked as a teacher. A few years later he created a photographic essay of Ellis Island immigrants. He left teaching to work with the National Child Labor Committee to document horrendous child labor practices in sweatshops, mills, mines, and other industries. His efforts sometimes put him in danger; companies often denied putting children to work (by lying about their ages)—or putting them at risk (by lying about the working conditions). Hine secretly compiled evidence of ages to prove that very young children were laboring. Of his work on behalf of children, he later said, "I wanted to show the thing that had to be corrected."

He documented the plight of refugees during World War I as a member of the American Red Cross. He later documented the construction of the Empire State Building in 1930—sometimes taking photographs while dangling from a crane. These photographs were published in a book for children, *Men at Work* (1932). Although he kept busy documenting American situations and events until his death, it was his efforts to end abusive child labor that had the biggest impact. He died at Hastings-on-Hudson, New York.

SAMUEL ADAMS

Born September 27, 1722
Died October 2, 1803

Born at Boston, Massachusetts, Samuel Adams was a cousin of John Adams, who became the second president of the United States. Samuel Adams himself was one of the key political figures in the American colonies at the time of the Revolutionary War. He graduated from Harvard but was an unsuccessful businessman. He studied law briefly, ran a tavern, and had several other ventures, but when his business failed in 1764, he became a full-time politician. He was elected to the Massachusetts legislature, where he served in various capacities from 1765 to 1774. During this time, he became increasingly outspoken on issues relating to the growing discontent in the Colonies. He opposed the Sugar Act of 1764 and drafted a protest against the Stamp Act of 1765. He was one of the first American political leaders to advocate separation from England.

Along with John Hancock, he organized a group of men called the Sons of Liberty. In response to the passage of the Tea Act of 1773, which gave the East India Company a monopoly on the import of tea into the Colonies, he led the Sons of Liberty in a protest. On the night of December 16, 1773, they dumped a British cargo of tea into Boston Harbor. This night later became known as the Boston Tea Party.

Adams became a member of the First Continental Congress in 1774. He was one of the signers of the Declaration of Independence. He also helped frame the constitution of Massachusetts and served as lieutenant governor and then governor of that state from 1789 to 1797. He died at Boston.

EDWIN COLBERT

Born September 28, 1905
Died November 15, 2001

Paleontologist, teacher, curator, and author Edwin Colbert was born at Clarinda, Iowa. As a youth he once saw a mammoth skeleton, which prompted his lifelong inquiry into dinosaurs. He eventually earned a Ph.D. at Columbia University and taught there from 1945 to 1969. He also became a curator at the American Museum of Natural History in New York for more than thirty years.

Colbert wrote many popular books about dinosaurs for children and adults (including *The Dinosaur Book* and *A Fossil-Hunters Notebook*) while he continued to take an active part in dinosaur hunting. He discovered the rich fossil fields of Ghost Ranch in New Mexico, which gave forth thousands of *Coelophysis* skeletons—an eight-foot-long carnivorous dinosaur that walked on two legs. Colbert's fossil research helped prove the theory of continental drift: in 1969 he found a type of dicynodont in Antarctica that had also been found in Asia and South Africa. His book *Wandering Lands and Animals* (1973) explained this for the popular audience.

Colbert's contributions to the understanding of dinosaurs are immense. He found more than fifty new dinosaur species, and he proved that dinosaurs could hear. He died at Flagstaff, Arizona. A dinosaur—*Nedcolbertia*—was named for him in honor of his work.

ENRICO FERMI

Born September 29, 1901
Died November 28, 1954

Born and educated in Italy, Enrico Fermi was one of the great scientists of the twentieth century. He earned his doctorate from the University of Pisa in 1922 and was a lecturer at the University of Florence. He became a professor of theoretical physics at the University of Rome; there he did the work on the theory of neutrons that gained him the Nobel Prize in Physics "for discovery of new radioactive elements produced by neutron irradiation, and for the discovery of nuclear reactions brought about by slow neutrons." He received the Nobel Prize in 1938, just before he moved to the United States to escape Mussolini's fascist regime.

He was appointed professor of physics at Columbia University in New York and later moved to the University of Chicago in 1942. There he continued to study the nucleus of the atom. Isolating the particles that make up the nucleus was considered to be the first step in making a viable nuclear bomb. He developed the first atomic pile, and on December 2, 1942, he set off the first controlled nuclear chain reaction under a football field at the University of Chicago. He later became a member of the team of physicists assigned to the Manhattan Project, the scientists at Los Alamos, New Mexico, who developed the first atomic bomb. He continued to teach at the University of Chicago until his death, which occurred just days after he won the first special award for outstanding achievement in the field of atomic energy, given by the U.S. Atomic Energy Commission. One of the main research facilities in the United States, Fermilab in Batavia, Illinois, was named in his honor.

ELIE WIESEL

Born September 30, 1928

Witness to the Holocaust, author, speaker, teacher, and Nobel Peace Prize recipient Elie Wiesel has sought to make remembrance an active force for worldwide peace. He was born at Sighet (in what is now Romania) to a Jewish family. He had three sisters. In 1944 his entire family was deported to the Nazi concentration camps: his grandfather, father, mother, cousins, and one sister perished. Wiesel endured imprisonment at Auschwitz and Buchenwald before being freed in 1945 by American troops as World War II ended. "After Auschwitz," Wiesel stated, "the human condition is not the same, nothing will be the same."

After the war, Wiesel became a journalist in France. He was also a foreign correspondent for an Israeli newspaper. In 1960 he published his first book, an autobiographical novel entitled *Night*, in which the protagonist struggles over his faith during the horrors of the concentration camps. Since then Wiesel has published more than forty novels, memoirs, and nonfiction books and has traveled the world as "a messenger to mankind" (as the Norwegian Nobel Committee put it) about the dangers of forgetting the Holocaust and as a crusader for human rights. He was awarded the Nobel Peace Prize in 1986 and used the prize money to found the Elie Wiesel Foundation for Humanity. In his Nobel lecture, Wiesel spoke eloquently: "Remembering is a noble and necessary act."

OCTOBER

JIMMY CARTER

Born October 1, 1924

The thirty-ninth president of the United States was born James Earl Carter Jr. in Plains, Georgia. A graduate of the U.S. Naval Academy, he served in the Navy as a nuclear engineer. He was elected to one term as governor of Georgia (1971–1975). During his term as president, his significant foreign policy accomplishments included the Panama Canal treaties, the Camp David Accords (the peace treaty between Egypt and Israel), the SALT II weapons treaty with the Soviet Union, and the establishment of diplomatic relations with China. Carter championed human rights throughout the world. On the domestic side, Carter's administration created the departments of energy and education, as well as important environmental protection legislation.

Carter has been active since leaving the presidency. He created the Carter Center, a nonprofit organization affiliated with Emory University (Atlanta, Georgia) and dedicated to human rights, global conflict resolution, democracy, and health improvement. In 2002 Carter became only the third U.S. president to receive the Nobel Peace Prize for his accomplishments since leaving the office. Those accomplishments included monitoring elections in Africa, Asia, and Latin America; negotiating ceasefires in Bosnia and Sudan; and working for the eradication of guinea worm and river blindness. Carter also was awarded the Presidential Medal of Freedom—the highest civilian award given by the United States—and the first United Nations Human Rights Prize. He is also a teacher and published poet active with Habitat for Humanity, an organization committed to creating housing for low-income families.

MOHANDAS GANDHI

Born October 2, 1869
Died January 30, 1948

One of the greatest national leaders of the twentieth century, this political and spiritual guide achieved recognition for his use of nonviolent
resistance against the British in his quest for India's independence. He
was a member of the Indian National Congress. He launched a policy of
noncooperation with the British in 1920. Gandhi was repeatedly imprisoned by the British; he often resorted to hunger strikes. He also worked
to improve the status of the untouchable (India's lowest caste) and to
improve relations between the Hindu majority and Muslims and other
minorities. He believed in simple living and manual labor. He was known
by the title *Mahatma*, which means "great soul."

Born at Porbandar, India, Gandhi studied law in London and practiced in South Africa, where he developed his techniques of civil disobedience while agitating for the rights of the Indian community. Gandhi
was assassinated in his own New Delhi garden by a Hindu fanatic. His
birthday is commemorated as a public holiday in India. Gandhi's method
and philosophy of nonviolent confrontation was later adopted successfully in the 1950s and '60s by Martin Luther King Jr. and the civil rights
movement in the United States. "Nonviolence and truth," Gandhi wrote,
"are inseparable and presuppose one another. There is no god higher than
truth."

WILLIAM GORGAS

Born October 3, 1854
Died July 4, 1920

Physician William Gorgas was born at Mobile, Alabama. He obtained his medical degree from Bellevue Hospital Medical College in New York City. Joining the army, he rose to the rank of major general, and in 1898 he was named the army's chief sanitation officer. In 1914 he was appointed surgeon general of the United States Army. He mobilized the nation's medical personnel for World War I and arranged for every army inductee to have a complete medical examination. In this role he also battled yellow fever, first in Florida and Cuba and then at the Panama Canal. The French had tried to build a canal across Panama and had failed, partially because of the high rate of illness among their workers. Gorgas succeeded in ridding the area of yellow fever and malaria. His actions led to the successful completion of the canal—a huge engineering project and one that had a major impact on world trade.

Gorgas was president of the American Medical Association in 1909 and 1910. He was knighted by King George V. He died at London, England, and was given a funeral at St. Paul's Cathedral. He is buried at Arlington National Cemetery.

FREDERIC REMINGTON

Born October 4, 1861
Died December 26, 1909

This artist of the American West was born at Canton, New York. Remington's career as an artist began in the 1880s as an illustrator for *Harper's Weekly* and *Collier's*. Most of his work as an illustrator was done in pen and ink. In the 1880s he began to visit the West, working as a cowboy and following the U.S. cavalry on its campaigns during the Indian wars. In 1891 Remington set up his studio in New Rochelle, New York, where he painted soldiers, cowboys, and Indians. In 1895, after watching a sculptor at work, he began to model these figures in clay. His clay models were cast into bronze at art foundries. The resulting twenty-two bronze statues were immensely popular during his lifetime and have been widely reproduced.

During the Spanish-American War Remington was a correspondent in Cuba; he supplied war illustrations for magazines. The Wild West, which by this time was disappearing, remained his favorite subject, however. Remington died at his home in Ridgefield, Connecticut.

ROBERT GODDARD

Born October 5, 1882
Died August 10, 1945

Called the father of the modern space age, this American physicist laid the foundations for modern rocket technology. Goddard was born at Worcester, Massachusetts, and was a professor at Clark University. He experimented with improving solid-propellant rockets and later switched to liquid fuels. On March 16, 1926, at Auburn, Massachusetts, Goddard fired the first successful liquid-propellant rocket, which burned gasoline and liquid oxygen. It only rose to a height of 41 feet and then flew 184 feet, but it proved that the technology could work. Although not recognized at the time, this was a turning point in history. He then moved his work to Roswell, New Mexico, where he continued to build more powerful rockets.

During World War II, the U.S. government did not think that rockets were useful as weapons and instead put Goddard to work building rockets that could assist aircraft in taking off. Goddard eventually had more than 200 patents covering inventions in the field of rockets, guided missiles, and space exploration. He died at Baltimore, Maryland. NASA named its Goddard Space Flight Center in his honor.

THOR HEYERDAHL

Born October 6, 1914
Died April 18, 2002

Sailing a balsa raft (the *Kon-Tiki*) 4,300 miles from Peru to Raroia in the South Pacific in 1947, this Norwegian anthropologist, explorer, and author set out to prove that ancient Peruvian Indians could have settled in Polynesia. His success in the 101-day adventure won him popular fame, and his book *Kon-Tiki* was an international bestseller. In 1953 he led an archeological expedition to the Galapagos Islands, and in 1955 he led another to Easter Island. In 1970 he sailed from Morocco to the West Indies in a papyrus boat, *Ra II*, to prove that Egyptian mariners could have crossed the Atlantic. He thought this could account for the presence of pyramids in the New World. He made the journey from Iraq to the Indus Valley of Pakistan in a reed boat, the *Tigris* (1977–1978).

Today Heyerdahl's theories on the diffusion of cultures are rejected by many scientists on linguistic and other grounds, but his sense of curiosity and tenacity have been admired by fans the world over. Born at Larvik, Norway, he died at Italy.

YO-YO MA

October 7, 1955

A cellist and one of the world's bestselling recording artists in classical music, Yo-Yo Ma was born to Chinese parents living in Paris. He began to study the cello at age four. Later his family moved to New York City, where he studied at the Juilliard School. A graduate of Harvard University, his many-faceted career spans the globe. He has played as a soloist with orchestras around the world, and he regularly gives recitals and performs chamber music. His discography includes more than fifty albums, fourteen of them Grammy Award winners. He plays instruments that were crafted in the 1700s.

Yo-Yo Ma works to make music and creativity a part of children's lives. He has reached young audiences through appearances on such programs as *Sesame Street* and *Arthur*. He recently founded the Silk Road Project to promote the study of the culture and art along the ancient trade route from the Mediterranean to the Pacific. He has said, "We live in a world where we can no longer afford not to know our neighbors."

R. L. STINE

Born October 8, 1943

Robert Lawrence Stine is the bestselling children's author in history. Born at Columbus, Ohio, he began his writing career as editor of *Bananas*, a humor magazine for children. He also wrote joke books for children under the name Bob Stine. In 1986 he broke away from humor and wrote *Blind Date*, his first scary book. That year he also created *Fear Street*, the first horror series for teenagers, which sold 80 million copies. His greatest success came in 1992 when he launched the *Goosebumps* series for kids ages eight to twelve. The series sold more than 220 million copies, making Stine the bestselling author in the United States for three straight years. It was published in thirty-one other countries as well. It was also made into a television series for the Fox network.

In 1999 Stine's first hardcover collection of stories, *Nightmare Hour*, was on the *New York Times* bestseller list and won several awards as best horror/mystery book of the year. In 2000 Stine released the first title in his latest series, *The Nightmare Room*. It has an accompanying interactive website and was also the basis for a television series.

Stine has been active in promoting literacy among children and has been especially lauded for writing books that boys like to read.

JOHN LENNON

Born October 9, 1940
Died December 8, 1980

A member of the Beatles, a rock group that had a profound influence on the course of popular music, Lennon was born at Liverpool, England. Along with Paul McCartney, Ringo Starr, and George Harrison, Lennon and the Beatles gave the 1960s its musical flavor. "Love Me Do," their first single, released in 1962, shot them to the top of the British pop charts.

Beatlemania began in the United States with the release of "I Want to Hold Your Hand" in 1964. The Beatles' records sold in the millions and their films, *A Hard Day's Night* and *Help!*, were enthusiastically received.

Lennon and McCartney composed most of the group's songs. *Sergeant Pepper's Lonely Hearts Club Band* is generally considered their most successful album. Lennon's song "Give Peace a Chance" became an anthem for the U.S. antiwar movement. In 1970 the last Beatles album, *Let It Be*, was released and the group disbanded.

Lennon and his wife, artist Yoko Ono, moved to New York City in the 1970s, where they made albums and worked on various artistic endeavors. They garnered plenty of media attention for some of their more outrageous efforts. Their last album, *Double Fantasy*, was released one month before Lennon's death. He was killed by a deranged fan outside his New York apartment building.

GIUSEPPE VERDI

Born October 10, 1813
Died January 27, 1901

This composer, born near Parma, Italy, created twenty-six operas, some of them among the most popular of the modern repertoire. His first work, *Oberto*, was performed in 1839. In 1842 Verdi wrote his first successful opera, *Nabucco*. Thereafter he was sought by all the best opera houses in Italy. He went on to produce eighteen operas in fifteen years, including *Rigoletto*, *Il Trovatore*, and *La Traviata*. By then Verdi was internationally known, and he began to get commissions from theaters abroad. He wrote *La Forza del Destino* for St. Petersburg. *Aïda* was commissioned by the Khedive of Egypt to celebrate the opening of the Suez Canal; the opera premiered in Cairo in 1871. Verdi was a great patriot, and during this period he was elected to the first Italian parliament after the unification of his country. After going into semiretirement, Verdi was induced to compose two Shakespearean operas, *Otello* and *Falstaff*.

Verdi was the most important of the nineteenth-century composers of Italian opera, beginning with Rossini and ending with Puccini. He favored melodramatic librettos and composed arias that still thrill opera lovers today. Verdi died at Milan.

ELEANOR ROOSEVELT

Born October 11, 1884
Died November 7, 1962

Born at New York City, a niece of Theodore Roosevelt, Eleanor Roosevelt married her cousin, Franklin Delano Roosevelt, who went on to become the governor of New York and the thirty-second president of the United States. Mrs. Roosevelt changed the public's perceptions about what a First Lady could accomplish; she was the first presidential wife to have an independent life. She traveled widely and served as the eyes and ears of the president, who was crippled by polio. She was the first presidential wife ever to give a press conference in the White House (1933). She had her own radio program, and she wrote a daily syndicated newspaper column. She advocated for many humanitarian causes, including the civil rights of African Americans and women. Internationally known, she was affectionately called "the first lady of the world."

After her husband's death in 1945 she served as a member of the U.S. delegation to the United Nations, where she helped draft the United Nations Declaration of Human Rights. She ended her service to the United Nations in 1951, and in 1961 she served the presidency of John F. Kennedy by accepting the chair of the Commission on the Status of Women. An inspiration to many, she said, "You must do the thing you think you cannot do." She died at New York City.

RALPH VAUGHAN WILLIAMS

Born October 12, 1872
Died August 26, 1958

Born at Gloucestershire, England, composer Vaughan Williams studied in Europe, including a stint in Paris with Maurice Ravel, but he was not influenced by continental musical traditions. Instead he rooted his music in the cultural soil of his country. He is considered England's first great national composer. He crafted modern compositions using traditional English folk songs and Tudor music and themes, creating a uniquely English style. He wrote nine symphonies, operas, and music for stage and screen. He was also a distinguished composer of choral works, songs, hymns, and carols. His best-known works include the *Mass in G Minor* and the opera *The Pilgrim's Progress*.

At various points in his life, Vaughan Williams was active as a conductor, teacher, editor, and writer. He died at London, England.

MOLLY PITCHER

Born October 13, 1754
Died January 22, 1832

A heroine of the American Revolution, Molly Pitcher was born Mary Ludwig near Trenton, New Jersey. She accompanied her husband William Hays as a camp follower during the Philadelphia campaign and spent the winter of 1777–1778 with him at Valley Forge. At the Battle of Monmouth, New Jersey, on June 28, 1778, she was serving as a water carrier. Women who carried pitchers of water to thirsty soldiers were known as Molly Pitchers. After her husband was wounded, she distinguished herself by loading and firing the cannon where he had fallen. She was affectionately known as Sergeant Molly after General Washington issued her a warrant as a noncommissioned officer. (Molly Pitcher was the second woman to man a gun in the Revolution. Margaret Corbin took up a cannon when her husband was wounded at Fort Washington on Manhattan Island in 1776.)

At the close of the war, William and Mary Hays returned to their home in Pennsylvania. After her husband's death, Mary married John McCauley, another veteran. She was awarded a pension by the state of Pennsylvania, and in 1876 a marker noting her exemplary service was placed on her grave at Carlisle, Pennsylvania.

DWIGHT DAVID EISENHOWER

Born October 14, 1890
Died March 28, 1969

The thirty-fourth president of the United States, Eisenhower was born at Denison, Texas, but grew up in Abilene, Kansas. He graduated from West Point and served as supreme commander of the Allied forces in Europe during World War II. Having led the D-Day invasion of Normandy, France, which was the turning point in the Allies' favor in World War II, he returned from the war a hero. Nicknamed Ike, he held the rank of five-star general. After the war he served as president of Columbia University and military commander of NATO in Paris.

Urged by people from both parties to run for the presidency, Eisenhower was more receptive to the Republicans. "I like Ike" was his famous campaign slogan, and America *did* like Ike. He served two terms as president (1953–1961). Achievements during his administration include the interstate highway system—which made cross-country travel much easier—and the Saint Lawrence Seaway. In foreign policy, Eisenhower maintained a tough stance against communism during the Cold War. Relations with the USSR deteriorated during his administration. He concluded the Korean War with a truce. Eisenhower retired to a farm in Gettysburg, Pennsylvania, and died at Washington, D.C.

FRIEDRICH NIETZSCHE

Born October 15, 1844
Died August 25, 1900

This influential German philosopher was born at Saxony. He was a professor at the University of Basel in Switzerland until he was forced to resign in 1879 for reasons of ill health. In his most celebrated book, *Thus Spake Zarathustra,* he introduced the concept of the death of God. He attacked Christianity and democracy as being moralities for the weak. His superman (Übermensch), driven by the will to power, has the courage to live dangerously and celebrates life on Earth rather than in the hereafter. Nietzsche asserted that humans must learn to live without their gods, and thus his philosophy was a precursor of existentialism.

Nietzche's ideas were later distorted by the Nazis to justify their concept of a master race. In 1889 he suffered a mental breakdown from which he never recovered.

NOAH WEBSTER

Born October 16, 1758
Died May 28, 1843

Compiler of the first dictionary that distinguished American usage from British, Webster's name is part of the title of many of the dictionaries published in the United States today. Webster was born at West Hartford, Connecticut. He served in the American Revolution, then settled into teaching. He wrote textbooks, including a spelling book that standardized American spelling and sold millions of copies. His series of dictionaries culminated in the two-volume *American Dictionary of the English Language*, published in 1828, which contributed to the development of a national culture distinct from that of Britain. To create this influential work, Webster labored twenty years and studied twenty-six languages. The dictionary contained 70,000 entries.

Webster also wrote medical and scientific texts, served in the Massachusetts state legislature, and advocated uniform copyright laws. He practiced law after his dictionary publication and was the publisher of two magazines. He died at New Haven, Connecticut.

JUPITER HAMMON

Born October 17, 1711
Died sometime after 1790 (exact date unknown)

America's first published African-American poet was born into slavery at Long Island, New York. While little is known of his life, he obviously was taught to read and probably was allowed to use his owner's library. His eighty-eight-line broadside poem, "An Evening Thought: Salvation by Christ, with Penitential Cries," was published on December 25, 1760. In a later religious poem, "A Dialogue, Entitled, the Kind Master and the Dutiful Servant," the servant is a slave. Although on the surface the slave appears to offer his master obedience, his subtle rebellion against the master is the subtext. His last work, "An Address to the Negroes in the State of New-York," was published in 1787. In this essay he pictures a heaven in which black and white are equal and are judged in the same way. Hammon published four poems and four prose pieces, one of which has never been found.

Phillis Wheatley was long thought to be the first African-American poet but her first work wasn't published until 1770. While Hammon never met Wheatley, his poem "An Address to Miss Phillis Wheatley, Ethiopian Poetess in Boston" shows that he was aware of her. Hammon's birth date is now celebrated as Black Poetry Day. His date and place of death are unknown.

WYNTON MARSALIS

Born October 18, 1961

An accomplished jazz trumpeter and classical musician, Wynton Marsalis was born near New Orleans into a musical family. Surrounded by a father and brothers who could play a number of instruments and a mother who was a teacher and dedicated to helping her sons succeed, Marsalis grew up to excel at trumpet playing. He was a straight-A student in school and an Eagle Scout. He studied at Juilliard. He made his recording debut in 1982 and has made almost forty jazz and classical albums, nine of which have won Grammy Awards. In 1983 he became the first artist to win both a classical and jazz Grammy in the same year; he repeated this feat in 1984. Marsalis is the music director of the renowned Lincoln Center Jazz Orchestra; he spends more than half the year on tour. He is also the artistic director of the Jazz at Lincoln Center arts organization.

Marsalis is also a composer, and in 1997 he became the first jazz artist to be awarded a Pulitzer Prize for his work *Blood on the Fields.* Wynton's older brother Branford Marsalis, a gifted jazz saxophonist, is also a Grammy winner.

ANNIE SMITH PECK

Born October 19, 1850
Died July 18, 1935

This American mountaineer was born at Providence, Rhode Island. Peck made her first climb, of Mount Shasta in California, when she was thirty-eight. When she was forty-five she visited Europe and climbed the Matterhorn in the Swiss Alps. In 1897 she climbed two Mexican peaks. One of them was 18,600 feet high, the highest peak ever climbed by a woman at that time. In 1900 she represented the United States at the International Congress of Alpinism in Paris. On her return she helped found the American Alpine Club.

By then she was supporting herself on the lecture circuit. In 1908 she scaled the as-yet-unclimbed Mount Huascarán in Peru. Calculating the summit to be about 24,000 feet, she claimed to have climbed higher than any other woman. Later measurements showed Huascarán to be lower, but she still could claim the American record in the Western Hemisphere. At the age of sixty she climbed Peru's Mount Coropuna. A suffragette and feminist, she raised a banner on the summit that read "Votes for Women." Her last climb was at the age of eighty-two when she reached the top of Mount Madison in New Hampshire. She published several books before her death at New York City.

JOHN DEWEY

Born October 20, 1859
Died June 1, 1952

America's foremost philosopher of education, Dewey was born at Burlington, Vermont, and became the intellectual leader of the progressive movement. While head of the department of philosophy, psychology, and pedagogy at the University of Chicago, he established the Laboratory School as a testing ground for his theories of education. In 1904 he joined Columbia University's Teachers College, where he spent the rest of his career.

The progressive movement emphasized teaching students rather than subjects. Dewey advocated activities that encouraged students to learn from their experience. He persuaded teachers to abandon their reliance on drill and memorization and instead to allow students to learn by doing. Among his many books that provided the intellectual foundations of the progressive movement are *Democracy and Education* and *The School and Society*. Dewey died at New York City.

ALFRED NOBEL

Born October 21, 1833
Died December 10, 1896

This Swedish chemist, engineer, and industrialist is best known today as the founder of the Nobel Prize. Born at Stockholm to a prosperous family, Nobel trained as an engineer and worked in his father's explosives factory. Nobel was also an inventor and created detonators (including a blasting cap that made explosives much safer to handle). He established his own factory outside Stockholm to manufacture nitroglycerin, but when an explosion there killed five people including his younger brother, he looked for a process that would lessen its volatility. The resulting mixture he patented as dynamite in 1867. He made a fortune through the manufacture of the explosive in a series of factories throughout Europe. He also perfected blasting gelatin and ultimately held more than 355 patents.

He died at San Remo, Italy, of a heart ailment, leaving behind ninety factories. A pacifist, he left $8.5 million in his will for prizes to honor achievements benefiting mankind. The first Nobels were awarded in 1901. The prizes designated in Nobel's will were for physics, chemistry, physiology or medicine, literature, and peace. In 1969 a prize for economics was added. The recipients for most of the prizes are selected by the Royal Swedish Academy of Sciences and the Swedish Academy; the recipient of the Nobel Peace Prize is chosen by a committee appointed by the Norwegian Parliament.

GEORGE W. BEADLE

Born October 22, 1903
Died June 9, 1989

Born on a farm in Wahoo, Nebraska, Beadle was a pioneer in chemical genetics. A graduate of the University of Nebraska, he earned a Ph.D. at Cornell University. He did research at Cal Tech, became a professor of genetics at Harvard and Stanford, and returned to Cal Tech in 1946. He remained there until 1961, when he was appointed president of the University of Chicago (1961–1968).

With Edward L. Tatum, Beadle won the Nobel Prize (for physiology and medicine) in 1958. The two men had studied how genes control the basic chemistry of the living cell—specifically through the biochemistry of the genetics of the fungus neurospora. They found that all biochemical reactions are controlled by genes and that a mutation in a gene blocks these reactions. Beadle was a member of the National Academy of Sciences and received many honorary degrees. He was awarded the National Award of the American Cancer Society in 1959 and the Kimber Genetica Award of the National Academy of Science in 1960. He died at Pomona, California.

PELÉ

Born October 23, 1940

To fans of soccer worldwide, the name Pelé means soccer. This soccer superstar was born Edson Arantes do Nascimento at Tres Coracoes, Brazil, to an impoverished family. He began playing professional soccer with São Paulo Santos at the age of sixteen in 1956. Pelé then helped lead Brazil to three World Cup victories, in 1958, 1962, and 1970. He is the top Brazilian goal scorer of all time and holds the all-time world record of 1,281 goals in 1,363 matches. He played for Santos from 1956 to 1974. He then went to the United States to play for the New York Cosmos from 1975 to 1977. Pelé's aim in coming to America was to popularize soccer—the world's favorite sport—in a land where football and baseball were preeminent. In 1977 he retired from soccer, but he remains active in the sport behind the scenes and has remained an inspiration to his countrymen and the world.

In 1999 the National Olympics Committee named him the top athlete of the twentieth century (out of five nominated), even though he had never taken part in an Olympics. Behind Pelé came Muhammad Ali, Carl Lewis, Michael Jordan, and Mark Spitz. Pelé has described soccer as "the beautiful game," and his fans would agree that beauty was the hallmark of his playing style.

BELVA LOCKWOOD

Born October 24, 1830
Died May 19, 1917

This lawyer and advocate for women's rights was born at Royalton, New York. When her husband died in 1853, leaving her with a young daughter, Lockwood went to college and became a teacher. In 1866 she moved to Washington, D.C., and opened her own school. She studied law and was admitted to the District of Columbia Bar in 1873. She petitioned Congress to pass legislation allowing women to practice before all U.S. courts. The bill passed in 1879, and soon afterward Lockwood became the first woman admitted to practice before the U.S. Supreme Court.

Lockwood advocated equal pay for equal work and was a busy lecturer. She was active in the National Woman Suffrage Association. By adding amendments to statehood bills in 1903, Lockwood managed to get voting rights for women in Oklahoma, New Mexico, and Arizona. She also helped to achieve equal property rights for women. In 1884 and 1888 she was nominated as the presidential candidate of the National Equal Rights Party. She was the first woman ever to receive a formal nomination for the presidency. She died at Washington, D.C.

PABLO PICASSO

Born October 25, 1881
Died April 8, 1973

The most influential artist of the twentieth century, Picasso was born at Málaga, Spain. He moved to Paris in 1904. After World War II he moved to the south of France, where he spent the rest of his life. He refused to return to Spain as long as the fascist dictator Franco was in power; one of his best-known paintings, *Guernica*, powerfully shows the suffering of the Spanish people during their civil war. It hung in New York's Museum of Modern Art until Spain returned to democracy in 1975, at which point the painting was given its own museum in Madrid.

It is estimated that in his lifetime Picasso produced more than 1,800 paintings and thousands of drawings, prints, sculptures, and ceramics. Picasso's work can be grouped into several periods; his cubist paintings of the 1900s were inspired by African and pre-Christian Iberian art. Cubism became too limiting for Picasso, and through the 1930s he added elements of surrealism to his work. After the war he began to concentrate on lithography and ceramics. He never stopped experimenting with new materials and new means of expression. Picasso once said, "[Painting is] a way of seizing the power by giving form to our terrors as well as our desires." He died at Mougins, France.

MAHALIA JACKSON

Born October 26, 1911
Died January 27, 1972

Jackson was the most famous gospel singer of her time. Born at the musical city of New Orleans, she, like many other African-American singers before and since, started her career by singing in a church choir. However, unlike Aretha Franklin and others who moved into pop music, Jackson sang gospel music throughout her career. In 1928 she moved to Chicago and sang with the Johnson Gospel Singers. Thomas A. Dorsey, the father of gospel music, became her musical adviser and accompanist from 1937 to 1946. She made her first recording in 1937. By the 1950s Jackson was heard more in concert halls than in churches.

A strong supporter of the civil rights movement, Jackson sang at the 1963 March on Washington rally where Dr. Martin Luther King Jr. made his famous "I Have a Dream" speech. King described Jackson's voice as "one heard once in a millennium." She sang at the inauguration of President John F. Kennedy.

She first toured Europe in 1952; she sang in Africa, India, and Japan in 1970. While Jackson was not the first gospel singer, it was through her that people all over the world came to know gospel music. When she died at Chicago, Illinois, more than 50,000 people came to view her casket. Her body was then sent on to New Orleans, where the funeral procession through the city was thronged with mourners.

JAMES COOK

Born October 27, 1728
Died February 14, 1779

This English navigator was the greatest explorer of the eighteenth century. He made three important voyages to the Pacific Ocean. In 1768 he left England on the ship *Endeavour* with a team of scientists and artists. One of his goals was to see if a major southern continent existed. They reached Tahiti and then sailed westward, rediscovering New Zealand (which originally had been discovered in 1642) and sailing along the unexplored eastern coast of Australia. His second voyage, in 1772, again accompanied by scientists and artists, proved that no great continent existed in the temperate part of the Pacific, but Cook became convinced that there was an Antarctic continent. On his third trip, he sailed east to look for the Northwest Passage from the Pacific side. On the way, he discovered the Hawaiian Islands (which he called the Sandwich Islands after the Earl of Sandwich). He then sailed north into the Arctic Ocean but found the way blocked by ice and had to turn back. The ship returned to Hawaii for repairs. Cook was killed there by Polynesian inhabitants.

Cook charted many thousands of miles of coastline and opened the American northwest to trade and colonization. He was loved by his crews and was a model leader in a time known for the cruelty of British Navy officers. Cook was adamant about diet aboard his vessels, with the result that he lost no personnel to scurvy—while the Navy lost hundreds of men each year to the dreaded and misunderstood ailment. The U.S. space shuttle *Endeavour* is named for Cook's first ship.

JONAS SALK

Born October 28, 1914
Died June 23, 1995

Salk, the microbiologist who was the developer of the first vaccine against polio, was born at New York City. At that time polio caused paralysis in many children and adults (Franklin D. Roosevelt had the disease). People with severe cases sometimes lost the ability to breathe and spent their lives in machines called iron lungs. In 1953, the year after a polio epidemic claimed more than 3,300 lives in the United States, Salk announced the creation of a successful vaccine. He and his associates had developed a vaccine that used an inactivated form of the virus, which was given in the form of an injection. Mass inoculations began across the country in 1955. The result was that polio deaths were soon reduced by 95 percent. In 1960 Albert Sabin developed a live virus vaccine that could be taken orally. It largely replaced Salk's vaccine.

   Salk founded the Salk Institute for Biological Studies in La Jolla, California, and spent the last ten years of his life doing AIDS research. He died at La Jolla.

HARRIET POWERS

Born October 29, 1837
Died 1911

The quilting folk artist and seamstress Harriet Powers was born into slavery at Athens, Georgia. Little is known of her slave life except that she spent her youth on a plantation outside of the city. At eighteen she married another slave, Armstead Powers, and they eventually had eight children. Upon achieving freedom after the Civil War, the Powers family struggled to make a living; Armstead Powers hired out as a farmhand and grew cotton.

Harriet Powers was an excellent seamstress known for her story quilts, which retold biblical or community stories through appliquéd pieces of fabric in a colorful tableau. This folk tradition was especially popular among African-American quilters. At the 1886 Athens Cotton Fair, Powers exhibited a story quilt that, in eleven panels and 229 pieces of fabric, recounted diverse tales from the Bible and from life in the Athens community. Financial hardship forced Powers to sell her masterpiece, but the woman who bought it recognized it as a work of art and displayed it at other fairs. As a result, faculty wives at Atlanta University commissioned Powers to create an even grander quilt, this one depicting the Leonid meteor shower of 1833, Noah and the flood, and other events. Both quilts now reside in museums (the first one at the Smithsonian) and are recognized as two of the greatest examples of the quilting tradition. Powers lived quietly as a seamstress until her death.

JOHN ADAMS

Born October 30, 1735
Died July 4, 1826

John Adams, born at Quincy, Massachusetts, was one of the founding fathers of the United States. In the 1760s he became a leader among Massachusetts radicals agitating for independence from Great Britain. In a diary entry of 1773 on the Boston Tea Party he wrote, "The people should never rise without doing something to be remembered— something notable and striking."

A delegate to the Continental Congress, he helped draft the Declaration of Independence. Along with John Jay and Benjamin Franklin, he was sent to Britain to negotiate with the British for recognition of American independence at the end of the Revolution. He was then appointed the first ambassador to Britain. He returned to the United States to be elected the first vice president of the new nation under George Washington. He later served as the second president of the United States (1797–1801). He was the father of John Quincy Adams, who became the sixth American president.

Adams was followed in the presidency by Thomas Jefferson, with whom he corresponded for many years later in his life. The two men died on the same day: the Fourth of July, the fiftieth anniversary of American independence.

JOHN KEATS

Born October 31, 1795
Died February 23, 1821

One of England's greatest poets, Keats was born at London, England. After studying to be a surgeon, he was encouraged by a friend to write. This friend, Leigh Hunt, introduced him to many of the most famous poets of the day, including Percy Bysshe Shelley. Keats wrote the sonnet "On First Looking into Chapman's Homer" in 1816.

In 1818 he found out he was suffering from tuberculosis. However, he continued to produce such masterpieces as "Ode on a Grecian Urn" (which features the immortal lines "Beauty is truth, truth beauty,—that is all/Ye know on earth, and all ye need to know") and "Ode to a Nightingale." He also wrote epic poetry, such as *The Fall of Hyperion*. In 1820 he moved to Rome in an attempt to slow the progression of his disease. He died there at the age of twenty-five. His friend Shelley drowned at Italy little more than a year later.

Between the ages of eighteen and twenty-four, Keats wrote poems that rank among the greatest of the English language. Together with Lord Byron and Shelley, he formed the second generation of British romantic poets.

NOVEMBER

STEPHEN CRANE

Born November 1, 1871
Died June 5, 1900

A journalist by profession, Stephen Crane was born at Newark, New Jersey. While struggling to make a living as a writer in New York, he published his first novel, *Maggie: A Girl of the Streets* (1893), a brutally realistic story of a prostitute. It was too shocking for the times and consequently it sold poorly. His 1895 Civil War tale, *The Red Badge of Courage*, forms the basis of his reputation. It was the first realistic novel about the war to achieve both popularity and critical acclaim. In it Crane describes the conflict through the eyes of a soldier who strives to overcome his fear in battle. This was a remarkable accomplishment in view of the fact that Crane had never been involved in combat.

Two later novels were not very successful. In 1897 Crane was shipwrecked for two days on a gun-running expedition to Cuba. This resulted in the magnificent short story, "The Open Boat." Crane covered the Greco-Turkish War of 1897 and the Spanish-American War of 1898 as a war correspondent. He later recorded his experiences in works of nonfiction. He died at Germany at the age of twenty-eight while seeking a cure for his tuberculosis.

JAMES POLK

Born November 2, 1795
Died June 15, 1849

The eleventh president of the United States was born at North Carolina, but his family moved to Tennessee when he was a boy. He was elected to the U.S. House of Representatives in 1825. He spent seven terms there. He was speaker of the House from 1835 to 1839. He then spent one term as governor of Tennessee.

In 1844 Polk won the Democratic nomination for president on the ninth ballot. He then won a narrow victory over Henry Clay. During his term as president, the border of the United States was expanded to the Pacific Ocean with the signing of the Oregon Treaty with the British. Polk personally planned American strategy during the Mexican War; that victory resulted in the cession of California and New Mexico to the United States and the recognition of U.S. claims to Texas. However, opponents of slavery viewed the conflict as a plan to bring additional slave states into the Union. This reopened the controversy over slavery that ultimately led to the Civil War. Polk died at Nashville, Tennessee, three months after finishing his term as president.

WALKER EVANS

Born November 3, 1903
Died April 10, 1975

This influential documentary photographer was born at St. Louis, Missouri. In 1926, intending to become a writer, he moved to Paris. He returned to New York a year later and worked as a stockbroker until the Wall Street crash. He then took up photography. His first published photographs appeared in the poet Hart Crane's *The Bridge*. Evans shared an apartment in Greenwich Village with artist Ben Shahn. He traveled to Cuba to shoot illustrations for a book.

In 1935 he made his first trip to the American South. During the Depression, Evans worked for the Farm Security Administration, a government agency, photographing rural poverty. In 1936 Evans shot the photographs for James Agee's brilliant 1941 book about tenant farmers in Alabama, *Let Us Now Praise Famous Men*. When the Museum of Modern Art mounted a show of Evans's photographs in 1938, it was the first exhibition the museum had ever devoted to a single photographer. Evans worked as a photographer for *Fortune* and *Time* magazines and taught photography at Yale University. Today his work is on display in museums around the United States. He died at New Haven, Connecticut.

STERLING NORTH

Born November 4, 1906
Died December 21, 1974

Born at Edgerton, Wisconsin, author Sterling North wrote books that appealed to both children and adults. After graduating from the University of Chicago, he became a journalist, writing for newspapers in Chicago and New York and for magazines such as *Reader's Digest* and *Esquire*.

In 1947 he wrote *So Dear to My Heart*, a bestseller that was translated into twenty-six languages. The story of a young boy and his lamb was set in 1903. It was made into a movie by Disney in 1949. The combination live-action/animation film starred Burl Ives. North later wrote an autobiographical book, *Rascal*, about a boy raising a raccoon; it was published in 1963 and has since sold more than two and a half million copies. The book was translated into eighteen languages and made into a Disney film starring Bill Mumy as young Sterling North. North's final book, *The Wolfling*, was published in 1969. It tells the story of raising a wild wolf pup in rural Wisconsin in the 1870s.

IDA TARBELL

November 5, 1857
Died January 6, 1944

Tarbell, the first great American woman journalist, was born at Erie County, Pennsylvania. After working as an editor for the *Chautauqua*, she spent some time in Paris. In 1894 she was hired as an editor by *McClure's* magazine. In the pages of that publication she campaigned against corruption in politics and business. She became famous as a muckraker as a result of her well-documented articles. (Muckrakers were writers such as Upton Sinclair and Lincoln Steffens whose exposés led to important reforms.) From 1906 to 1915 Tarbell continued this work as an editor and writer at the *American* magazine.

Her two-volume *History of the Standard Oil Company*, published in 1904, led to federal action to break up John D. Rockefeller's giant corporation. She also wrote a biography of Abraham Lincoln and two feminist books before her death at Bethel, Connecticut.

JOHN PHILIP SOUSA

Born November 6, 1854
Died March 6, 1932

A composer and bandleader born at Washington, D.C., Sousa was known as the March King because of the enormous popularity of the 136 marches he wrote. He commanded the U.S. Marine Band from 1880 to 1892. Then he left to form his own band, which became the most successful in the nation. His foreign tours with the band brought him worldwide celebrity. He is remembered for such stirring marches as "Semper Fidelis," "El Capitan," and "The Washington Post March," which was associated with a new dance, the two-step. His most famous march, "Stars and Stripes Forever," was first performed in Philadelphia on May 14, 1897, at the unveiling of a statue of George Washington.

Sousa also wrote operettas and arranged more than 300 songs. He was the author of seven books. When the United States entered World War I in 1917, Sousa reenlisted and this time led the Navy Band. He remained active in music until the time of his death at Reading, Pennsylvania.

MARIE CURIE

Born November 7, 1867
Died July 4, 1934

This chemist and physicist, the first woman to win a Nobel Prize in the sciences, was born at Warsaw, Poland. She moved to France and later received degrees in mathematics and physics from the Sorbonne. She joined her husband Pierre Curie in his laboratory, where they discovered two naturally radiating elements, which they named polonium and radium. Along with another colleague they were awarded the Nobel Prize in 1903 for their discovery of radioactivity. Pierre Curie was killed in an accident in 1906, and his wife became head of his laboratory at the Sorbonne and the first woman lecturer at the university. In 1908 she was appointed a professor there. Marie Curie won a second Nobel Prize (this time in physics) in 1911 for her isolation of radium.

During World War I, Curie worked on the use of x-rays in medicine. For the rest of her life her research was devoted to the medical applications of radioactive materials. She died at France from leukemia that had been caused by her long exposure to radiation.

EDMOND HALLEY

Born November 8, 1656
Died January 14, 1742

Halley was an astronomer and mathematician born at London, England. He discovered the motion of stars and the periodicity of comets. He observed the great comet of 1682, which is now named for him, and was the first to realize that it would reappear periodically and predicted that it would appear again in 1758 (sixteen years after his death), which it did. He cataloged the positions of about 350 Southern Hemisphere stars and observed a transit of Mercury. At the Royal Observatory he devised a means for determining longitude at sea by lunar observation. A member of the Royal Society, Halley was a friend of Isaac Newton and was instrumental in the publication of Newton's work on gravitation, *Principia Mathematica*. Halley was a professor at Oxford University and served as Astronomer Royal from 1721 until his death at Greenwich, England, the site of the Royal Observatory.

Halley's Comet appears about once every generation—the average time between appearances is seventy-six years. The comet is expected to next be visible in 2061.

BENJAMIN BANNEKER

Born November 9, 1731
Died October 9, 1806

This American astronomer, clockmaker, and surveyor was born at Ellicot's Mills, Maryland. He was a free black tobacco farmer, though his father had been a slave. He studied at a Quaker school. In 1753 he borrowed a watch from a neighbor and took it apart. After making drawings of all the parts, he reassembled it. He used the drawings to carve large wooden copies of each part. From these he made a clock that kept accurate time for many years.

At age fifty-eight he took up the study of astronomy. He compiled tables of eclipses and phases of the moon and used them for an almanac he published from 1791 to 1802. He assisted in surveying the new boundaries for the District of Columbia in 1791. When the architect Pierre L'Enfant quit his job in anger, taking the plans for the city with him, Banneker was able to reconstruct them from memory.

Banneker was a man of wide interests. He performed a study of the seventeen-year cycle of the locust. He also became a pamphleteer for the antislavery movement. Unfortunately, a fire that started during his funeral destroyed his home and library in Baltimore, along with his clocks and virtually all documents related to his life.

MARTIN LUTHER

Born November 10, 1483
Died February 18, 1546

The founder of the Protestant Reformation was born at Saxony, in what is now Germany. He had been an Augustinian monk, a theologian, and a professor of scripture. The practice of the sale of indulgences by the church, with its mechanical view of redemption from sin, angered Luther. On October 31, 1517, he tacked his ninety-five theses, "On the Power of Indulgences," to the door of Wittenberg Castle's church. Luther asserted that the Bible was the sole authority of the church; he denied the supremacy of the Pope and called for the reformation of abuses in the Roman Catholic Church. Salvation by faith alone was the central tenet of his doctrine. Luther was tried for heresy by the church and excommunicated by a papal bull. During subsequent years, he translated the Bible into German, composed hymns (of which "A Mighty Fortress Is Our God" is the most famous), and wrote sermons, tracts, and biblical commentaries.

Luther started a movement that quickly spread throughout the Western world. By the time of his death, a large part of northern Europe had left the Roman Catholic Church. His doctrines are shared by many Protestant churches today, one of which, the Lutheran Church, is named for him.

FYODOR DOSTOYEVSKY

Born November 11, 1821
Died February 9, 1881

This novelist born at Moscow is perhaps the most important of all Russian authors. His first book, *Poor Folk*, was published in 1846. A political liberal, he was arrested and sentenced to death in 1849 for his participation in a subversive group. Instead he was exiled to a Siberian prison for ten years. In 1859 he returned to St. Petersburg and began the most important phase of his literary career.

His *Notes from the Underground*, published in 1864, is considered to be a prologue to his great tragic novels. His masterful *Crime and Punishment*, published in 1866, took as its theme redemption through suffering. In 1867 Dostoyevsky moved abroad where he wrote *The Idiot* and *The Possessed*. He returned to Russia in 1871 and in 1880 completed his final novel, *The Brothers Karamazov*. One of the triumphs of world literature, it essentially summarizes Dostoyevsky's beliefs. His motif of the underground hero who rejects modern advances has influenced many twentieth-century novelists. He died at St. Petersburg.

ELIZABETH CADY STANTON

Born November 12, 1815
Died October 26, 1902

This American reformer and a founder of the women's rights movement was born at Johnstown, New York. Stanton was active in the temperance and antislavery movements. Her husband, Henry B. Stanton, was an abolitionist. With Lucretia Mott she organized the first women's rights convention, which was held at Seneca Falls, New York, in 1848. There she drafted a Declaration of Sentiments that paralleled the Declaration of Independence ("all men and women are created equal"). She insisted on the adoption of a resolution calling for votes for women.

With Susan B. Anthony she edited the feminist newspaper *The Revolution*. She called for more liberal divorce laws, coeducation, and the right of married women to control their own property. She was the first president of the National Woman Suffrage Association. A prolific author, she coauthored the six-volume *History of Woman's Suffrage*.

ROBERT LOUIS STEVENSON

Born November 13, 1850
Died December 3, 1894

Born at Edinburgh, Scotland, Stevenson was a novelist, poet, travel writer, and essayist. A case of tuberculosis as a young man prompted his first extensive trip to France, which inspired his *Travels with a Donkey in the Cévennes*. Stevenson reached a wide audience with his essays in the *Cornhill Magazine*. In 1879 he traveled to the United States to join an American woman with whom he had fallen in love, Fannie Van de Grift Osbourne. After their marriage the following year, they began their travels in search of a better climate for his health. His romantic adventure story *Treasure Island* was written at a Swiss health resort. That classic novel, introducing the villainous Long John Silver, has colored most people's ideas about what pirates were like. It also introduced the notion of pirates burying their treasure.

Many of his novels, such as *Kidnapped* and *Master of Ballantrae*, are set in Scotland. His collection of poems, *A Child's Garden of Verses*, written in 1885, remains popular with children today. *Doctor Jekyll and Mr. Hyde* is a psychological thriller set in London, which has become a horror classic with many movie adaptations.

Still plagued by tuberculosis, Stevenson and his wife moved to the islands of the South Pacific in 1888. He died at Samoa.

AARON COPLAND

Born November 14, 1900
Died December 2, 1990

This prolific American composer was born at Brooklyn, New York. Copland incorporated American folk music into his compositions. He is best known for his ballet scores for *Billy the Kid*, *Rodeo*, and *Appalachian Spring*, for which he won a Pulitzer Prize. He was a leading composer of film scores and won an Academy Award for his soundtrack for *The Heiress*. His orchestral works include *Fanfare for the Common Man* and *A Lincoln Portrait*, which contains spoken portions from Abraham Lincoln's speeches interspersed with the music.

Copland taught and lectured widely, wrote several books, and conducted some of his own music. By writing in a specifically American musical idiom he made contemporary music accessible to a wide audience.

GEORGIA O'KEEFFE

Born November 15, 1887
Died March 6, 1986

American modernist painter Georgia O'Keeffe was born on a farm in Sun Prairie, Wisconsin. After studying at the Art Institute of Chicago, she moved to New York in 1905 to study at the Art Students League, where the curriculum was based on imitative realism. While she mastered this style and even won a prize for her work, she felt she could never achieve distinction by painting this way; she gave up art for a period of four years. After being exposed to some of the theories of abstract art, she created a series of charcoal drawings. Photographer Alfred Stieglitz encountered her work and arranged for her first one-woman show at his New York gallery in 1917. In 1924 they were married, and, until his death in 1946, Stieglitz worked to promote O'Keeffe's art. He also took photographic portraits of her during this period.

O'Keeffe usually took her subjects from nature, including flowers and landscapes. Her famous flower paintings of the mid-1920s (especially *Red Poppies*) were characterized by their large scale and simplicity of form. She also did a series of city scenes. In 1929 she first visited New Mexico. She moved there in 1949 and lived there until the end of her life. Her later paintings reflected the scenery of the American desert. A well-known work from this period shows a series of austere studies of animal bones against a plain background. She died at New Mexico.

W. C. HANDY

Born November 16, 1873
Died March 28, 1958

Composer, bandleader, and bluesman William Christopher Handy was born at Florence, Alabama. He displayed an interest in music as a child, but his family and church frowned upon the playing of musical instruments. When he saved his money and bought a guitar, his father made him take it back and exchange it for a dictionary. Handy worked as a teacher and in a pipe works; in his free time he organized an orchestra. In 1896 he joined a minstrel group and traveled around the country playing the cornet. In 1903 he got a job directing a band in Clarksdale, Mississippi.

Handy and his band moved to Memphis in 1909. There he wrote "Memphis Blues." It was such a huge hit that he published it in 1912. His most famous composition was "St. Louis Blues," published in 1914. He formed his own publishing company and became one of the first to publish music by black composers. In 1918 he moved to New York City and continued to compose and work as a music arranger for Broadway, film, and radio. When he died, an estimated 150,000 people lined the funeral route. By synthesizing elements of ragtime, Latin American, and Southern music, Handy had popularized the blues for white audiences.

NICOLAS APPERT

Born November 17, 1749
Died June 3, 1841

This French chef and inventor revolutionized our previously seasonal diet by devising a system of heating food and sealing it in airtight jars. Called the father of canning, Appert made it possible for people to eat fruits and vegetables in the winter. During the Napoleonic wars, more soldiers died from scurvy and malnutrition than from enemy guns. In 1795 the French government offered an award of 12,000 francs to anyone who could develop a method of preserving food.

Appert, a baker and brewer, experimented for fourteen years before winning the prize in 1809 for his invention. While he didn't understand the scientific theory behind the process, the application of heat to the food in jars stopped bacterial spoilage. Appert wrote a book, *The Art of Preserving*, and with his prize money opened the world's first commercial cannery. Tin-plated steel cans first patented by an Englishman in 1810 solved the problem of in-transit breakage. In 1804 Appert also created the bouillon tablet, a concentrated form of meat flavor used to make stock for soup. He died near Paris. His company remained in business until 1933.

ALAN SHEPARD

Born November 18, 1923
Died July 21, 1998

The first American in space, Alan Shepard was born at East Derry, New Hampshire. He was a graduate of the U.S. Naval Academy and worked as a naval test pilot. In 1959 he was one of the original seven astronauts picked by NASA for Project Mercury. The Soviets had launched *Sputnik* in 1957, and the United States was hurrying to catch up in the space race.

Shepard's first flight was a suborbital one in 1961 aboard *Freedom 7*, which was the first manned Mercury flight and made him the first U.S. astronaut in space. He made his second flight as commander of *Apollo 14* in 1971, the third manned mission to the moon. Five days after launch, Shepard and Edgar Mitchell landed on the moon in the lunar module *Antares*. Shepard spent four hours exploring the surface of the moon, making him one of only twelve Americans to have walked on the moon. He was the only lunar golfer; he practiced his drive in space with a six iron! Shepard was chief of the astronaut office at the Johnson Space Center until his retirement in 1974. He was awarded the Congressional Space Medal of Honor in 1979. He died at Monterey, California.

ROY CAMPANELLA

Born November 19, 1921
Died June 26, 1993

One of the first black major leaguers and a star of one of baseball's greatest teams, the Brooklyn Dodgers "Boys of Summer," Campanella was born at Philadelphia. Campy, as he was known, was named the National League's Most Valuable Player in 1951, 1953, and 1955. In 1953 he established three single-season records for a catcher: most home runs, most putouts, and most runs batted in. During his career, which lasted from 1948 to 1957, he hit 242 home runs and batted in 856 runs.

His career was cut short in 1958 when an automobile accident left him paralyzed and in a wheelchair. In 1959 the Dodgers and the Yankees held an exhibition game in his honor, which drew a crowd of 93,103, which remains a baseball record. After his accident he served as a spokesman for the disabled. He was named to the Baseball Hall of Fame in 1969.

EDWIN HUBBLE

Born November 20, 1889
Died September 28, 1953

Astronomer Edwin Hubble was born at Marshfield, Missouri. His development of the concept of an expanding universe has been described as the most important astronomical discovery of the twentieth century. Hubble earned a Ph.D. at the University of Chicago. After World War I he worked at the Mount Wilson Observatory in California, where he demonstrated that the Andromeda nebula was far outside our galaxy. He composed the classification scheme for the structure of galaxies that is still used today. The founder of extragalactic astronomy, he formulated Hubble's law, from which Hubble's constant on the velocity–distance relationship of galaxies is derived. Using this constant, he estimated the upper limit of the age of the universe.

As a tribute, the Hubble Space Telescope, deployed in 1990 from the U.S. Space Shuttle *Discovery*, was named for him. This telescope, which is still in orbit, allows astronomers to see farther into space than they ever could from telescopes on Earth.

Hubble died at San Marino, California.

HETTY GREEN

Born November 21, 1835
Died July 3, 1916

Hetty Green was the richest woman in the world in her day. Born Henrietta Howland Robinson at New Bedford, Massachusetts, she inherited a whaling and trade fortune of $7.5 million. By shrewd investments in stocks and real estate, she increased it to $100 million at the time of her death. That would be worth more than $1.5 billion today! Because of her success in an exclusively male domain, she was called the witch of Wall Street by her rivals.

Green was married to a banker and had two children. She was frugal to a fault—she is rumored to have spent hours searching for a two-cent stamp she had lost. Her unwillingness to pay for a doctor to treat her son's leg injury led to an amputation. After her death, her son and daughter gave much of her money away to charitable institutions, including to Wellesley College for the administration building named in her honor, Hetty Green Hall. In 1998 Green was ranked by *Fortune* magazine as the thirty-sixth richest American in history.

ABIGAIL ADAMS

Born November 22, 1744
Died October 28, 1818

Abigail Adams was the wife of John Adams, the second president of the United States, and the mother of John Quincy Adams, the sixth president. She was born Abigail Smith at Weymouth, Massachusetts, and was educated at home. She married John Adams in 1764 and over the next ten years gave birth to three sons and two daughters. Long separations kept the Adamses apart, as he worked as a circuit judge, a delegate to the Continental Congress, and an envoy to Great Britain to negotiate an end to the American Revolution. A prodigious letter writer during these separations, she is credited with having an influence on her husband's career. Her plea in a letter to her husband that Congress should "remember the ladies" was her request that the new American government should guarantee women's rights.

In 1784 Abigail joined her husband at his diplomatic post in France and then in Great Britain. In 1788 they moved to Washington, D.C., when Adams was elected the first vice president of the new United States. They remained there until the end of his term as president in 1801. They then retired to their farm in Massachusetts, where she died eight years before John Adams. Abigail and her husband had been happily married for fifty-four years.

BORIS KARLOFF

Born November 23, 1887
Died February 2, 1969

Although his name became synonymous with Frankenstein, Boris Karloff was actually a quiet London-born Englishman whose original name was William Henry Pratt. He moved to North America in 1909 and acted with touring theatrical companies. He made his Hollywood debut as an extra in a 1916 film. By the 1920s he had changed his name and was playing supporting roles in dozens of movies. In 1931 *Dracula* star Bela Lugosi turned down the *Frankenstein* role, and it was offered to Karloff. His other horror roles in the 1930s included those in *The Mummy*, *The Bride of Frankenstein*, *The Body Snatcher*, and *The Raven* (with Bela Lugosi). In the 1940s and 1950s Karloff worked exclusively in horror films and thrillers.

He fared better on Broadway (where he earned a Tony nomination in 1956 for his dramatic role in *The Lark*) and on TV. He provided the voice for the Grinch in the 1966 animated film, *Dr. Seuss' How the Grinch Stole Christmas*. Karloff appeared on two stamps issued by the U.S. Postal Service. Both stamps were in honor of movie monsters.

SCOTT JOPLIN

Born November 24, 1868
Died April 1, 1917

An African-American composer famous for his ragtime music, Joplin grew up in Texarkana, Texas. Although from a poor family, he studied classical music as a child. He published his first composition in 1895. His "Maple Leaf Rag," written in 1899, was the most popular piano rag of the day. A royalty on this song produced a small but steady income for him for the rest of his life. In 1903 he wrote an opera, *A Guest of Honor*, that depicted Booker T. Washington's dinner with President Roosevelt at the White House—the first time that an African American had ever been a guest there. Unfortunately, no copies of the opera survive.

Joplin published a total of sixty compositions, most of them rags (melodies featuring strong syncopation) but also marches and the opera *Treemonisha*. This opera was published in 1911, but Joplin was never to see a completely staged version of it in his lifetime. He was not acknowledged as a serious composer, and at the time of his death he had almost been forgotten. However, his opera was successfully revived in 1968. His music was used as the score for the movie *The Sting* in 1973, and he was awarded the Pulitzer Prize for music posthumously in 1976.

ANDREW CARNEGIE

Born November 25, 1835
Died August 11, 1919

The philanthropist who funded Carnegie libraries for 2,500 communities in the United States and Great Britain was born at Dunfermline, Scotland. Poor and nearly uneducated, he moved to Pennsylvania with his family in 1848. He worked in a factory and then for the Pennsylvania Railroad. In 1865 he went into the iron and steel business and became a prime mover in creating the steel industry. He bought out the Homestead Steel Works and consolidated all his holdings into the Carnegie Steel Company.

In 1901 Carnegie sold his company to the United States Steel Company, which was owned by J. P. Morgan, and spent the rest of his life giving his money away. In addition to funding libraries through the Carnegie Corporation of New York (founded to promote "the advancement and diffusion of knowledge"), he founded the Carnegie Institute of Pittsburgh (a museum), the Carnegie Institution of Washington (which supports scientific research by operating observatories and laboratories), the Carnegie Endowment for the Advancement of Teaching, and the Carnegie Endowment for International Peace. He also donated the funds to build Carnegie Hall in New York City.

CHARLES SCHULZ

Born November 26, 1922
Died February 12, 2000

Born at St. Paul, Minnesota, Charles Schulz was the most widely read cartoonist in the world. His "Peanuts" comic strip debuted in seven newspapers in 1950, and by the time of his death the strip ran in more than 2,500 newspapers worldwide. Characters such as Charlie Brown, Snoopy, Linus, and Lucy became an indelible part of American culture. Though these characters were all children, Schulz expressed adult ideas in the strip. Several TV specials were animated spin-offs of the strip, including *A Charlie Brown Christmas* and *It's the Great Pumpkin, Charlie Brown*. A feature-length film and a long-running musical were based on Schulz's characters. These characters were licensed for everything from stuffed animals to books to jewelry to greeting cards.

When Schulz became ill in 1999, he decided he didn't want another cartoonist to continue the strip. The "Peanuts" gang last appeared in newspapers on February 13, 2000, the day after Schulz died at California and almost fifty years after the strip had first appeared.

BRUCE LEE

Born November 27, 1940
Died July 20, 1973

Actor and martial artist Bruce Lee was born at San Francisco, where his parents were performing with a touring Chinese opera company. They returned to their home in Hong Kong when Bruce was a year old. He became a child actor. As a teenager, Lee began to study kung fu. In 1959 he returned to the United States for college and started to teach martial arts. Eventually he opened kung fu schools in Seattle, Washington, and Oakland, California. A producer who was looking to cast a part for a TV series saw Lee at the International Karate Championships. In 1966 Lee debuted in *The Green Hornet*, playing the part of Kato. He moved to Los Angeles and opened a kung fu school there.

In 1971 he returned to Hong Kong and starred in movies that featured martial arts displays. *Fists of Fury* was released in the United States that year. In 1973, after completing the filming of *Enter the Dragon*, Lee was preparing to return to the United States for a publicity tour when he died suddenly of a cerebral edema. His final movie was released a month later in Hollywood, and Lee achieved worldwide fame.

WILLIAM BLAKE

Born November 28, 1757
Died August 12, 1827

This English poet, artist, and philosopher began his career as an engraver. He exhibited his first artwork in 1780. Blake produced and published his works himself by engraving both text and illustrations on copper plates and then coloring the printed volumes by hand. He also executed numerous watercolors and paintings. In order to support himself, he also did engravings for the books of others.

His earliest well-known work is *Songs of Innocence*, to which he later appended *Songs of Experience*. For the most part, he concentrated on producing longer works. He wrote lengthy symbolic poems influenced by the Bible. In his visions of the "Daughters of Albion" he offered radical views on sex, politics, and religion. The first of the great English romantic poets, Blake's work was not well known during his lifetime. Today he is appreciated for both his art and his poems.

LOUISA MAY ALCOTT

Born November 29, 1832
Died March 6, 1888

Louisa May Alcott's father, Bronson Alcott, was a transcendentalist philosopher and was involved in several utopian projects. After her birth at Philadelphia, the family moved to Massachusetts, where they had as neighbors and friends Thoreau, Hawthorne, and Emerson. Because her family was always in need of money, Louisa turned to writing. She sold her first story in 1852. In 1854 she published a book of fairy tales. She was a regular contributor to the *Atlantic Monthly*. A nurse during the Civil War, her letters were published as *Hospital Sketches*.

Alcott became financially successful with the 1868 publication of her largely autobiographical *Little Women*, the classic story of sisters Meg, Jo, Beth, and Amy. Sequels soon followed. Her novels for adults were less successful. Alcott was an abolitionist and also gave her support to women's suffrage and the temperance movement. She died at Boston on the day of her father's funeral.

MARK TWAIN

Born November 30, 1835
Died April 21, 1910

Born Samuel Clemens at Florida, Missouri, this celebrated American gained worldwide fame during his lifetime as an author, lecturer, and humorist. Twain grew up in Hannibal, Missouri, on the Mississippi River, and worked as a journalist and printer. He adopted the name Mark Twain in 1863. (He borrowed the name from a Mississippi River call that meant the water was deep enough for a steamboat.) Twain first achieved a measure of national fame with *The Celebrated Jumping Frog of Calaveras County and Other Sketches*. His trip to Europe and the Holy Land resulted in *The Innocents Abroad*, which won international acclaim.

In 1871 Twain moved to Hartford, Connecticut, and gave up journalism to devote all his attention to writing. Here he wrote *The Adventures of Tom Sawyer*, his classic tale of boyhood, in 1875. Many books followed, including *Life on the Mississippi* in 1883 and his masterpiece, *Adventures of Huckleberry Finn*, in 1884. Financial problems then forced Twain to go on a world lecture tour. After the death of one of his daughters and his wife, his writing became more pessimistic. Twain is considered to be the first writer to achieve a uniquely American voice. He died at Connecticut. In a message to the Young People Society in Brooklyn, he said, "Always do right. That will gratify some people and astonish the rest."

DECEMBER

MINORU YAMASAKI

Born December 1, 1912
Died February 7, 1986

Yamasaki was born at Seattle, Washington. After studying architecture at the University of Washington, he moved to New York City and worked as a designer for several firms. In 1949 he founded his own firm, Minoru Yamasaki and Associates, in Troy, Michigan, where he practiced architecture until his death. In 1951 he designed the St. Louis Airport and in 1955 the Pruitt-Igoe public housing project (also in St. Louis). He designed two buildings that were constructed in Saudi Arabia as well as a hotel in Los Angeles, a synagogue in Michigan, a performing arts center in Tulsa, Oklahoma, and the Woodrow Wilson School at Princeton University. These buildings are linked by their textile-like facades.

His most famous buildings were the twin towers of the World Trade Center in New York City, which he designed along with Emery Roth starting in 1962. These buildings changed the Manhattan skyline. Yamasaki's original plan called for two ninety-story buildings, but the developer insisted that they contain 10 million square feet of office space so the buildings were expanded to 110 stories, which made them the tallest buildings in the world. These New York icons were destroyed by terrorists on September 11, 2001.

Yamasaki died at Detroit, Michigan.

GEORGES SEURAT

Born December 2, 1859
Died March 29, 1891

This French neo-impressionist painter was known for his style of painting called Pointillism. Seurat studied in Paris (his birthplace) at the Ecole des Beaux Arts and became interested in color theory and the science of optics. His approach to standard Impressionism, which he found too subjective, was more direct, systematic, and scientific. In Pointillism (or divisionism, as it was also called at the time), a painting is created with small dots of color that fuse in the viewer's eye and give the work a sense of vibrancy and luminosity.

Seurat was the founder of neo-impressionism, a movement in painting that included Paul Signac. Seurat and Signac first exhibited their work in Paris in 1884 at the Groupe des Artistes Independant. The movement was short-lived and had only a modest impact on other painters. Seurat died at the age of thirty-one in Paris.

The Stephen Sondheim musical *Sunday in the Park with George* is based on Seurat's most famous painting, *A Sunday Afternoon on the Island of La Grande Jatte*, which today is part of the permanent collection at the Art Institute of Chicago.

JOSEPH CONRAD

Born December 3, 1857
Died August 3, 1924

A Pole who became one of greatest writers in the English language, Conrad was born Jósef Teodor Konrad Korzeniowski to Polish parents in the Ukraine. He learned English during the sixteen years he spent as a sailor on British ships. His voyages to Asia and Africa later provided the subject matter for his writing. In 1895 he gave up the sea to be a writer. Although he objected to being described as a writer of sea stories, many of his novels and short stories were set on ships. *Lord Jim* was based on a story he heard of a crew deserting their ship, and the short story "The Secret Sharer" was derived from a voyage he had taken from Bangkok to Singapore.

The novella *Heart of Darkness* is set in the Congo and based on a trip Conrad had once made there on a river steamer. Like most of Conrad's writing, it explored complex moral issues and the nature of evil. This work served as the thematic basis for the 1979 film *Apocalypse Now*, which is set in Vietnam. One of the main characters in both the book and film is named Kurtz.

The Secret Agent, published in 1907, relates the story of a bomb plot that took place in London in 1894. Conrad had received critical praise as a writer, but it was only with his 1913 novel *Chance* that he became a bestselling author. He died at Canterbury, England.

WASSILY KANDINSKY

Born December 4, 1866
Died December 13, 1944

Born at Moscow, Russia, Kandinsky is considered to be the founder of abstract art, in which the manner and means are the subject of the painting rather than the representation of any object. Trained as a lawyer, he moved to Munich in 1896 to study art. On trips to Paris he became familiar with the work of Paul Gauguin and the neo-impressionists. He began exhibiting his paintings in Germany in 1907 and in 1910 executed his first abstract painting. In 1912 he published a theoretical study of nonrepresentational painting. With artists Paul Klee and Franz Marc he founded Der Blaue Reiter (The Blue Rider) group. They held exhibitions in Munich and Berlin and published a book of essays surveying music, art, literature, and theater. With the outbreak of World War I, the group disbanded; Kandinsky returned to Russia.

He returned to Germany after the war and became a teacher at the Bauhaus, a famous school of architecture and design. When the Nazis closed the school in 1933, Kandinsky moved to Paris, where he spent the rest of his life. Kandinsky's paintings and theoretical writings exhibited a strong influence on the development of modern art.

WALT DISNEY

Born December 5, 1901
Died December 15, 1966

Born at Chicago, animator Walt Disney is best remembered as the creator of Mickey Mouse. Disney grew up in Missouri. In Kansas City, he founded an animation studio, which failed in 1923. He then moved to Hollywood and founded another studio there. In 1928 the character Mickey Mouse made his debut in "Steamboat Willie," the first sound cartoon. By the mid-1930s Disney films were in color and featured such beloved characters as Donald Duck and Goofy. Disney made the world's first feature-length animated film, *Snow White and the Seven Dwarfs*, in 1938. It was a box-office smash and was followed by such movies as *Fantasia* and *Bambi*.

In the 1950s Disney Studios began to make films with live characters, such as *Mary Poppins*. Disney films have won more than thirty Academy Awards. The Disney corporation also made nature films and films for TV, such as the Davy Crockett series. Disneyland, the company's first theme park, opened in Anaheim, California, in 1955. Walt Disney World opened in Orlando, Florida, in 1971. By the time of Disney's death, he had created an empire. Disney theme parks later opened in France and Japan, and the name Disney became synonymous with American culture for much of the world.

IRA GERSHWIN

Born December 6, 1896
Died August 17, 1983

This Pulitzer Prize–winning lyricist was born at New York City. With his composer brother, George, he wrote two dozen scores for Broadway and Hollywood, which contain many songs that remain familiar today. Gershwin's first Broadway score was written with Vincent Youmans. The first popular song the Gershwins wrote together was "Swanee," which Al Jolson made into a smash hit. The Gershwins wrote the music for such shows as *Lady Be Good*, *Girl Crazy*, and *Of Thee I Sing*, which won the Pulitzer Prize for drama in 1931. Their shows contained such songs as "I Got Rhythm," "Someone to Watch Over Me," and "Funny Face." In 1935 George Gershwin wrote *Porgy and Bess*, an opera based on a book by DuBose Heyward. Ira Gershwin and Heyward wrote the lyrics. With such classic songs as "Summertime," it remains the most popular of American operas.

George Gershwin died of a brain tumor in 1937 at the age of thirty-eight. Ira Gershwin continued to write lyrics with other composers. He wrote the lyrics to accompany Kurt Weill's music for *Lady in the Dark* and collaborated with Jerome Kern and Harold Arlen on *A Star Is Born*. Ira Gershwin died at California at the age of eighty-six.

WILLA CATHER

Born December 7, 1873
Died April 24, 1947

Willa Cather was born at Winchester, Virginia, but when she was nine her family moved to Red Cloud, Nebraska, where six of her twelve novels are set. After graduation from the University of Nebraska, she worked as a journalist and teacher in Pittsburgh, Pennsylvania. From 1906 to 1912, she was an editor for *McClure's Magazine* in New York City, where she spent the rest of her life. In 1912 she first visited the Southwest, where she would later set her historical novel *Death Comes for the Archbishop*.

The Nebraska of Cather's childhood was a place where immigrants living in sod houses struggled to raise crops in the dry soil. She portrayed this in a series of books that recounted the pioneer experience, including *O Pioneers!*, *My Ántonia*, and *A Lost Lady*. *One of Ours*, which won the Pulitzer Prize for fiction in 1923, tells the story of a young man from Nebraska who goes off to World War I. Cather also wrote short stories and essays. Her fiction is characterized by a strong sense of place. She is considered to be one of the most important writers of the first half of the twentieth century.

DIEGO RIVERA

Born December 8, 1886
Died November 25, 1957

The murals of this Mexican painter ignited controversy in the United States. Born at Guanajuato, Mexico, Rivera traveled to Europe as a young man. There he was influenced by the work of Paul Cézanne and Pablo Picasso. He painted some cubist works, but by the time he returned to Mexico in 1921 he was committed to depicting contemporary Mexican life and the struggle between the classes. His Marxist views were reinforced by a visit to the Soviet Union in 1927. On his return he painted ideologically oriented murals at the Ministry of Education, the National Palace of Fine Arts, and the Hotel Reforma in Mexico City. When Trotsky fled to Mexico, Rivera became one of his supporters and in so doing fell out of favor with the Mexican Communist party. His increasing fame in the 1930s led to invitations to paint murals in San Francisco and at the Detroit Institute of Art. A mural at Rockefeller Center was later destroyed because it contained an image of Lenin.

In 1954 Rivera was readmitted to the Communist party, and he visited the Soviet Union again in 1955. Rivera was married (twice) to the surrealist Mexican painter Frida Kahlo. It was a tempestuous relationship. Rivera died at Mexico City.

JEAN DE BRUNHOFF

Born December 9, 1899
Died October 16, 1937

This children's author and illustrator was born at Paris. De Brunhoff's wife told their son, Laurent, a story about a little elephant. De Brunhoff decided to illustrate the tale, which was published as *The Story of Babar* in 1931 in France and in 1933 in the United States. De Brunhoff wrote six more books in the series, including *Babar and His Children*. In one of them, he sent Babar to the center of the Earth, in the tradition of Jules Verne. His books are warm depictions of family life, but tragedy is not absent: in the first book, Babar sees his mother killed by hunters. De Brunhoff had tuberculosis; his failing health may have caused him to write about sorrow in a sober manner to prepare his son for the inevitable. Babar's adventures are rooted in two different realities: the private life of the author and the literary traditions of France.

Laurent was twelve when his father died at Switzerland. He studied art and in the 1950s began to continue the series. He has since written and illustrated many Babar stories. Some critics consider these books to be pale imitations of the originals, but Laurent de Brunhoff has continued the saga of Babar, Celeste, Arthur, and the rest of his father's creations for children around the world.

EMILY DICKINSON

Born December 10, 1830
Died May 15, 1886

One of America's most famous poets, Emily Dickinson lived her entire life at Amherst, Massachusetts. She began writing poetry in the 1850s. In 1862 she wrote to a popular critic asking for advice about her poems. Because of their unusual form and content, he advised against publication. She continued to write in the same style, but by the late 1860s she had withdrawn from any contacts beyond her family circle. This reclusiveness appears to have been a deliberate choice; it resulted in the freedom she needed to create her bold, imaginative poems. She lived out her inner life in her work.

Fearing that she would be misunderstood, Dickinson published only seven poems during her lifetime. After her death, her sister discovered almost 2,000 more poems locked in a bureau. These poems were published gradually over the next fifty years. Her lines are now well known: " 'Hope' is the thing with feathers," "I'm Nobody! Who are you?," or "There is no Frigate like a Book . . ." Today, she is hailed, with Walt Whitman, as one of the two foremost American poets of the nineteenth century.

ALEKSANDR SOLZHENITSYN

Born December 11, 1918

This author, born at Rostov-on-Don, USSR, exposed the Soviet Union's system of labor camps—the gulag—in three novels and one work of nonfiction. After serving in the Soviet army during World War II, he was arrested for some critical remarks he had written in a personal letter. He was sentenced without trial to eight years of hard labor in a prison camp. During the period of de-Stalinization, Solzhenitsyn was pronounced "rehabilitated" and allowed to return to Moscow in 1956. The short novel *One Day in the Life of Ivan Denisovich* was published in the Soviet Union in 1962. Because its subject was Stalin's forced labor camps, he was no longer able to publish his work there.

His problems with the government increased when he published *The First Circle* and *The Cancer Ward* abroad. In 1970 he received the Nobel Prize for literature. After publication of the first volume of his nonfiction work *The Gulag Archipelago* he was exiled by the Soviet authorities in 1974. He settled first in Zurich and then moved to the United States, where he completed the second volume of the work. He was not happy in America, however, and with the fall of communism he returned to Russia in 1994.

JOHN JAY

Born December 12, 1745
Died May 17, 1829

American statesman John Jay was born at New York City. Active in pre-Revolutionary politics, he was largely responsible for writing New York's first state constitution of 1777. He also served as New York's first chief justice. A delegate to the Continental Congress, he was its president in 1778. He was then appointed minister to Spain, where he failed to win Spanish recognition of American independence. In 1782 he went to Paris with Benjamin Franklin and John Adams to negotiate the treaty that ended the American Revolution. With Alexander Hamilton and James Madison he wrote the influential Federalist Papers, a series of eighty-five essays published in New York newspapers to persuade voters to support ratification of the new U.S. Constitution.

In 1789 Jay was appointed the first chief justice of the U.S. Supreme Court, where he established procedures still used today. In 1794 he was sent to England to settle outstanding differences between Great Britain and the United States with the treaty that bears his name. In 1795 he resigned from the Supreme Court to serve as governor of New York. After finishing his term in 1801, Jay refused further public office.

MARY TODD LINCOLN

Born December 13, 1818
Died July 16, 1882

The wife of the sixteenth president of the United States, Mary Todd Lincoln was born at Lexington, Kentucky. In 1839 she went to live with her sister in Springfield, Illinois, where Abraham Lincoln was a prominent lawyer and a member of the state legislature. They married in 1842. In 1847 the Lincolns moved to Washington, D.C., where Abe served one term in the House of Representatives. He did not run for reelection, and he and Mary returned to Springfield. In 1860, when Lincoln was elected to the presidency, the family returned to Washington. During the Civil War Mary Lincoln was seen as a traitor by Southerners and was suspected of treason by those loyal to the Union. One of her four sons had already died in Illinois and another died while they were in Washington.

Mary Todd Lincoln was shattered by her husband's assassination. After her third son, Tad, died in 1871 she was plagued by delusions. Her surviving son, Robert Todd Lincoln, had her committed to a sanitarium in 1875, but after less than a year she was declared sane. She died at Springfield at her sister's home.

MARGARET CHASE SMITH

Born December 14, 1897
Died May 29, 1995

Born at Skowhegan, Maine, Smith was the first woman to serve in both the U.S. House of Representatives and the Senate. Her husband, Clyde Smith, had been elected to the House from Maine in 1936. Upon his death in 1940 she succeeded him. After serving four terms, she was elected to the Senate in 1948 and served there until 1973. Smith gained national attention in 1950 when she was the first member of the Senate to denounce Senator Joseph McCarthy with her "Declaration of Conscience" speech. McCarthy had alleged that the State Department was full of members of the Communist party and expanded his accusations to other areas of government. The Senate didn't vote to condemn him until 1954.

In 1964 Senator Smith ran in several Republican presidential primaries. She took her candidacy to the Republican National Convention, where she became the first woman in either party ever to have her name placed in nomination for the presidency; but she lost the nomination to Barry Goldwater. After thirty-two years in Congress, Smith lost reelection in 1972. She returned to Maine and began planning the library that now bears her name. It opened in Skowhegan in 1982.

ALEXANDRE-GUSTAVE EIFFEL

Born December 15, 1832
Died December 28, 1923

Eiffel, born at Dijon, France, designed the tower that bears his name for the Paris International Exposition of 1899. Eiffel was an engineer who had gained a reputation as a builder of bridges and viaducts. In 1884 he designed the iron pylon for the inside of the Statue of Liberty. The Eiffel Tower was built to celebrate the technical achievements of its age. The 984-foot structure consists of a base resting on four separate legs or pylons and a slender tower created as the pylons taper upward to emerge in a single column. It is constructed of open-lattice wrought iron and weighs more than 7,000 tons. An elevator leads to a platform from which all of Paris can be seen. It was the tallest building in the world until the Empire State Building was constructed in 1931.

Eiffel was the leading expert of his day on the aerodynamics of tall buildings. The curve of the pylons in the Eiffel Tower was precisely calculated to transform the forces of the wind into forces of compression. In 1913 Eiffel wrote a book, *The Resistance of the Air*. Today the Eiffel Tower is a landmark that signifies the city of Paris to people all over the world.

LUDWIG VAN BEETHOVEN

Born December 16, 1770
Died March 26, 1827

Beethoven, one of the world's greatest composers, was born at Bonn, Germany. At the age of twelve he was an assistant organist, and in 1792 he moved to Vienna to study with Joseph Haydn. Vienna was his home for the rest of his life. He supported himself by teaching piano, giving concerts, and selling his compositions. In 1809 three members of the Viennese aristocracy guaranteed him a steady income.

During the early part of his career, Beethoven wrote mostly for piano and chamber groups. The first of his sixteen string quartets dates from 1798. By the early 1800s he began to notice the onset of deafness. He composed thirty-two piano sonatas in addition to five piano concertos and an opera, *Fidelio*. His nine symphonies include the *Eroica* (1804) and culminated in the great *Ninth Symphony* (1824), which contains the well-loved "Ode to Joy." By this time Beethoven was totally deaf. His music had a major impact on the next generation of composers (such as Schubert, Berlioz, and Mahler) and continues to hold a central place in the world's concert repertory.

DEBORAH SAMPSON

Born December 17, 1760
Died April 29, 1827

Born at Plympton, Massachusetts, Deborah Sampson (some sources spell her name Samson) spent her childhood as an indentured servant. On May 21, 1782, at the age of twenty-one, she enlisted in the Fourth Massachusetts Regiment as Robert Shurtleff. She was the first American woman to impersonate a man to join the army and take part in combat. She was tall for her age and had bound her breasts. Older soldiers teased her for not having to shave, but rather than finding her out they simply assumed she was a young boy.

She was wounded in the leg in a battle in New York and cared for the wound herself so as not to be detected. However, she developed a fever in Philadelphia, and a doctor, discovering she was a woman, arranged for her to leave the army. She received an honorable discharge in 1783. After returning home, she married a farmer and had three children. Sampson later traveled throughout New England and New York, lecturing on her experiences in the military. She was awarded army pensions by Massachusetts and the U.S. government for her service in the Revolution. A military pension was provided to her heirs after her death at Sharon, Massachusetts.

STEPHEN BIKO

Born December 18, 1946
Died September 12, 1977

Biko was a martyr for the anti-Apartheid cause in South Africa. Apartheid was a system that required the racial classification of all South Africans at birth. Nonwhites could not vote and were limited as to residence and occupation. Biko attended the University of Natal (black section) but was expelled for his political activities. He helped form the South African Students' Organization in 1968 and served as its president. He was also a founder of the Black People's Convention and other organizations and was an active speaker and writer. In March 1973 he was officially banned by the white government, which meant it was illegal for him to make public speeches. It was also illegal for others to quote anything he said—even in private conversations.

He was arrested on August 18, 1977, at a roadblock and detained. He suffered a major head injury while in police custody, and no medical treatment was offered. He died at Pretoria, South Africa. He was thirty years old.

Biko's story was told in the 1987 film *Cry Freedom* in which Denzel Washington played the part of Biko. Apartheid finally came to an end in South Africa in 1994. For the first time, nonwhites were allowed to vote, and Nelson Mandela was elected president of the country.

CARTER G. WOODSON

Born December 19, 1875
Died April 3, 1950

This African-American historian, born at New Canton, Virginia, is known as the father of black history. The son of former slaves, he received a Ph.D. from Harvard University in 1912. As a professor of history at Howard University, he encouraged the serious academic study of African-American and African history. He founded the Association for the Study of Negro Life and History to train black historians and to preserve and publish documents on black history. He established the *Journal of Negro History*, the first scholarly journal in the field, and served as its editor for thirty-five years. He also created a publishing company to issue books on black life and culture. In 1926 he organized the first Negro History Week, which later became Black History Month, to disseminate this information to a wider public, both black and white.

The NAACP awarded him the Spingarn Medal for his contributions to black history. An author of many books, Woodson was working on the *Encyclopedia Africana* when he died at Washington, D.C.

SACAGAWEA

Birth date unknown
Died December 20, 1812

Sacagawea was a young Shoshone Indian woman who traveled with the Lewis and Clark expedition. She was born in the 1780s; there is controversy about her death date, with some sources saying December 12 and others saying December 22. (At one point she was confused with another Indian woman who died April 9, 1884, and some references still list that as her death date.) In 1800, when she was still a young girl, Sacagawea was kidnapped by a band of Hidatsa Indians and taken from her home in what is now Idaho to North Dakota. There she was later sold to a French Canadian fur trader who made her his wife. In 1804 the Corps of Discovery, led by Lewis and Clark, arrived in North Dakota and built Fort Mandan. Sacagawea gave birth to a son there the following year.

The expedition required horses to cross the mountains on the way to Oregon. The leaders needed a translator to negotiate to buy the horses from the Shoshone. Although she didn't speak English, Sacagawea spoke Hidatsa with her husband who then spoke French to a member of the Corps. So Sacagawea and her husband were hired as translators and with their infant son accompanied the thirty-three members of the expedition to the West Coast, arriving back in North Dakota in 1806. In addition to serving as a translator, Sacagawea gathered plants for food and medicine. In 1812 she gave birth to a daughter and died not long afterward at about the age of twenty-five. In 2000 the U.S. Mint issued a coin in honor of Sacagawea.

JOSEPH STALIN

Born December 21, 1879
Died March 5, 1954

One of the most powerful and feared men of the twentieth century, Stalin was born at Georgia, near the Black Sea. In 1898 he became involved in radical political activity as a full-time revolutionary organizer. He was a member of the Bolshevik Central Committee and edited the party's newspaper, *Pravda*. Between 1902 and 1913 he was arrested numerous times. In 1913 he was exiled to Siberia by the czarist government but returned to Moscow in 1917 after the Russian Revolution deposed the czar. In 1922 he was appointed by Lenin to the powerful position of general secretary of the Communist party.

After Lenin's death in 1924, Stalin crushed any opposition within the party, and by 1929 he was the undisputed leader of the Soviet Union. He began a program of industrialization through a series of five-year plans. He eliminated any real or perceived threats to his authority through purges, which killed thousands.

He served as a skillful leader during World War II. At the end of the war, Stalin was at the height of his power as a complete dictator, and his rule became even more repressive. It is estimated that millions of people died during Stalin's regime, either from starvation or by execution. After his death in Moscow, many of his crimes were revealed to the Soviet people.

GIACOMO PUCCINI

Born December 22, 1858
Died November 29, 1924

This composer of some of the world's best-loved operas was born into a musical family at Lucca, Italy, and studied at a conservatory in Milan. Inspired by Verdi's *Aida*, he began to write operas in 1883. His first two efforts were not successful, but with the next two, *Manon Lescaut* and *La Boheme*, he won fame and fortune. His operas *Tosca* and *Madama Butterfly* were not critical successes but were extremely popular with the public, and Puccini was hailed as the successor to Verdi. Though he was not the musical innovator that Verdi was, Puccini had great theatrical gifts.

His opera *The Girl of the Golden West* was written for the Metropolitan Opera in New York and was presented there in 1910. His last great opera, *Turandot*, was presented after his death at Brussels. Puccini's operas, like those of Verdi, remain part of the standard repertory for opera companies around the world.

SARAH "MADAME C. J." WALKER

Born December 23, 1867
Died May 25, 1919

The first self-made American woman millionaire, Madame Walker was born Sarah Breedlove to former slaves at Delta, Louisiana. With money she had saved from her work as a washerwoman, she started a business making hair and skin care products for the African-American community. In 1910 she built a factory in Indianapolis to manufacture her products. Her approach to beauty became known as the Walker Method. She invented the curling iron and a hot comb for straightening hair. She used a network of door-to-door sales agents and advertised in black newspapers. Eventually she employed hundreds of people. She moved her company to Harlem in New York City. By 1918 she had sales exceeding $250,000 a year. Her products were sold in the Caribbean and Central America as well as all over the United States.

Madame Walker was an advocate of women's economic independence. She was known for her philanthropy, making large contributions to the NAACP, black colleges, and other charities.

HOWARD HUGHES

Born December 24, 1905
Died April 5, 1976

Born at Houston, Texas, Howard Hughes never graduated from high school. His wealthy father arranged for him to attend classes at Cal Tech, however, by donating money to the school. Hughes inherited the Hughes Tool Company at the age of eighteen. As a young man, with an estimated income of $2 million, he became a Hollywood producer of such films as *The Front Page, The Outlaw,* and *Scarface.* In 1932 Hughes founded the Hughes Aircraft Company, which pioneered many advances in aviation technology. In 1935 he set a new speed record flying a plane he had designed, and he broke Lindbergh's New York–Paris record in 1938.

With the approach of World War II, Hughes turned his business interests to building military aircraft. The Hughes Flying Boat, mockingly called the "Spruce Goose" because it was built out of laminated wood, was the biggest aircraft ever built and only flew once. After the war, Hughes was a majority owner of TWA and Air West airlines. He established the Hughes Medical Institute, a research facility, as his only philanthropy.

In his later years, living in Las Vegas where he owned much of the hotel and nightclub business, Hughes became an eccentric, reclusive hypochondriac. At the time of his death, he had not been seen in public in twenty years. After his death on a plane en route from Acapulco to Houston, there was a great controversy about the disposal of his $2 billion estate and the legitimacy of various wills.

CLARA BARTON

December 25, 1821
Died April 12, 1912

This nurse and philanthropist was born at Oxford, Massachusetts. After working as a teacher, she became a clerk in the U.S. Patent Office in Washington. She resigned from her job at the beginning of the Civil War to collect supplies for soldiers. In 1862 she received permission to deliver these supplies directly to the front. In 1864 she was given the position of superintendent of Union nurses and became known as the "Angel of the Battlefield." She helped gather identification from the dead and after the war headed up a government agency that helped families locate missing soldiers. She lectured about her experiences at the front and worked with the suffragist movement.

After a breakdown in 1869, she traveled to Europe to regain her health. During this time, she learned of the Treaty of Geneva, which prescribed rules for the treatment of captured and wounded soldiers. The United States had not signed this treaty. She also became familiar with the Red Cross, which had been founded in Switzerland in 1863 by Henri Dunant. When she returned to the United States she lobbied for the adoption of the Treaty of Geneva. Her tactics were successful. The United States signed the treaty in 1882. Barton founded the American Red Cross in 1881 and became its first president. She expanded its mandate to include caring for the victims of disasters as well as wars. The last relief operation she supervised was for the victims of the Galveston hurricane of 1900, the worst natural disaster in U.S. history at that time.

LAURENT CLERC

Born December 26, 1785
Died July 18, 1869

The first teacher of the deaf in America, Clerc was born at LaBalme, France, and was deaf himself. He studied at the Royal Institution for the Deaf in Paris and stayed on to teach.

At this time there were no schools for the deaf in the United States. Thomas Gallaudet had gone to Europe in 1815 seeking information on educating the deaf. He met Clerc, who taught him sign language. Clerc agreed to come to the United States, with the understanding that he would only stay a short time.

Gallaudet and Clerc founded what is now the American School for the Deaf in Hartford, Connecticut, in 1817. There Clerc trained pupils in the use of sign language and teachers in methods of teaching the deaf for forty-one years. A respected teacher, he appeared before the U.S. Congress and met President James Monroe. He married one of his pupils and had a family. He never did return to France.

LOUIS PASTEUR

Born December 27, 1822
Died September 28, 1895

This French chemist is considered the founder of microbiology, the study of organisms such as bacteria and viruses that cannot be detected by the naked eye. In 1854 Pasteur became professor of chemistry at the Lille Faculty of Science. He studied fermentation, proving that yeast is a microorganism that converts sugar into alcohol. He laid the foundation of the germ theory of disease by suggesting that just as each kind of fermentation is caused by a particular kind of microorganism or germ, many diseases are caused by specific germs. He also concluded that the spoilage of food could be controlled by killing microorganisms with controlled heat. This process, called pasteurization in his honor, is still used today to treat milk and other perishable food products.

Pasteur discovered the anthrax bacillus and showed that immunization was possible with a weakened form of the disease. In 1882 he proved that rabies is caused by a virus and developed a vaccine against it. With this he laid the foundation for the study of viruses. He also campaigned for better standards of sanitation and sterilization, which contributed greatly to the field of immunology. In 1888 he became the first director of the Pasteur Institute in Paris. He suffered a paralyzing stroke at the age of forty-six, but he continued his work until his death twenty-seven years later.

WOODROW WILSON

Born December 28, 1856
Died February 3, 1924

The twenty-eighth president of the United States was born at Staunton, Virginia. A professor of political science at Princeton, in 1902 Wilson became the university's president. In 1910 he was persuaded to run for governor of New Jersey. His success as governor got him the Democratic nomination for the presidency in 1912.

In his two terms as president he achieved an impressive record of reforms. His administration saw the beginning of the Federal Reserve system and the Federal Trade Commission. The Child Labor Act, which limited children's work hours, was passed. After the outbreak of World War I in Europe in 1914, Wilson struggled to maintain American neutrality, but when Germany renewed submarine warfare against American ships, he asked Congress for a declaration of war in 1917. During the war, Wilson promulgated his Fourteen Points as a basis for a just peace and called for a postwar association of nations. The Paris Peace Conference that ended the war created the League of Nations, but Wilson was unable to get the United States to join. In 1919 he suffered a major stroke and was incapacitated for the remainder of his term in office. He was awarded the Nobel Peace Prize for 1919.

ANDREW JOHNSON

Born December 29, 1808
Died July 31, 1875

The seventeenth president of the United States was born at Raleigh, North Carolina. Like Abraham Lincoln before him, he was self-educated. Johnson moved to Tennessee and by the 1830s was an important figure in politics in the state. He served in the state legislature, as governor and then in the U.S. House of Representatives. Although Johnson represented the nonslaveholding farmers of the hill country of eastern Tennessee, he defended slavery. However, when the Southern states began to secede, he tried to keep Tennessee in the Union and was the only Southern senator who did not resign from Congress.

Johnson was chosen as the running mate for Abraham Lincoln's second presidential campaign. After Lincoln's assassination, Johnson tried to restore the Union by following Lincoln's Reconstruction plans. However, as a proponent of states' rights, he felt that Congress should not intervene in the internal affairs of the Southern states. He clashed with Congress over protecting the rights of former slaves and other issues. In 1868 he was impeached by the House of Representatives, but the Senate found him not guilty by a slim margin. However, his power as president had been weakened. He returned to Tennessee and was elected to the U.S. Senate one more time in 1875. He died shortly thereafter.

TIGER WOODS

Born December 30, 1975

Golfer Tiger Woods was born Eldrick Woods at Cypress, California, to an African-American father and a Thai mother. His father taught him to play golf. At age two he appeared on television, putting with Bob Hope. He entered Stanford University in 1994 and won ten collegiate golf events, concluding with the NCAA title. Woods had one of the most impressive amateur records, winning six USGA national championships before turning professional in 1996. In his first year as a professional, Woods became the youngest-ever number one golfer in the Official World Golf Ranking. He was twenty-one.

Since then he has won more than fifty tournaments, including the 1997, 2001, and 2002 Masters Tournaments; the 1999 and 2000 PGA Championships; the 2000 and 2002 U.S. Opens; and the 2000 British Open. With his second Masters victory in 2001, he became the first person ever to hold all four major championships at the same time. He is the youngest (and only fifth) person to complete the career Grand Slam of major professional championships. Woods has won more than $40 million worldwide playing golf. He was named Sportsman of the Year by *Sports Illustrated* in 1996 and 2000 and Male Athlete of the Year by the Associated Press in 1997, 1999, and 2000.

GEORGE C. MARSHALL

Born December 31, 1880
Died October 16, 1959

This American army officer and diplomat was born at Uniontown, Pennsylvania. A staff officer in France in World War I, he was later an aide to General John J. Pershing and by 1939 was the chief of staff of the army. During World War II he directed U.S. forces in both Europe and the Pacific and became general of the army in 1944. President Truman sent him to China in 1945, where he unsuccessfully tried to negotiate a settlement in the civil war between the nationalists and the communists.

In 1947 Marshall was appointed secretary of state. During his tenure, he created the European Recovery Plan, later known as the Marshall Plan, which provided economic and technical assistance to sixteen war-ravaged European countries. The program succeeded in restoring the economies of these nations. For this work he won the Nobel Peace Prize in 1953.

In 1950 Marshall was appointed secretary of defense during the Korean War. He is the only person ever to have served as both secretary of state and secretary of defense. He died at Washington, D.C.

INDEX

Aaron, Henry "Hank," 38
Abbott, Berenice, 208
Abolitionists. *See also* Civil rights leaders
  John Brown, 136
  William Ellery Channing, 102
  Harriet Beecher Stowe, 173
Actors. *See also* Dancers; Filmmakers
  Fred Astaire, 137
  Mikhail Baryshnikov, 28
  LeVar Burton, 49
  Charles Spencer Chaplin, 111
  Tom Hanks, 200
  Lena Horne, 189
  Boris Karloff, 342
  Bruce Lee, 346
  Marcel Marceau, 85
  Patricia Neal, 21
  Christopher Reeve, 280
  Paul Robeson, 104
  Johnny Weissmuller, 161
Adams, Abigal, 341
Adams, Ansel, 53
Adams, John, 317
Adams, Samuel, 2, 281
Adventurers. *See* Explorers
African Americans
  Henry "Hank" Aaron, 38
  Marian Anderson, 60
  Louis Armstrong, 227
  Benjamin Banneker, 328
  Mary McLeod Bethune, 201
  Willa B. Brown, 23
  LeVar Burton, 49
  Roy Campanella, 338
  Wilt Chamberlain, 244
  Charles Waddell Chesnutt, 179
  Bessie Coleman, 23
  Countee Cullen, 157
  Thomas A. Dorsey, 192
  W. E. B. DuBois, 56
  Marian Wright Edelman, 165
  Alex Haley, 234
  Jupiter Hammon, 304
  W. C. Handy, 335
  Matthew A. Henson, 231
  Langston Hughes, 34
  John Hurt, 194
  Mahalia Jackson, 313
  Robert Johnson, 135
  Scott Joplin, 343
  Ernest Just, 237
  Meadowlark Lemon, 120
  Bobby McFerrin Jr., 74
  Malcom X, 146
  Wynton Marsalis, 303
  Thurgood Marshall, 193
  Toni Morrison, 51
  Jessie Owens, 267
  Leroy "Satchel" Paige, 198
  Mary Ann "Aunt Mary" Prout, 47
  Paul Robeson, 104
  Wilma Rudolph, 182
  Alice Walker, 42
  Maggie Walker, 47
  Sarah "Madame C. J." Walker,
    374
  Mary Wells, 140
  Phillis Wheatley, 304
  Roy Wilkins, 253
  Granville T. Woods, 118
  Tiger Woods, 381
  Carter G. Woodson, 370
Airy, George Biddell, 218
Albright, Madeleine, 142
Alcott, Louisa May, 348
Alger, Horatio, 14
American politicians. *See also* U.S. Presidents
  Madeleine Albright, 142
  Henry Clay, 107
  Millicent Fenwick, 57
  Benjamin Franklin, 18
  John Jay, 363
  Clare Booth Luce, 73
  George C. Marshall, 382
  Claude Denson Pepper, 263
  William Henry Seward, 143
  Margaret Chase Smith, 365
  Daniel Webster, 19

Index

Amundsen, Roald, 207
Andersen, Hans Christian, 97
Anderson, Marian, 60
Appert, Nicolas, 336
Architects. *See also* Engineers
 Daniel Hudson Burnham, 259
 Pierre Charles L'Enfant, 225
 Frank Lloyd Wright, 167
 Minoru Yamasaki, 352
Armstrong, Lance, 273
Armstrong, Louis, 227
Artists. *See also* Cartoonists; Illustrators
 Ansel Adams, 53
 Fred Astaire, 137
 John James Audubon, 121
 Thomas Bewick, 235
 William Blake, 347
 Gutzon Borglum, 88
 Mary Cassatt, 149
 George Catlin, 217
 Thomas Gainsborough, 141
 Paul Gauguin, 166
 Jim Henson, 279
 George Herriman, 245
 George Inness, 128
 Wassily Kandinsky, 355
 Emanuel Leutze, 151
 Michelangelo, 69
 Alice Neel, 29
 Georgia O'Keefe, 106, 334
 Maxfield Parrish, 216
 Pablo Picasso, 312
 Harriet Powers, 316
 Rembrandt van Rijn, 206
 Frederick Remington, 291
 Diego Rivera, 359
 Norman Rockwell, 36
 Maurice Sendak, 169
 Georges Seurat, 353
 Vincent van Gogh, 93
 Grant Wood, 46
Astaire, Fred, 137
Astronauts
 Jeannette Ridlon Piccard, 6
 Sally Kristen Ride, 153
 Alan Shepard, 337
 Donald "Deke" Slayton, 64
 Kathryn Sullivan, 153
Astronomers
 George Biddell Airy, 218
 Benjamin Banneker, 328
 Nicolaus Copernicus, 52
 Edmond Halley, 327
 Caroline Lucretia Herschel, 79
 Edwin Hubble, 339
 Marquis Pierre-Simon de Laplace, 86
 Maria Mitchell, 224

Athletes
 Henry "Hank" Aaron, 38
 Lance Armstrong, 273
 Bonnie Blair, 81
 Roy Campanella, 338
 Wilt Chamberlain, 244
 George Foreman, 11
 Meadowlark Lemon, 120
 Jessie Owens, 267
 Leroy "Satchel" Paige, 198
 Arnold Palmer, 265
 Annie Smith Peck, 306
 Pelé, 310
 Mary Lou Retton, 25
 Cal Ripken Jr., 247
 Wilma Rudolph, 182
 Helen Candaele St. Aubin, 76
 Albert Spaulding, 257
 Junko Tabei, 277
 Jim Thorpe, 155
 William Toomey, 11
 Johnny Weissmuller, 161
 Tiger Woods, 381
Audubon, John James, 121
Authors. *See* Poets; Writers
Aviators
 Willa B. Brown, 23
 Bessie Coleman, 23, 27
 Amelia Earhart, 215
 Howard Hughes, 375
 Anne Morrow Lindberg, 181
 Charles Lindberg, 37
 Jacques-Étienne Montgolfier, 8
 Juan T. Trippe, 185

Bach, Johann Sebastian, 84
Bacteriologists
 Alexander Fleming, 229
 Louis Pasteur, 378
Baez, Joan, 10
Banneker, Benjamin, 328
Barton, Clara, 376
Bartram, John, 150
Baryshnikov, Mikhail, 28
Bascom, Florence, 205
Baseball players
 Henry "Hank" Aaron, 38
 Roy Campanella, 338
 Leroy "Satchel" Paige, 198
 Cal Ripken Jr., 247
 Helen Candaele St. Aubin, 76
 Albert Spaulding, 257
 Jim Thorpe, 155
Basketball players
 Wilt Chamberlain, 244
 Meadowlark Lemon, 120
Beadle, George W., 309

Beard, Mary Ritter, 228
Beethoven, Ludwig van, 367
Begin, Menachem, 239
Bell, Alexander Graham, 66
Bethune, Mary McLeod, 201
Bewick, Thomas, 235
Biko, Stephen, 369
Biologists
    Charles Robert Darwin, 45
    Ernest Just, 237
    Jonas Salk, 315
Blair, Bonnie, 81
Blake, William, 347
Bliss, Lizzie "Lillie," 106
Bly, Nellie, 132
Bombeck, Erma, 54
Booth, William, 105
Borglum, Gutzon, 88
Botanists
    John Bartram, 150
    Charles Robert Darwin, 45
Boycott, Charles Cunningham, 75
Boyle, Robert, 26
Brahms, Johannes, 133
Braille, Louis, 5
Brown, John, 136
Brown, Willa B., 23
Burbank, Luther, 70
Burnham, Daniel Hudson, 259
Burroughs, Edgar Rice, 256
Burton, LeVar, 49
Business leaders
    Andrew Carnegie, 344
    Ole Evinrude, 114
    Henry Ford, 221
    Hetty Green, 340
    John Harvey Kellogg, 59
    Howard Hughes, 375
    André Michelin, 17
    John Pierpont Morgan, 112
    Alfred Nobel, 308
    Ferdinand Porsche, 258
    John Cecil Rhodes, 196
    Albert Spaulding, 257
    Leland Stanford, 72
    Sarah "Madame C. J." Walker, 374
Butts, Alfred M., 108

Campanella, Roy, 338
Capra, Frank, 145
Carnegie, Andrew, 344
Carson, Rachel, 154
Carter, Jimmy, 288
Cartoonists. *See also* Artists; Humorists
    George Herriman, 245
    Charles Schulz, 345
Cassatt, Mary, 149

Cather, Willa, 358
Catlin, George, 217
Cavoukian, Raffi, 199
Chamberlain, Wilt, 244
Channing, William Ellery, 102
Chaplin, Charles Spencer, 111
Chavez, Cesar, 94
Chemists
    Robert Boyle, 26
    Marie Curie, 326
Chesnutt, Charles Waddell, 179
Chess players
    Judit Polgar, 214
Child, Lydia Maria, 44
Civil rights leaders. *See also* Abolitionists
    Mary McLeod Bethune, 201
    Stephen Biko, 369
    William Ellery Channing, 102
    W. E. B. DuBois, 56
    Marian Wright Edelman, 165
    John Howard Griffin, 175
    Martin Luther King Jr., 16
    Malcolm X, 146
    Bayard Rustin, 80
    Roy Wilkins, 253
Clay, Henry, 107
Clemens, Samuel. *See* Twain, Mark
Clerc, Laurent, 377
Colbert, Edwin, 283
Coleman, Bessie, 23, 27
Composers. *See also* Musicians; Singers
    Johann Sebastian Bach, 84
    Joan Baez, 10
    Ludwig van Beethoven, 367
    Johannes Brahms, 133
    Raffi Cavoukian, 199
    Aaron Copland, 333
    Arcangelo Corelli, 50
    Thomas A. Dorsey, 192
    Stephen Foster, 195
    Ira Gershwin, 357
    Edvard Grieg, 174
    W. C. Handy, 335
    Patty Smith Hill, 90
    Scott Joplin, 343
    Cole Porter, 168
    Giacomo Puccini, 373
    Franz (Peter) Schubert, 32
    John Philip Sousa, 325
    Giuseppe Verdi, 297
    Ralph Vaughan Williams, 299
Comte, Auguste, 20
Conrad, Joseph, 354
Conservationists. *See* Naturalists
Cook, James, 314
Copernicus, Nicolaus, 52
Copland, Aaron, 333

Index

Corelli, Arcangelo, 50
Cousteau, Jacques, 170
Crane, Stephen, 320
Crockett, Davy, 240
Cullen, Countee, 157
Curie, Marie, 326
Cyclists
    Lance Armstrong, 273

Dancers. *See also* Actors
    Fred Astaire, 137
    Mikhail Baryshnikov, 28
    Martha Graham, 138
Darrow, Clarence Seward, 113
Darwin, Charles Robert, 45
De Brunhoff, Jean, 360
De Brunhoff, Laurent, 360
De Forest, Lee, 249
Dewey, John, 307
Dickinson, Emily, 361
Disney, Walt, 356
Dix, Dorothea, 99
Doctors. *See* Health-care leaders
Dorsey, Thomas A., 192
Dostoyevsky, Fyodor, 330
DuBois, W. E. B., 56

Earhart, Amelia, 215
Earp, Wyatt, 82
Ecologists. *See* Naturalists
Economists
    Milton Friedman, 222
    John Stuart Mill, 147
    Adam Smith, 164
Edelman, Marian Wright, 165
Edison, Thomas, 70
Educators
    Mary McLeod Bethune, 201
    Laurent Clerc, 377
    John Dewey, 307
    W. E. B. DuBois, 56
    Thomas Gallaudet, 377
    William Holmes McGuffey, 278
    Anne Sullivan Macy, 109
    Horace Mann, 131
    Maria Montessori, 254
    Jean Piaget, 232
    John T. Scopes, 226
    Carter G. Woodson, 370
Eiffel, Alexandre-Gustave, 366
Einstein, Albert, 77
Eisenhower, Dwight D., 301
El-Hajj Malik el Shabazz (Malcom X), 146
Emerson, Ralph Waldo, 152
Engineers. *See also* Architects
    Alexandre-Gustave Eiffel, 366
    Lord Kelvin, 185

Environmentalists. *See* Naturalists
Evans, Walker, 322
Evinrude, Ole, 114
Explorers
    Roald Amundsen, 207
    Nellie Bly, 132
    James Cook, 314
    Jacques Cousteau, 170
    Matthew A. Henson, 231
    Thor Heyerdahl, 293
    Edmund Hillary, 211
    Meriwether Lewis, 241
    John Muir, 116
    Robert E. Peary, 133
    John Wesley Powell, 87
    James Clark Ross, 110
    Ernest Shackleton, 48
    Jedediah Strong Smith, 183

Feminists. *See also* American
        politicians; Athletes; First ladies;
        Poets; Writers
    Joan Baez, 10
    Mary Ritter Beard, 228
    Mary McLeod Bethune, 201
    Willa B. Brown, 23
    Lydia Maria Child, 44
    Bessie Coleman, 23, 27
    Millicent Fenwick, 57
    Anne Morrow Lindbergh, 181
    Belva Lockwood, 311
    Harriet Martineau, 171
    Alice Neel, 29
    Jeannette Ridlon Piccard, 6
    Mary Lou Retton, 25
    Eleanor Roosevelt, 31
    Deborah Sampson, 368
    Margaret Chase Smith, 365
    Elizabeth Cady Stanton, 331
    Laura Ingalls Wilder, 40
Fenwick, Millicent, 57
Fermi, Enrico, 284
Filmmakers. *See also* Actors
    Frank Capra, 145
    Jacques Cousteau, 170
    Walt Disney, 356
    Rudolf C. Ising, 230
    Darryl F. Zanuck, 260
Financiers. *See* Business leaders
First ladies
    Abigal Adams, 341
    Mary Todd Lincoln, 364
    Eleanor Roosevelt, 31
Fleming, Alexander, 229
Ford, Henry, 221
Foreman, George, 11
Foster, Stephen, 195

Franklin, Benjamin, 18
Friedman, Milton, 222

Gainsborough, Thomas, 141
Gallaudet, Thomas, 377
Gandhi, Mohandas, 289
Gannett, Frank, 270
Gauguin, Paul, 166
Gauss, Carl Friedrich, 125
Geisel, Theodore Seuss ("Dr. Seuss"),
    65
Geneticists
    George W. Beadle, 309
Geologists
    Florence Bascom, 205
    James Hutton, 162
    John Wesley Powell, 87
George III, king of Great Britain, 163
Gershwin, Ira, 357
Getz, Stan, 35
Goddard, Robert, 292
Goethe, Johann Wolfgang von, 251
Golding, William Gerald, 274
Golfers
    Arnold Palmer, 265
    Tiger Woods, 381
Goodall, Jane, 98
Gorgas, William, 290
Graham, Martha, 138
Grahame, Kenneth, 71
Grant, Ulysses Simpson, 122
Green, Hetty, 340
Gregory, Isabella Augusta, 78
Grieg, Edvard, 174
Griffin, John Howard, 175
Gutenberg, Johannes, 57
Gymnasts
    Mary Lou Retton, 25

Haley, Alex, 234
Halley, Edmond, 327
Hammon, Jupiter, 304
Hancock, John, 2, 24
Handy, William Christopher, 335
Hanks, Tom, 200
Health-care leaders
    Clara Barton, 376
    Dorothea Dix, 99
    Alexander Fleming, 228
    William Gorgas, 290
    Edward Jenner, 144
    Hans Adolf Krebs, 248
    Joseph Lister, 100
    Florence Nightingale, 139
    Louis Pasteur, 378
    Walter Reed, 268
    Jonas Salk, 315

Benjamin Spock, 129
Rosalyn Yallow, 210
Hemingway, Ernest, 212
Henry, O. (William Sydney Porter), 266
Henry, Patrick, 156
Henson, Jim, 279
Henson, Matthew A., 231
Herriman, George, 245
Herschel, Caroline Lucretia, 79
Heyerdahl, Thor, 293
Hill, Patty Smith, 90
Hillary, Sir Edmund, 211
Hine, Lewis, 281
Hirohito, 124
Hitler, Adolf, 115
Holly, Buddy, 262
Hoover, Herbert, 232
Horne, Lena, 189
Horticulturists
    Luther Burbank, 70
Hubble, Edwin, 339
Hughes, Howard, 375
Hughes, Langston, 34
Humorists. *See also* Cartoonists
    Erma Bombeck, 54
    Ogden Nash, 242
    Mark Twain, 349
Hurt, John, 194
Hutton, James, 162

Ibsen, Henrik, 83
Illustrators. *See also* Artists
    Thomas Bewick, 235
    Jean de Brunhoff, 360
    Theodor Seuss Geisel ("Dr. Seuss"), 65
    Maxfield Parrish, 216
    Norman Rockwell, 36
    Maurice Sendak, 169
Immunologists
    Alexander Fleming, 229
    Edward Jenner, 144
Independent Order of St. Luke, 47
Industrialists. *See* Business leaders
Inness, George, 128
Inventors
    Nicolas Appert, 336
    Alexander Graham Bell, 66
    Louis Braille, 5
    Alfred M. Butts, 108
    Lee De Forest, 249
    Ole Evinrude, 114
    Benjamin Franklin, 18
    Johannes Gutenberg, 57
    Rudolf C. Ising, 230
    John Harvey Kellogg, 59
    Gerhardus Mercator, 68
    Mark Middlemark, 271

Index

Alfred Nobel, 308
Granville T. Woods, 118
Ising, Rudolf C., 230

Jackson, Mahalia, 313
Jackson, Thomas "Stonewall," 22
Jay, John, 363
Jenner, Edward, 144
Johnson, Andrew, 380
Johnson, Robert, 135
Jones, John Paul, 197
Joplin, Scott, 343
Journalists
    Nellie Bly, 132
    Ida Tarbell, 324
Just, Ernest, 236

Kandinsky, Wassily, 355
Karloff, Boris, 342
Keats, John, 318
Keller, Helen, 109
Kellogg, John Harvey, 59
Kelvin, Lord (William Thompson), 185
King, Martin Luther, Jr., 16
Kings
    George III, 163
Krebs, Hans Adolf, 248

Labor leaders
    Cesar Chavez, 94
    Julia C. Lathrop, 188
    Rose Schneiderman, 101
Lafayette, Marquis de, 261
Laplace, Pierre-Simon, Marquis de, 86
Lappé, Frances Moore, 43
Lathrop, Julia C., 188
Lawyers. See also Supreme Court justices
    Clarence Seward Darrow, 113
    Belva Lockwood, 311
Lee, Bruce, 346
Lemon, Meadowlark, 120
L'Enfant, Pierre Charles, 225
Lenin, Vladimir Ilyich, 117
Lennon, John, 296
Leopold, Aldo, 12
Leutze, Emanuel, 151
Lewis, Meriwether, 241
Lincoln, Abraham, 364, 380
Lincoln, Mary Todd, 364
Lindbergh, Anne Morrow, 181
Lindbergh, Charles, 37
Lister, Joseph, 100
Lockwood, Belva, 311
London, Jack, 13
Longfellow, Henry Wadsworth, 2
Luce, Clare Booth, 73
Luther, Martin, 329

McCartney, Paul, 177
Macdonald, Betty, 89
McFerrin, Bobby, Jr., 74
McGuffey, William Holmes, 278
Macy, Anne Sullivan, 109
Malcolm X (El-Hajj Malik el Shabazz), 146
Mandela, Nelson, 209
Mann, Horace, 131
Marceau, Marcel, 85
Marley, Bob, 39
Marsalis, Wynton, 305
Marshall, George C., 382
Marshall, Thurgood, 193
Martineau, Harriet, 171
Mathematicians
    George Biddell Airy, 218
    Carl Friedrich Gauss, 125
    Edmond Halley, 327
    Lord Kelvin, 175
    Marquis Pierre-Simon de Laplace, 86
    Blaise Pascal, 178
Mather, Increase, 180
Meir, Golda, 130
Mercator, Gerhardus, 68
Michelangelo, 69
Michelin, André, 17
Middlemark, Mark, 271
Military leaders
    Dwight D. Eisenhower, 301
    Ulysses Simpson Grant, 122
    Thomas "Stonewall" Jackson, 22
    John Paul Jones, 197
    George C. Marshall, 382
    Bernardo O'Higgins, 243
    Oliver Hazard Perry, 246
    Casimir Pulaski, 67
    James Wolfe, 3
Mill, John Stuart, 147
Mitchell, Maria, 224
Monroe, James, 123
Montessori, Maria, 254
Montgolfier, Jacques-Étienne, 8
Morgan, John Pierpont, 112
Morris, Lewis, 103
Morrison, Toni, 51
Mountaineers
    Edmund Hillary, 211
    Annie Smith Peck, 306
    Junko Tabei, 277
Muir, John, 116
Musicians. See also Composers; Singers
    Louis Armstrong, 227
    Raffi Cavoukian, 199
    Stan Getz, 35
    W. C. Handy, 335
    John Hurt, 194
    Robert Johnson, 135

Wynton Marsalis, 305
Charlie Parker, 252
Yo-Yo Ma, 294
Mussolini, Benito, 220

Nash, Ogden, 242
Native Americans
Sacagawea, 371
Jim Thorpe, 155
Naturalists
Ansel Adams, 53
John James Audubon, 121
Rachel Carson, 154
Jacques Cousteau, 170
Jane Goodall, 98
Aldo Leopold, 12
John Muir, 116
Andrei Dmitrievich Sakharov, 148
Neal, Patricia, 21
Neel, Alice, 29
Neumann, Saint John, 91
Nietzsche, Friedrich, 302
Nightingale, Florence, 139
Nobel, Alfred, 308
Nobel Prize winners
George W. Beadle, 309
Menachem Begin, 239
Jimmy Carter, 288
Marie Curie, 326
Albert Einstein, 77
Enrico Fermi, 284
Milton Friedman, 222
William Gerald Golding, 274
Ernest Hemingway, 212
Martin Luther King Jr., 16
Hans Adolf Krebs, 248
Nelson Mandela, 209
George C. Marshall, 382
Toni Morrison, 51
Linus Pauling, 61
Ivan Petrovich Pavlov, 269
Andrei Dmitrievich Sakharov, 148
Albert Schweitzer, 15
Aleksandr Solzhenitsyn, 362
Wole Soyinka, 204
Mother Theresa, 250
Elie Wiesel, 285
Woodrow Wilson, 379
Rosalyn Yallow, 210
North, Sterling, 323
Nurses. *See also* Health-care leaders
Clara Barton, 376
Dorothea Dix, 99
Florence Nightingale, 139

Oakley, Annie, 236
O'Higgins, Bernardo, 243

O'Keefe, Georgia, 106, 334
Orwell, George, 184
Owens, Jessie, 267

Paige, Leroy "Satchel," 198
Palmer, Arnold, 265
Parker, Charlie, 252
Parnell, Charles Stewart, 75
Parrish, Maxfield, 216
Pascal, Blaise, 178
Pasteur, Louis, 378
Pauling, Linus, 61
Pavlov, Ivan Petrovich, 269
Peale, Norman Vincent, 158
Peary, Robert E., 133
Peck, Annie Smith, 306
Pelé, 310
Pepper, Claude Denson, 263
Perry, Oliver Hazard, 246
Philanthropists
Clara Barton, 376
Lizzie "Lillie" Bliss, 106
Andrew Carnegie, 344
Alfred Nobel, 308
John Cecil Rhodes, 196
John D. Rockefeller Jr., 30
Philosophers
William Blake, 347
Auguste Comte, 20
John Dewey, 307
Ralph Waldo Emerson, 152
Johann Wolfgang von Goethe, 251
John Stuart Mill, 147
Friedrich Nietzsche, 302
Blaise Pascal, 178
Jean-Jacques Rousseau, 187
Adam Smith, 164
Henry David Thoreau, 152, 203
Photographers
Berenice Abbott, 208
Ansel Adams, 53
Walker Evans, 322
John Howard Griffin, 175
Lewis Hine, 281
Physicians. *See* Health-care leaders
Physicists
Marie Curie, 326
Albert Einstein, 77
Enrico Fermi, 284
Robert Goddard, 292
Lord Kelvin, 185
Blaise Pascal, 178
Piaget, Jean, 232
Picasso, Pablo, 312
Piccard, Jeannette Ridlon, 6
Pilots. *See* Aviators
Pitcher, Molly, 300

Index

Poets. *See also* Writers
  William Blake, 347
  Countee Cullen, 157
  Emily Dickinson, 361
  Johann Wolfgang von Goethe, 251
  Jupiter Hammon, 303
  Langston Hughes, 34
  John Keats, 318
  Emma Lazarus, 213
  Anne Morrow Lindbergh, 181
  Ogden Nash, 242
  Carl Sandburg, 7
  Sir Walter Scott, 238
  Phillis Wheatley, 304
  William Butler Yeats, 172
Polgar, Judit, 214
Politicians. *See* American politicians; World
  leaders
Polk, James, 321
Porsche, Ferdinand, 258
Porter, Cole, 168
Porter, William Sydney (O. Henry), 266
Potter, Beatrix, 219
Powell, John Wesley, 87
Powers, Harriet, 316
Presidents. *See* U.S. Presidents
Presley, Elvis, 9
Prout, Mary Ann "Aunt Mary," 47
Publishers
  Benjamin Franklin, 18
  Frank Gannett, 270
Puccini, Giacomo, 373
Pulaski, Casimir, 67

Quinlan, Karen Ann, 92

Ram, Jagjivan, 96
Reed, Walter, 268
Reeve, Christopher, 280
Religious leaders
  William Booth, 105
  William Ellery Channing, 102
  Martin Luther, 329
  Increase Mather, 180
  Saint John Neumann, 91
  Norman Vincent Peale, 158
  Mother Theresa, 250
  John Wesley, 176
  Brigham Young, 160
Rembrandt van Rijn, 206
Remington, Frederick, 291
Retton, Mary Lou, 25
Revere, Paul, 2
Revolutionary War heroes
  John Adams, 317
  Samuel Adams, 2, 281
  Benjamin Franklin, 18

  John Hancock, 24
  Patrick Henry, 156
  John Paul Jones, 197
  Marquis de Lafayette, 261
  Lewis Morris, 103
  Molly Pitcher, 300
  Casimir Pulaski, 67
  Paul Revere, 2
  Deborah Sampson, 368
  George Washington, 55
Rhodes, Cecil John, 196
Ride, Sally Kristen, 153
Ripken, Cal, Jr., 247
Rivera, Diego, 359
Robeson, Paul, 104
Rockefeller, John D., Jr., 30
Rockwell, Norman, 36
Roosevelt, Eleanor, 31, 60, 298
Roosevelt, Franklin Delano, 31
Ross, James Clark, 110
Rousseau, Jean-Jacques, 187
Rudolph, Wilma, 182
Runners
  Jesse Owens, 267
  Wilma Rudolph, 182
  William Toomey, 11
Rustin, Bayard, 80

Sacagawea, 371
St. Aubin, Helen Candaele, 76
Sakharov, Andrei Dmitrievich, 148
Salk, Jonas, 315
Salvation Army, the, 105
Sampson, Deborah, 368
Sandburg, Carl, 7
Schneiderman, Rose, 101
Scholars
  August Comte, 20
  Jean Piaget, 232
  Carter G. Woodson, 370
Schubert, Franz (Peter), 32
Schulz, Charles, 345
Schweitzer, Albert, 15
Scientists
  George Biddell Airy, 218
  Benjamin Banneker, 328
  John Bartram, 150
  Florence Bascom, 205
  George W. Beadle, 309
  Robert Boyle, 26
  Luther Burbank, 70
  Edwin Colbert, 283
  Marie Curie, 326
  Charles Robert Darwin, 45
  Albert Einstein, 77
  Enrico Fermi, 284
  Alexander Fleming, 229

Carl Friedrich Gauss, 125
Robert Goddard, 292
Jane Goodall, 98
James Hutton, 162
Edward Jenner, 144
Ernest Just, 237
Lord Kelvin, 185
Hans Adolf Krebs, 248
Blaise Pascal, 178
Louis Pasteur, 378
Linus Pauling, 61
Ivan Petrovich Pavlov, 269
Jeannette Ridlon Piccard, 6
Jonas Salk, 315
Scopes, John T., 226
Scott, Sir Walter, 238
Scrabble, 108
Sendak, Maurice, 169
Seurat, Georges, 353
Seward, William Henry, 143
Shackleton, Ernest, 48
Shepard, Alan, 337
Sinclair, Upton, 275
Singers. *See also* Composers; Musicians
    Marian Anderson, 60
    Joan Baez, 10
    Buddy Holly, 262
    Lena Horne, 189
    Mahalia Jackson, 313
    Robert Johnson, 135
    John Lennon, 296
    Paul McCartney, 177
    Bobby McFerrin Jr., 74
    Bob Marley, 39
    Elvis Presley, 9
    Paul Robeson, 104
    Mary Wells, 140
    Hank Williams, 272
Skaters
    Bonnie Blair, 81
Slayton, Donald "Deke," 64
Smith, Adam, 164
Smith, Jedediah Strong, 183
Smith, Margaret Chase, 365
Soccer players
    Pelé, 310
Solzhenitsyn, Aleksandr, 362
Sousa, John Philip, 325
Soyinka, Wole, 204
Spaulding, Albert, 257
Spock, Benjamin, 129
Stalin, Joseph, 372
Stanford, Leland, 72
Stanton, Elizabeth Cady, 331
Stevenson, Robert Louis, 332
Stine, R. L. (Robert Lawrence), 295
Stowe, Harriet Beecher, 173

Sullivan, Kathryn, 153
Supreme Court justices. *See also* Lawyers
    John Jay, 363
    Thurgood Marshall, 193
Swimmers
    Johnny Weissmuller, 161

Tabei, Junko, 277
Tarbell, Ida, 324
Teachers. *See* Educators
Theresa, Mother, 250
Thompson, William (Lord Kelvin), 185
Thoreau, Henry David, 152, 203
Thorpe, Jim, 155
Tolkien, J. R. R., 4
Tolstoy, Leo, 264
Toomey, William, 11
Trippe, Juan T., 185
Twain, Mark (Samuel Clemens), 349

U.S. Presidents. *See also* American politicians
    John Adams, 317
    Jimmy Carter, 288
    Dwight D. Eisenhower, 301
    Ulysses Simpson Grant, 122
    Herbert Hoover, 232
    Andrew Johnson, 380
    Abraham Lincoln, 364, 380
    James Monroe, 123
    James Polk, 321
    Franklin Delano Roosevelt, 31
    George Washington, 55
    Woodrow Wilson, 379

van Gogh, Vincent, 93
Verdi, Giuseppe, 297
Verne, Jules, 41

Walker, Alice, 42
Walker, Maggie, 47
Walker, Sarah "Madame C. J.," 374
Warren, Robert Penn, 119
Washington, George, 55
Webster, Daniel, 19
Webster, Noah, 303
Weissmuller, Johnny, 161
Wells, H. G., 276
Wells, Mary, 140
Wesley, John, 176
Western heroes (U.S.)
    Davy Crockett, 240
    Wyatt Earp, 82
    Annie Oakley, 236
    Jedediah Strong Smith, 183
Wheatley, Phillis, 304
White, E. B., 202
Wiesel, Elie, 285

Index

Wilder, Laura Ingalls, 40
Wilkins, Roy, 253
Williams, Hank, 272
Williams, Ralph Vaughan, 299
Wilson, Woodrow, 379
Wolfe, James, 3
Women's rights leaders. *See* Feminists
Wood, Grant, 46
Woods, Granville T., 118
Woods, Tiger, 381
Woodson, Carter G., 370
World leaders
  Menachem Begin, 239
  Mohandas Gandhi, 289
  Hirohito, 124
  Adolf Hitler, 115
  Vladimir Ilyich Lenin, 117
  Nelson Mandela, 209
  Golda Meir, 130
  Benito Mussolini, 220
  Jagjivan Ram, 96
  Andrei Dmitrievich Sakharov,
    148
  Joseph Stalin, 372
Wright, Frank Lloyd, 167
Writers. *See also* Poets
  Louisa May Alcott, 348
  Horatio Alger, 14
  Hans Christian Andersen, 97
  Mary Ritter Beard, 228
  Thomas Bewick, 235
  Erma Bombeck, 54
  Edgar Rice Burroughs, 256
  Willa Cather, 358
  Charles Waddell Chesnutt, 179
  Lydia Maria Child, 44
  Edwin Colbert, 283
  Joseph Conrad, 354
  Stephen Crane, 320
  Jean de Brunhoff, 360
  Laurent de Brunhoff, 360
  Fyodor Dostoyevsky, 330
  Ralph Waldo Emerson, 152
  Theodore Seuss Geisel ("Dr. Seuss"),
    65
  Johann Wolfgang von Goethe,
    251
  William Gerald Golding, 274
  Kenneth Grahame, 71

  Isabella Augusta Gregory, 78
  John Howard Griffin, 175
  Alex Haley, 234
  Ernest Hemingway, 212
  O. Henry, 266
  Langston Hughes, 34
  Henrik Ibsen, 83
  Frances Moore Lappé, 43
  Anne Morrow Lindbergh,
    181
  Jack London, 13
  Clare Booth Luce, 73
  Betty Macdonald, 89
  Toni Morrison, 51
  John Muir, 116
  Sterling North, 323
  George Orwell, 184
  Norman Vincent Peale, 158
  Beatrix Potter, 219
  Carl Sandburg, 7
  Albert Schweitzer, 15
  Sir Walter Scott, 238
  Upton Sinclair, 275
  Aleksandr Solzhenitsyn, 362
  Wole Soyinka, 204
  Robert Louis Stevenson, 332
  R. L. Stine, 295
  Harriet Beecher Stowe, 173
  Ida Tarbell, 324
  Henry David Thoreau, 203
  J. R. R. Tolkien, 4
  Leo Tolstoy, 264
  Mark Twain, 349
  Jules Verne, 41
  Alice Walker, 42
  Robert Penn Warren, 119
  Noah Webster, 303
  H. G. Wells, 276
  E. B. White, 202
  Elie Wiesel, 285
  Laura Ingalls Wilder, 40

Yallow, Rosalyn, 210
Yamasaki, Minoru, 352
Yeats, William Butler, 78, 172
Young, Brigham, 160
Yo-Yo Ma, 294

Zanuck, Darryl F., 260